ELECTION DAY

ELECTION DAY

A Documentary History

Robert J. Dinkin

An Oryx Book

GREENWOOD PRESS
Westport, Connecticut • London

Library of Congress Cataloging-in-Publication Data

Election day : a documentary history / [edited by] Robert J. Dinkin.
   p. cm.
   Includes bibliographical references and index.
   ISBN 0–313–32220–1 (alk. paper)
   1. Elections—United States—History—Sources. 2. Election Day—History—
Sources. I. Dinkin, Robert J.
   JK1965.E426 2002
   324'.973—dc21   2002024481

British Library Cataloguing in Publication Data is available.

Library of Congress Catalog Card Number: 2002024481
ISBN: 0–313–32220–1

First published in 2002

Greenwood Press, 88 Post Road West, Westport, CT 06881
An imprint of Greenwood Publishing Group, Inc.
www.greenwood.com

Printed in the United States of America

The paper used in this book complies with the
Permanent Paper Standard issued by the National
Information Standards Organization (Z39.48–1984).

10 9 8 7 6 5 4 3 2 1

Contents

Preface

Election Day, from the beginning of the republic to the controversial outcome in 2000, has usually been seen as a time of great importance, a time of renewal, a time of reaffirming our democratic traditions, a time of choosing our country's political leaders, and, perhaps, as signal of a change in government policies and national direction. Especially in connection with presidential contests, this day has marked the climax of a multifaceted ritual drama that has built up over many months, or in recent years even longer. Yet when one looks at studies of the election process past and present, almost none of them devote much space to the happenings on Election Day itself.[1] Most studies of elections seem primarily concerned with analysis of the results—why one side won and the other side lost, which groups supported which candidates and issues, and perhaps the size of the turnout. Such works virtually ignore other facets of Election Day—the public mood at the outset, the efforts to get out the vote, the actual casting of ballots with its consequent irregularities, the counting and reportage of the returns, plus the many forms of celebration and other postelection activity.

This volume seeks to correct that oversight by providing a close examination of Election Day activities in America from the eighteenth century to the present. After a general introduction, the book presents a series of documents that vividly describe specific contests or election practices and that collectively show how this eventful day has evolved over time. Original documents provide the reader with a better sense of the flavor and excitement of past election days than can be furnished through a narrative format or other means. In a number of cases the document chosen is the only account illustrating a particular aspect of the election process known to exist for that period. In making the selections, I have tried where possible to include material taken from actual participants—the voters, the candidates, the election officials—so the reader can experience the event directly through that individual's own words. Some of the most interesting descriptions come from foreign travelers in the United States, who often commented on aspects of Election Day ignored by native observers. However, when no useful primary source is available, later, secondary accounts of elections, reconstructed by journalists or historians, are used. In each instance, the document is put into historical context by a brief introduction, highlighting the importance of the subject matter being discussed. The book is divided chronologically into seven parts, the first few coinciding with such traditional political watersheds as the rise and fall of party systems, the later ones corresponding more to innovations in technology, particularly the advent of radio and television, and new methods of casting ballots.

While Election Day has held an exalted place in the nation's political tradition, what has happened on that day has not always shown American democracy in its best light, or shown the American people on their best behavior. Indeed, democratic ideals have often been lacking; some segments of the populace for a long time found themselves barred from the proceedings. Moreover, those who did participate sometimes circumvented the rules, producing results that undercut the wishes of the majority. In fact, fraud and violence have been frequent components of elections in the United States, and some of the country's most admired political leaders have at times gained public office through nefarious means. Yet, as a few of the commentators cited below point out, the negative aspects of elections have perhaps been exaggerated and the more positive facets ignored. After looking at all the material presented here, the reader can make his or her own judgment on this matter.

Election Day in America has had a long and interesting history, characterized by considerable change in terms of what transpired and the public's reaction to it. It went from being primarily celebratory and of limited political importance (in the colonial era) to a time, starting with the independence movement and continuing through the nineteenth century, when it was both highly celebratory and politically significant for a large majority of citizens. Then, over the course of the twentieth century, while still the biggest date on the political calendar, it became less celebratory and less politically meaningful to a growing part of the population. The percentage of people voting and the level of celebration have followed along the same curve. Both have risen with the emergence of competitive politics, reaching their zenith in the late nineteenth century, before falling to some degree in the initial decades of the twentieth century and then somewhat farther after 1960. Attempts to reverse the drop in turnout have not necessarily centered on restoring the primacy of Election Day. The trend in many states in recent decades has been toward "early voting," through expanded use of absentee balloting or balloting by mail, as well as actual casting of ballots in the weeks beforehand. Furthermore, as we enter the new millennium, there is serious consideration of the idea of giving people the option to vote at home via the Internet. How the nation has reached this point will be carefully explored both in the introduction and through the documents.

In producing this work, I have been assisted by numerous librarians at California State University, Fresno, and at many other institutions I have visited, especially the University of California, Berkeley, and Duke University, where I spent my sabbatical leave for the academic year 1998–99. Several colleagues at Fresno State have read parts of the manuscript, including Don Broyles and David Provost of the Political Science Department and David Hudson of the History Department. I would also like to thank my chairman Malik Simba and Dean Ellen Gruenbaum of the College of Social Sciences for supporting my research efforts, Alice Ricardo and Julie Watson for their secretarial help, and Judy Bonander of the Academic Innovation Center for solving various computer problems. Cynthia Harris and her staff at Greenwood Press did their usually fine job in editing the manuscript. Most helpful has been my wife Roxane Head Dinkin, who read numerous drafts and offered many suggestions for improving the text.

NOTE

1. An exception is Kate Kelly, *Election Day: An American Holiday, An American History* (New York: Facts on File, 1991).

Introduction

It is perhaps difficult today, in a period of limited enthusiasm for partisan politics, declining voter turnout, and scaled-down postelection events to realize that for a considerable part of our country's history Election Day was a momentous occasion. It was a day on which few people stayed home. It was a day that combined significant political decision making with national celebration. In former times, the public had a greater trust in government and a higher degree of patriotism, creating a solid core of voters eager to go to the polls. For many Americans, voting defined citizenship, and in the pretelevision age, when political parties were more central to what transpired, casting a party vote affirmed a sense of identity. Unlike the bland atmosphere that has frequently surrounded elections in recent years, a high level of excitement existed prior to an impending contest regardless of how competitive it was anticipated to be. Before scientific polling, much more doubt and suspense were associated with the outcome of electoral encounters than is currently the case. Straw polls and other earlier methods of forecasting the results generally lacked reliability. Therefore, it was more logical for people to believe that their favored side had a chance to win and that one's vote would count regardless of what results had been predicted. Party workers and rival candidates were more likely to be in an optimistic mood as well, thus further encouraging potential voters to take part.

The perception of an uncertain outcome also sparked a bigger surge of gambling, not necessarily in the amount of money put forth but in the proportion of the public involved in such transactions, than is true nowadays. As election contests had marked similarities to sporting events, many men enthusiastically debated the odds and then vigorously wagered on the candidates they expected to win. From the early nineteenth century onward, commentators often remarked about this aspect of the race as it reached its climax. "Wild Scramble To Place Bets On The Election—Hundreds Of Thousands Of Dollars To Change Hands" was at one time a typical big-city newspaper headline on the morning of the vote.[1] Along with concern over the betting odds, there was a great deal of anxiety about how the weather would affect the turnout. Partisan GOP sources commonly referred to Republican weather as "cool and fair," while describing Democratic weather as "rainy" or worse—it was believed that a bad day favored the Democratic "machine" candidates, who would turn out regardless of the elements, whereas a clear day favored the Republican side. (In recent times, the reverse situation has prevailed, as the Republican faithful have become the more highly committed voters.) Yet whatever the conditions, whatever the projected outcome, a far greater percentage of the eligible voters went to the polls throughout much of the past than is currently the case—when barely 50 percent take part in presidential elections and far less do so in other contests. Between 1840 and 1900 anywhere from 75 to 80 percent of those eligible participated regularly, and while the numbers declined somewhat over the next several decades, much of the spectacle and excitement remained. Even supposedly one-sided races a long time ago usually drew more voters than closely contested elections today. Indeed, many individuals went to great lengths to cast their votes, waiting in long lines for up to two hours, and, in the days before absentee ballots, returning home from distant points to take part. Traveling salesmen often left the road to go back to their hometowns for that purpose, as did large numbers of government employees situated in Washington, D.C. Without a doubt, previous generations took voting very seriously, seeing the benefits as clearly outweighing the costs.[2]

The act of voting was not the only element of the day's festivities in former times. After going to the polls early, many people celebrated in one way or another, taking the whole day off from work. In contrast to the serious, somber mood and lonely decision making associated with elections in modern times, those of yesteryear were open and lively community events. Describing what went on at such occurrences in the mid-nineteenth century, one scholar writes: "Election Day itself was festive, noisy, fiercely partisan, disruptive, and—like a celebration—extremely well attended. Banners, placards, fistfights, shouting matches, marching bands were the stuff of Election Day." It was, he adds, "a grand social occasion," with people coming together to meet their friends and neighbors. "The political parties sometimes rented taverns to entertain and give encouragement to potential supporters. Food and drink were free and everybody came."[3] The journal of an English traveler, Sir Charles Lyell, which records his observations of Trenton, New Jersey, and then Philadelphia, on Election Day in 1841, clearly confirms a substantial part of this assessment. The town of Trenton, Lyell exclaimed, was "in all the bustle of a general election. . . . Processions called 'parades' were perambulating the streets headed by bands of music, and carrying transparencies with lights in them, in which the names of different counties, and mottoes, such as Union, Liberty and Equality, were conspicuously inscribed." Philadelphia, he found, was "also in the ferment of an election, [with] bands of music placed in open carriages, each drawn by four horses, and each horse decorated by a flag, attended to its shoulder, which had a gay effect. All day a great bell tolls at the State house to remind electors of their duties."[4]

Election Day celebrations had some similarity to other holiday festivities, such as those connected with July 4—Independence Day. In each case, large public gatherings occurred in towns and cities, accompanied by much hoopla. A number of the elements described in the paragraph above could apply to both holidays—banners, parades, music, and bell ringing. Election Day, of course, had its own distinctive rituals, which, despite the extensive use of red, white, and blue, were always more partisan than patriotic. Its activities tended to be less formal and less family focused. Although women may have prepared food and watched the processions, men were clearly at the center of what went on, both as voters and celebrants. Each party sponsored separate events, and full public unity was found only in those communities heavily committed to one political persuasion. The announcement of victory elicited an enthusiastic response, though mainly from those favoring the winning side. For example, a newspaper report from New York City, after the election of Franklin Pierce as president in 1852, stated that "the joy of the Democracy was unbounded. They shouted, hurrahed, laughed, tossed their caps, and gave all sorts of indications of exultation." In Boston that same evening, a similar reaction among Democrats could be seen: "There was a pedestrian ovation with torches and drums in the streets."[5] Even normally staid businessmen took to jumping up and down or dancing with one another when informed of their party's success. Victorious local candidates might be carried along the main thoroughfares or serenaded at their homes and asked to deliver short statements. For those on the losing side, the celebrating abruptly ended, and many retired earlier than planned. Invariably, some of the revelers were too drunk to care about which ticket had won and continued to whoop it up.

By the end of the nineteenth century, much of the daytime pageantry had disappeared. All celebrations were pushed back into the evening, which were now more connected to the results than to the process of voting. Most voting occurred early in the morning, and afterward many people sought to get away from the tensions of the election (and of daily life in general) for several hours. Farmers left their farms and mingled with the townspeople. In some urban communities, stores and businesses shut down, as citizens flocked to ferry terminals or railway stations, seeking to go to the seashore or countryside for the day. As one French visitor to New York City reported, "Election day is a holiday in the United States. Offices and factories close. Only such employees as are indispensable for guarding property and performing necessary services remain on duty. The downtown business centre and its narrow streets, gloomy in the shade of gigantic sky scrapers[,] . . . ordinarily such a hive of hurrying humanity, are deserted and dead."[6] Still, plenty of activity could be seen around the polling place, as party functionaries sought to get latecomers to cast their ballots and prevent those on the other side from doing so. Arguments and fistfights sometimes broke out, but overall there were fewer disruptive incidents and fewer people milling around than in years gone by.

If daytime celebrating had declined, nighttime celebrating was in its ascendance at the turn of the twentieth century, particularly as urban locales acquired electricity. Once the polls closed and all the sojourners had returned from outlying areas, huge crowds gathered downtown awaiting the results and engaging in all sorts of "hijinx." Noise-making instruments abounded—according to one Chicago reporter, "horns, cowbells, and rattles were used by about every fifth person in hotels and on the streets." Indeed, as a time of public celebration it became similar to New Year's Eve. The *Atlanta Constitution* talked about a "Carnival Night" in 1912, reporting the goings-on in that city in reaction to Woodrow Wilson's impending victory in the presidential race. A *Chicago Tribune* headline in 1920, describing the local response to Warren Harding's election, declared, "Twas Glorious Victoree! Whole Town on a Toot." Generally, on such occasions the well-to-do attended banquets at posh hotels and restaurants, while many party officials and the rank and file gathered at party headquarters. The average person often went to a large auditorium to hear telegraphed reports of the election's progress or milled about in the streets outside the main newspaper offices, where the most recent figures were conspicuously displayed on bulletin boards or special screens. In some major cities, searchlights flashed beams in different colors to show which side was ahead. Even after the names of the winners were announced, the revelry would generally go on for several more hours. Certain communities held torchlight parades, or, in later times, organized processions of honking automobiles to highlight the occasion. Sometimes, when the main contest was undecided, the victory parties had to be delayed for a day or two. Invariably, however, some partisans could not wait and started celebrating long before the results were known and continued for a long time afterward.[7]

By the end of the 1920s, the response to Election Day seems to have changed somewhat, as partisan politics began to occupy a less important place in people's lives. Political parties became less involved in recruiting voters, and other attractions increasingly competed for the public's attention. Although women's suffrage raised the overall number of ballots cast, the proportion of eligible voters coming to the polls declined during the decade. Newspapers reported greater peace and quiet around the polling places. Fewer businesses shut down, and stores remained open most of the day. Some followed the lead of Macy's in New York, holding special Election Day sales.[8] Evening celebrations continued but seemed less connected with the balloting just concluded. People out and about on election night were more likely to be seeking entertainment than the latest returns. As former New York governor and Democratic presidential candidate Al Smith observed in his autobiography, *Up to Now* (1929), public attitudes had changed from the years of his youth, when enthusiasm for politics had been much greater and everyone had avidly awaited the news bulletins being posted outside the newspaper offices. In contrast, he wrote, "On election night nowadays places of amusement are packed to the doors. Moving-picture houses and theaters have their gala night of the year."[9] In one location at least—the small Midwestern town of Algona, Iowa—an attempt was made to combine on-screen entertainment with a presidential victory celebration. On election night in 1928 a "big extra special frolic" was scheduled at the local "opera house." To those attending the regular movie performance, the management said, confetti, balloons, and noisemakers would be furnished to be used when results of the contest between Smith and Herbert Hoover came in, presumably around midnight.[10] In such a setting though it is hard to know how much political meaning was associated with the celebration.

One of the biggest changes in Election Day behavior—or, more accurately, election night behavior—in that era came with the advent of radio. Thanks to the existence of radio, people had less need to go downtown in the evening and await the results. Of course, numerous individuals continued to do so, but even they increasingly gathered near radios if they could. A reporter in San Francisco during the 1928 presidential contest exclaimed, "Every place where a radio announced counts boasted its cluster of humanity."[11] Radio broadcasts of the returns had existed on a small scale from the beginning of the 1920s, though not until 1928 could their impact really be felt nationwide. By that point, thanks to improvements in transmitting facilities and home reception, radio started to reach vast numbers of people. The two leading networks, NBC and CBS, controlled 168 stations with a potential cumulative audience of fifteen to twenty million. On election night from then on, the networks used their enormous news-gathering resources to bring their listeners the latest information on the various races being contested. One could hear not only the up-to-the-minute results but also prominent political commentators providing instant analysis. Radio audiences on election night would continue to grow over the next two decades, while the crowds downtown gradually diminished. On the day after the general election in 1948, one northern California newspaper, the *San Rafael Independent*, reported that the local streets had been quiet the previous evening—"Residents Stay Home to Listen to Returns on Radio."[12]

By the 1950s, even more people were staying home on election night, thanks to the emergence of television. Television, which had initiated political reporting on a small scale in the previous decade, began to broadcast election returns on an extensive basis starting in 1952. Each of the main networks would have its leading commentators "anchoring" a team of reporters that would provide the latest results and analysis, intercut with speeches from prominent candidates and interviews with party officials. Coverage commenced at about 7:00 P.M. eastern time, and stations remained on the air until the contest was decided, sometimes not before the early morning hours. The television networks improved the speed and accuracy of earlier tabulations, employing large computers to calculate results more quickly. As the networks competed for viewers, each sought to outdo the others in projecting the winners of major races, sometimes doing so before the balloting had concluded and not always with perfect accuracy. Many people complained that this practice interfered with the freedom of elections and rendered many votes meaningless.[13] The controversy would reach its highest level during election night 2000, when the networks prematurely predicted a victory in Florida for Vice President Al Gore and then withdrew it, and later claimed Governor George W. Bush had won the entire election though the count in several states seemed still in doubt. However, if members of the public have been unhappy with the networks' handling of this matter, they have not turned off their TV sets and returned to the downtown streets. Indeed, the vast majority of the American public has continued to watch election night proceedings on their home screens. With television, one could be an eyewitness to dramatic moments—major upsets, critical speeches— taking place all over the country. Even when people attended local party get-togethers, a TV set was often to be found playing in the background.[14]

While Election Day has attracted widespread interest over the centuries, not everyone in the country became caught up in the festivities. Quite a few Americans have always been indifferent toward or disgusted with traditional politics and have wanted no part in the machinations of elections. Throughout our history, certain reformers have seen the elective process as subverting democracy and benefiting only a few special interests. To such critics, Election Day created false hopes and eventual disenchantment among large segments of the populace. Even those who did not go as far in their criticism often saw elections as frivolous exercises, contributing little to the public good. The nineteenth-century New England moralist Henry Thoreau once wrote, "All voting is a sort of gaming, like chequers or backgammon, with a slight moral tinge to it." He added, "Even voting *for the right* [cause] is *doing* nothing for it." By the time the majority of people got to vote against slavery, he asserted, the issue would no longer be important.[15] For those on the political extremes—whether on the Left or the Right—there has always been great doubt as to whether societal change can come about through the ballot box. Anarchists such as Emma Goldman and labor agitators like "Mother" Mary Jones usually downplayed the significance of the vote, seeing it as having little value in the struggle for workers' rights.[16] Such radicals have generally been more interested in strikes and other forms of protest than in trying to win elections. They knew minor parties could make little headway under our winner-take-all voting system, which makes no provision for proportional representation.

Others have ignored or avoided Election Day for different reasons. Among the foreign born, especially those coming from nondemocratic and non–English speaking countries, election festivities have probably seemed somewhat strange and not at all relevant to their lives. Except for a few groups like the Irish, it would take immigrants a long time to play meaningful parts in the political realm, if they ever did. They would always have lower turnout rates than people who grew up within our political culture. Yet over the course of the nation's history even numerous native-born Americans have found the political system unresponsive to their needs and not worth bothering about. As a result, they have looked upon voting as a waste of energy and upon election results as meaningless, and they have not shown much interest in them. Having been barred from the vote for centuries left many women, blacks, and members of certain other minorities largely indifferent to the electoral process for a long time. In fact, even today that legacy has not totally disappeared.

But for the majority of homegrown adult white males, Election Day was for most of the past three centuries a meaningful and exciting moment. As we have seen, in many places it was considered a holiday— one of the few notable events on the calendar. A woman traveler in her description of Connecticut in the early 1700s noted, "Their Cheif [*sic*] Red Letter day is St. Election."[17] The electors not only had a chance to deliver a vote and perhaps meet the candidates but could frequently find pleasing alternatives to the routine matters of daily life. Going to the polling place offered a good excuse for visiting with friends, enjoying free food and drink, and perhaps engaging in sports and games. In certain colonies, Election Day coincided with a militia training or a meeting of the county court. The day that elections were held, declared the Rev. Henry Muhlenburg of Pennsylvania in the 1760s, was "the most turbulent day in the whole year.... [T]he towns are crowded and noisy."[18] Even in later times, when Election Day no longer meant an entire day off and men had to cast a vote either before or after their daily toil, much activity could still be observed. Besides the qualified electors, young men under twenty-one, below the existing voting age, were usually close at hand, drinking, shouting, and, like quite a number of their elders, acting in a generally rowdy manner.

Indeed, the consumption of alcoholic beverages was often a major component of Election Day and its celebrations. In many places, before the advent of restrictive legislation, the candidates and their supporters offered free drinks and other treats to the electors as an incentive to come out and vote. The famous as well as the not so famous indulged in this practice. Even George Washington spent lavishly on liquid refreshments on the occasion of his numerous elections to the House of Burgesses in Virginia. Washington generally made an effort to see that all voters were treated alike, even those who voted against him; certain office seekers, however, provided drinks only to their own backers, leading to charges of bribery.[19] By the early nineteenth century, several states had passed laws making it illegal to offer "spiritous liquors" to prospective voters, but various enterprising politicians sought to get around such legislation. In order to allay charges of impropriety, candidates in some locales got together with their adversaries to furnish alcoholic beverages jointly to all participants after the contest ended. As one rural Alabaman, E.A. Powell, remembered the scene of his first general election in 1832, "In a dry-goods store there was improvised, outside the regular counters, a board reaching clear across the room. On that board was ranged in regular order, fine decanters filled with Whiskey, Brandy, Wine, Rum, etc.— each handsomely labeled, 'Col. James K. Anderson,'—'Major James Moore,' and so on through the entire list of candidates." Some of the voters, Powell recalled, "were very liberal" and "drank all around the board."[20] Such arrangements continued to flourish in parts of the country through the rest of the nineteenth century.

Although free drinks were a strong enticement, those partaking in the offer could suffer some unpleasant consequences. On one occasion in Lexington, Kentucky, during the Jacksonian era, when the winners placed a barrel of punch near the voting site, in the middle of Limestone Street, a member of the opposition secretly inserted some tartar emetic in the punchbowl. As one bystander wrote, "Such a scene as ensued beggars all description, and could hardly be limned with the pencil of a Hogarth. The retching and heaving, the sputtering, and spewing, and spouting with 'The two and seventy stenches / All well defined, and several stinks,' which assailed the olfactories of the passers-by was due notice to give the participants in the debauch a wide birth."[21] In many locales during this period, the experience of drunkenness led to fighting among the spectators, sometimes unrelated to the contest at hand, but frequently not.

In fact, physical violence has been closely associated with America's election history from nearly the beginning. It was so common in certain places that it was considered the norm rather than an aberration. To understand its evolution, one must distinguish at least three separate categories. The first is generally associated with the pre-party period of the eighteenth century, especially in the upper South and middle colonies—Virginia, Maryland, Delaware, New York and Pennsylvania. Violence here was mostly spontaneous, perhaps arising from small incidents that got out of hand, and linked to momentary conflict between the supporters of rival candidates or factions who may have overindulged in the offerings of free whiskey. Rarely did it cause anyone much permanent damage. As historian Edmund S. Morgan has written in his prize-winning book, *Inventing the People* (1988), "Fighting to kill was not part of the script. Seldom do we find any mention of firearms in the accounts of violence. There might be clubs and cleavers but not guns, there might be bruises and blood, but no dead bodies. If anyone was dangerously injured it was by accident. Hence the reluctance of the courts to punish those at fault; election brawls were not to be taken seriously once the election was over."[22]

A second category of violence is linked to the growth of vigorous competition between the major political parties in the nineteenth century, especially after 1830. This violence, in contrast to the initial type, was frequently planned in advance; a party would hire a gang of "toughs" to prevent voters favoring the other side from reaching polling places. Sometimes just a few individuals were beaten and bloodied as a warning to others to stay away. Sometimes a full-scale riot developed as those in the opposing camp retaliated with equal force, leaving many of the brawlers in need of medical attention. Such episodes were common particularly in the large cities of the Middle Atlantic states like New York, Philadelphia, and Baltimore, and they often involved clashes between nativist elements and recent immigrants, especially Irish Catholics. Though these confrontations produced more bloodshed than the election skirmishes of the earlier period, few participants died, and few kept grudges after the contest had ended.[23]

While violence and intimidation remained parts of the election landscape into the next century, albeit at a lower rate, the greatest amount of such behavior from the post–Civil War years onward was of a third type. It took place primarily in the former slave states, as conservative whites formed armed groups, like the Ku Klux Klan, to prevent recently freed black males from exercising their newly won voting rights. Even after many southern states had effectively disenfranchised most African Americans through literacy tests, poll taxes, and other manipulative practices, violence continued to be employed against individuals who sought to defy the racial ban. Sometimes even black men who were prominent in their communities would be beaten or even murdered for trying to vote. The number of such incidents declined in the first four decades of the twentieth century, as fewer blacks saw much gain in risking their lives for the privilege of voting. Yet as the civil rights movement assumed a more militant stance after World War II and made access to the ballot box a major goal, acts of violence against those attempting to go to the polls rose once again.[24]

From the preceding paragraphs one might get the impression that virtually all the nation's early political contests must have been accompanied by some form of brutal or riotous behavior. Indeed, an unsuspecting individual of those times, after listening to all the preelection diatribes on behalf of rival candidates, might assume that physical conflict at the polling place was all but inevitable. Yet as Alexander Mackay, a mid-nineteenth-century British observer of American politics, insisted, such was not usually the case. The inexperienced stranger might wake up on Election Day believing that "not a throat will be left uncut—not a bone unbroken," he wrote. "But to his surprise the whole evaporates in smoke, the poll proceeding in the quietest possible manner; and a President of the United States, or a Governor of a State, or some other officer, is peaceably made or unmade, by men who can look one another very kindly in the face, after having, but yesterday, said such hard things of each other." Citing the example of the much-ballyhooed presidential race in 1840 between William Henry Harrison and Martin Van Buren, in which many unpleasant words were exchanged, Mackay noted that "not a life was lost at that election, while scarcely a drop of blood was drawn," among the two million men casting ballots. Admittedly, in certain contests, he added, "fatal affrays sometimes take place, but they are rare considering how numerous the occasions on which they might arise, and are invariably confined to large towns, where it is not always easy to keep the dregs of the rabble in subjection."[25]

Often (but not necessarily) connected with violence and intimidation of voters in the past was a great deal of election fraud. As one political scientist who carefully analyzed the subject prior to the 1950s put it, "A study of the history of American elections will reveal a fairly large number of irregularities and occasionally even sensational frauds." Election fraud was especially widespread in the late nineteenth and early twentieth centuries, when partisan conflict was strong and federal authority remained weak. It was particularly noticeable in parts of the South, where the dominant Democrats sought to prevent the emerging Republicans and minor parties like the Populists from gaining political clout. As one-party states emerged, fraud was most evident in primary elections, where the entrenched leadership sought to squash any opposition to its long-term rule. Besides the South, election fraud was especially common in the immigrant-filled cities of the Northeast. "Where political bosses and machines batten themselves on the people there is almost always a certain amount of corruption in elections," the same writer has stated. "The stakes are high and scruples are lacking, hence anything goes." Especially when opponents rose up against the power of the machine, all sorts of mischief might prevail. "Repeating is likely to reach large proportions; the buying of votes will be commonplace; corrupt election officials will tamper with the ballots, mutilating those of opponents, adding spurious ones that favor their candidates, and occasionally totally disregarding the sentiments of the voters by falsifying returns."[26] Gradually, stricter laws and closer observation by poll watchers helped reduce the problem. Yet even in recent years, election fraud, though in decline, has continued to exist. This was made clear in the aftermath of the presidential contest in 2000, when many allegations of improprieties were reported. In addition to some traditional methods such as ballot destruction, more recent episodes have involved tampering with registration lists and the use of fraudulent absentee ballots.[27]

As can be imagined, the level of interest in Election Day and the amount of revelry and nefarious activity engaged in varied from region to region and according to a locale's size, the composition of its people, and the competitiveness of its politics. In the aforementioned cities of the Middle Atlantic states or a place like Chicago, where the population was religiously and ethnically mixed and partisan division was strong, public participation was quite high, as were reports of rowdy behavior. The day after the presidential contest in 1916, a headline in the *Chicago Tribune* exclaimed: "Election Enthusiasts Keep Firemen on Jump—False Alarms, Bonfires, and Disturbances Frequent Where Battles Were Bitterest."[28] In the small towns of more homogeneous New England, Election Day, while politically important, did not produce so much excitement or discord. Also, in those areas of the country where politics was normally one-sided and not very competitive, like parts of the Deep South in former epochs, the results were often such a foregone conclusion that elections did not arouse much public interest. Of course, regardless of where one resided, attitudes toward participation varied among the individuals involved in the day's proceedings. Some took part in an enthusiastic manner, cheerfully exercising their political privileges and engaging in postelection festivities, whereas others saw voting as a civic obligation and had nothing to do with the goings-on afterward. Naturally, elections mattered most to those people directly connected to politics and personally affected by the outcome. This included party officials, civil servants, representatives of various interest groups, and, of course, the candidates and their families.[29]

Just who constituted the bulk of participants at the polls and at other election-related events in the past is difficult to ascertain. In recent years, as we know from numerous behavioral studies, interest in politics and level of voting has been higher among the well-to-do than among the less affluent; in college graduates and professionals compared to the less educated and less skilled; in the native born compared to the immigrant; and in the middle aged compared to the young. But was this now common pattern—particularly the greater rate of participation among the rich—true in earlier times? The answer is unclear. In some instances it may have been the case, but in others the opposite seems to have occurred. In the mid-eighteenth-century colonies, for example, several British officials bemoaned the absence of the gentlemanly class at election meetings where ballots were cast. One royal governor, William Shirley of Massachusetts, claimed that the better sort found it "irksome to attend . . . except upon very extraordinary occasions," so that legislative contests were dominated by men of the lowest orders.[30] In the nineteenth century too a number of commentators complained of elections in the eastern cities being controlled by "low-born Irish emigrants."[31] However, later on, observers often played down the differences in economic background among the electors. One Atlanta newspaperman in 1892 described those taking part in the balloting process this way: "The voting," he declared, "was not confined to any class but was participated in by all. The mechanic was as eager to get to the ballot box through the mud and slush as was his wealthy neighbor who was driven to the polls in his carriage."[32] Actually, it would seem that for much of our history, where turnout was high it would be hard to find any groups of white men who did not vote regularly, other than transients, military personnel, felons, and the legally insane.

While Election Day started out essentially as an all-white-male experience, not all white males possessed the voting franchise at first. In colonial times, aliens, religious dissenters, indentured servants, and those without much property—perhaps one-fifth to one-half of all white men— were ineligible. However, during and after the American Revolution, lawmakers removed many of the previous barriers to eligibility. Property qualifications were reduced or replaced by taxpaying alternatives, and religious requirements modified or eliminated. With the continuing growth of democracy in the first half of the nineteenth century, further reforms were implemented, and universal white manhood suffrage was more or less achieved. Strict racial and gender requirements nevertheless remained. Only a handful of northern states permitted free black men the right to vote before the Civil War, and none allowed it to all adult women. (In 1776, the state of New Jersey began admitting single, property-owning women to cast ballots but abruptly ended this practice a few decades later.) Formerly enslaved black men first became eligible to vote under the Fifteenth Amendment to the Constitution but found it difficult to exercise their newly obtained rights, as many southern states found ways to keep the freedmen from voting for a long, long time. For women the suffrage struggle was a long and arduous one as well. Though women gained the franchise in a few western states in the late nineteenth century, not until 1920 was the gender restriction removed nationwide. Not until the middle to late 1960s were most African Americans accepted as voters throughout the country. Native Americans, although given full citizenship in 1924, were also denied the vote in some states until the 1940s and '50s.[33]

Election Day probably grew more meaningful to many people not only as the franchise was expanded but as more high offices became elective in the new republic. When Americans lived under British rule, usually just the lower houses of the legislatures and certain local positions lay open to the popular vote. Almost all governors and members of the upper houses were appointed. Only Rhode Island and Connecticut possessed charters allowing their inhabitants to elect their own governors and upper houses. After 1776, five states had elective governors, and the number gradually rose over the next half-century to include almost all. By the early to mid-nineteenth century, most states had also introduced popular election of their upper houses, though not before 1916 was the national upper house—the U.S. Senate—popularly elected. Other high state positions—for instance, lieutenant governor, state treasurer, attorney general, and even judgeships—began to be elective in the second quarter of the nineteenth century. The most important development, however, was the growing public demand to participate in the election of the U.S. president. The president, under the Constitution, was supposed to be chosen by a separate electoral college, whose members were at first designated mainly by the state legislatures. In 1792, only three states chose their presidential electors by popular vote on a statewide, general-ticket basis. But by the 1820s an upsurge of reform had helped expand this figure dramatically. At the end of the decade, all states (with the exception of South Carolina) had adopted this method, leading to much higher turnouts in the ensuing general elections.[34]

Neither in colonial times nor in the early republic was the idea of casting ballots on a single day at regular intervals widely established. Prior to the middle of the nineteenth century, little standardization existed, which meant that the months and dates for holding elections varied considerably. In many of the colonies, elections were called at the discretion of the governor and were held infrequently or irregularly—sometimes at three, or five, or seven-year intervals. Only the New England colonies, Delaware, and Pennsylvania had frequent (annual) elections. However, beginning in 1776, under the new state constitutions, the concept of regular and frequent elections started to spread elsewhere. But there remained sharp variations regarding the specific months and dates, especially according to region. Northern states, such as New Hampshire and Massachusetts, scheduled their statewide contests in March and April; the Middle Atlantic states of Pennsylvania, Delaware, and Maryland set their dates in October; while the southern states of South Carolina and Georgia chose late November or early December for their contests. Later on, the new states of Tennessee, Louisiana, and Mississippi instituted election days in July and August. The particular time of the month varied too. Some states designated the first day, some the last; others picked the first or second Monday or Tuesday. It would take quite a while to establish the principle that all national elections should take place on a single day, and how this was accomplished is not altogether clear. For a long time in certain states the polls remained open more than one day, in a few instances as many as five days.[35]

There was also little consistency in the early republic regarding the number of hours for the polls to be open on the day of election. In most cases, the decision was left to the officials in charge, who, while usually allowing the voters to cast ballots throughout the daylight hours, sometimes ended contests abruptly and arbitrarily. Following independence, a few states established uniform hours for voting. Starting in 1777, New York stipulated that voting be permitted from one hour after sunrise until sunset, while Georgia called for balloting to proceed from 9:00 A.M. to 6:00 P.M. Pennsylvania decreed that the polls should remain open till seven in the evening but allowed votes to be accepted in the city of Philadelphia for an additional hour so that late-working laborers might be able to participate. The question of extra voting hours for workingmen continued to be an issue throughout the next century. The Democratic party, which normally depended on votes from the laboring class in urban areas, always wished to extend the polling hours, while the Whigs and later Republicans generally sought to pass "sunset" laws to limit the duration of voting time. By the late nineteenth century, most states had passed laws keeping the polls open from early morning to early evening, roughly 6:00 A.M. to 6:00 P.M., and in subsequent periods the polls in most jurisdictions remained open to 7:00 or 8:00 P.M.[36]

The need for long hours and additional voting days in the early period of our history stemmed partly from the fact that voters often had to travel great distances to get to polling places. Outside of New England, where voting had always occurred at the local town meetinghouse, men needed to go to the county seat to cast their ballots. This could mean a ride of five, ten, even twenty miles. In most of the South, voting only at the county courthouse prevailed through the first half of the nineteenth century. The Middle Atlantic states, in contrast, moved to establish local

election districts of varying kinds. As early as 1778, the New York legislature ordered that all future balloting be arranged "not by counties
but by boroughs, towns, manors, districts, and precincts." New Jersey
and Pennsylvania soon made similar reforms. The rise in the number of
voting districts led to a wider variety of structures being used as polling
places, including taverns, mills, churches, and private residences. In the
nineteenth century, schools and firehouses would be added. Gradually,
other states went about creating smaller districts or precincts. By the first
half of the twentieth century, voting precincts usually contained from
three hundred to eight hundred voters, depending on the density of the
population. Some precincts might hold more than a thousand and some
less than a hundred. In certain rural jurisdictions there might be only a
handful of eligible voters. The establishment of smaller districts, as one
historian has noted, greatly facilitated access to the ballot box and reduced the necessity of holding elections over a span of several days.[37]

From the ratification of the U.S. Constitution onward, the trend was
generally toward fewer polling days and consolidation of state and federal contests. This resulted partly from the passage of laws dealing with
federal elections. Early in the new republic, Congress designated the initial Wednesday in December as the day when electors were to cast ballots for president and vice president, and it stipulated that these electors
be chosen within thirty-four days prior to that date. The states were now
forced to choose electors within a particular time frame, and as a result
early November soon became the most popular period for holding federal elections. Certain states established the first Monday or Tuesday,
others the second Monday or Tuesday, and two assigned the Friday
nearest November 1st. But as elections were still scheduled on different
days in different states, illegal voting grew increasingly common, especially during the vigorous party struggle of the Jacksonian era. Partisan
leaders often herded gangs of men across state lines to vote, taking advantage of scheduling differences. Finally, in 1845, after one Midwestern
congressman had made an issue of such election fraud, a law was passed
setting a specific date for choosing all presidential electors nationwide—
the first Tuesday after the first Monday in November. A generation later,
in 1872, Congress required that all House members be elected on that
date as well, unless a state's constitution said otherwise. Around a dozen
years after that (1884–85), almost all statewide elections—for selecting
the governor, legislature, etc.—began to be held on this date too, though
Maine continued down to the year 1960 its old tradition of having separate state contests in the month of September. In a related development,
states that had originally held annual elections of their officials started
in the late nineteenth century to move toward biennial elections, and
ultimately to quadrennial ones. As much as anything else, it was the

high cost and inconvenience of frequent elections that put an end to most annual and biennial contests.[38]

Local elections for offices such as mayor and city council were usually kept separate from national races. They were often held at a different time of year, or in alternate years, from federal elections. In fact, sometimes there were deliberate attempts to keep the two kinds of election separate. That was the case especially at the turn of the twentieth century, when the Republican party, which was dominant nationally, sought to influence local results by consolidating municipal with federal contests, and strong Democratic opposition to the idea arose. The Democrats, who controlled many urban "machines" in the Northeast and Midwest, naturally did not want any outside interference or potential loss of voting strength. Therefore, they fought hard in the state legislatures to stop any such consolidation. Eventually, the division of municipal and federal elections was assured. This was accomplished partly through the efforts of urban reformers (ironically, many of them were Republicans) who wished to improve the quality of local government and believed the separation of local from national voting would help bring it about. With reductions of local party competition at the polls, they thought, less corruption and fraud would occur.[39]

Another move toward uniformity came in the realm of actual balloting. It was a slow process, however. Voice voting—following the English tradition—was the dominant mode in the South and would remain so in some places down to the Civil War, and in Kentucky until 1890. Elsewhere, by the early nineteenth century, paper balloting had become the prevailing method, the individual voter frequently preparing his own ticket before going to the polls. With the rise of permanent political organizations, printed ballots, often of distinctive colors, began to be furnished to prospective voters by "party hawkers" at the polling site. These ballots were by no means secret, and this practice could lead to fraud as bogus tickets—listing the names of some Democratic candidates on a seemingly Republican ballot or vice versa—were given to the unwary. When this happened the opposition party urged voters to be on the lookout; for example, a GOP handbill in San Francisco in 1880 warned: "Let every Republican carefully examine his ticket before voting today, and ascertain whether it is accurate in every particular. The regular Republican ticket contains a scroll with the words 'Regular Republican Ticket,' beneath which are vignettes of Garfield and Arthur, with a shield surmounted by an American eagle between them, and the words, 'Free Ballot and An Honest Count,' in a small scroll running from one vignette to the other."[40] Such warnings were not always heeded, which meant that members of the opposing side sometimes wound up being wrongfully elected.

Finally, in the 1890s, efforts made to end the abuses finally paid off.

Reformers were able to convince the vast majority of states to adopt the so-called Australian ballot (used successfully to combat voter corruption in that country since the 1850s). As the political scientist Jerrold Rusk has written, "The Australian ballot was the exact opposite of the earlier party ballots. It is official (being prepared and distributed by the government rather than by the political parties), consolidated (placing the candidates of both major parties on the same ballot instead of on separate ballots), and secret (eliminating the 'public vote')." Not only did it limit the amount of voter fraud, but it facilitated the possibility of split-ticket voting, something hard to accomplish with printed party tickets. Even with the gradual introduction of the voting machine, the basic principles of the Australian ballot remained intact; the voting machine became in essence "a mechanical Australian ballot."[41]

Indeed, this new machine proved to be one of the most important innovations in election history. The voting machine was a complex electromechanical interlocking device, designed to help ensure secrecy, accuracy, and rapidity in the reporting of results. The first such machines were created in the middle of the nineteenth century, though none were employed in an actual election until a type invented by Jacob Myers came into use in Lockport, New York, in 1892. Mechanical voting was thereafter established on a broader basis in the large cities of upstate New York, such as Buffalo and Rochester, and soon spread elsewhere. Its reception, however, was not universally favorable. Despite the machines' advantages and the fact that in the long run they reduced costs, critics pointed to the disadvantages: initial high investment, frequent breakdowns, difficulties in operation. When first introduced in Chicago in 1912, it was reported that many people seemed afraid of them. There were complaints that learning to operate the devices made the voting process too slow. In fact, on that first occasion in Chicago, only 19 percent of the voters in the precincts where they were available consented to use them.

Gradually, of course, mechanical voting became more acceptable to the public. By mid-century, almost half of the electorate, particularly in large cities, was voting by machine. Over the years several different models would be developed. The most common for a long time was the Automatic Voting Machine, first manufactured in 1898. It had a horizontal ballot arrangement, with the candidates listed in party rows beneath the title of the office. An attendant activated the machine for each voter, who then indicated his or her choices by pulling a straight-party lever or turning individual pointers. The Shoup Voting Machine, launched in the early 1930s, had a vertical ballot arrangement. Here the candidates' names appeared vertically under the title of the office. The Coleman Vote Tally System, starting in 1962, had the voter mark the ballot with a special stamp that contained fluorescent ink so that counting could be done

easily at a data-processing center. A bigger breakthrough came about
with the Coyle Electronic and Harris Votomatic voting machines, which
entered the field in 1959 and 1964, respectively. These two machines
allowed voters to make their selections on punch-card ballots that could
be more quickly tabulated than ballots of any previous mode. By the
1980s, punch-card ballots, which could be fed into computers, were employed in more than one-third of all jurisdictions and were used by more
than half of all participants in any major contest.[42]

While later on a few new methods began being introduced, including
optical scanning and touch-screen voting, the majority of electors at the
end of the twentieth century were still using well-worn equipment and
older formats, which after many decades had started to reveal crucial
flaws. The older methods and machines remained satisfactory in one-
sided races where absolute accuracy was not essential, but the presidential election of 2000, particularly in the state of Florida, clearly showed
their inadequacy in close contests. Counting machines did not necessarily
sense and record all the punch cards, especially those that had not been
cleanly punched. Ballots containing any irregularities, such as choosing
two candidates for the same office, were completely discarded. As these
shortcomings became publicized after the 2000 election, many citizens
began to wonder whether their ballots really counted. Representatives
of foreign countries joked about the inadequacies of the system and seriously questioned whether the United States was living up to its democratic ideals. All this criticism subsequently led to strident calls for
voting reform and the adoption of new technology in some local jurisdictions.[43]

Whatever the method of balloting, from the outset elections have generally been overseen by a number of officials, which differed in kind
according to region. In New England, where people voted on the township basis, the town councilors known as "selectmen" supervised the
process. In South Carolina, where the parish was the unit of election,
parish churchwardens presided. But in the majority of states the county
was the main local jurisdiction and the county sheriff the chief individual
in charge, though he might be assisted by several clerks. Over time, as
problems arose, some people began to complain about giving one person
absolute control of the proceedings. Eventually, New York and a number
of other states replaced the sheriff with a group of locally elected judges
and inspectors, and this became the norm. Yet it did not reduce the
number of accusations of impropriety. Whoever served as a community's
election officials, conflict and partisanship often characterized the conduct of elections—for, as a historian has recently pointed out, the presiding officers were invariably members of the locally dominant party.
Although they were supposed to rule impartially upon such matters as
voter qualifications and then make fair and accurate tallies of returns,

partisan feelings sometimes intruded. In many cases over the years, the blatant partisanship of election officials caused state legislatures to intervene. Committees formed to investigate at times recommended overturning the original results of suspect elections.[44]

As election officials went about their business supervising the proceedings, the candidates and their followers increasingly took steps to see that those eligible did indeed cast ballots. In the eighteenth century, only in the most hotly contested races does one find a major effort to "turn out the vote." But by the nineteenth century such endeavors were becoming more common. As the party system developed, it became the norm in many places to send out a horse and buggy or even a carriage to bring in stragglers. Men were dispatched to every neighborhood to find those who had not yet done their duty, and party leaders like Thurlow Weed of New York would exhort the rank and file not to wait long before doing so. Prior to the election of 1860, he insisted that they "bring up delinquents" early in the day. They were to consider every man a delinquent "who doesn't vote by 10 o'clock." At that hour, "Begin to Hunt Up Voters!"[45] By the early twentieth century, precinct captains in the major cities were responsible for delivering a certain number of votes at election time and would do whatever was necessary to make sure that the total was reached. As the automobile became widespread, voters unable to get to the polls were increasingly driven there by car. Often the drivers were women, who also volunteered to do chores, like babysitting, so that other members of their sex could vote. In addition, as more and more of the population owned telephones, phone banks were established at party headquarters, and staffers began placing calls to people who did not vote early in order to remind them to do so. Sometimes local parties distributed small amounts of cash to prospective voters who needed funds for transportation or baby-sitting. In recent years, the amount of such "street money" allotted in some areas has increased dramatically and, as a result, caused considerable controversy.[46]

Election Day saw not only vigorous get-out-the-vote efforts in many places but also significant amounts of actual campaigning. Election Day was supposedly reserved for the casting and counting of votes, but electioneering did not necessarily come to a screeching halt the night before the polls opened. Indeed, in the early years, when campaigns were brief, part of the vote-getting enterprise went on around polling places after the balloting had commenced. As previously noted, this sometimes included dispensing food and drink and various forms of intimidation.[47] In more recent times, less direct pressure has been applied, but there are still attempts to affect outcomes, as partisan volunteers hold up signs or hand out flyers—even shout out the names of favored candidates—as people arrive at the voting sites. Election laws today generally restrict such activities to at least seventy-five to one hundred feet from the polling place, but this has not stopped on-the-spot campaigning. Although most voters have probably made up their minds about which candidates to choose for major offices, these last-minute campaign ploys clearly affect decision making for minor offices and referendum measures.[48]

One way of influencing the selection process back in the eighteenth and nineteenth centuries, where voice voting existed, was to have prominent individuals from the district cast the initial votes for the candidate, hoping that many other electors present would then follow suit. In 1758, during George Washington's first major campaign for a seat in the Virginia House of Burgesses from Frederick County, Washington's patron, Thomas, Lord Fairfax, cast the first vote and helped establish a successful trend. Three years later, Washington, running for reelection together with his ally George Mercer, told an associate, "Could Mercer's Friends and mine be hurried in at the first of the Poll it might be an advantage." Indeed, it seemed to work out in that manner; fifteen of the initial twenty voters were for Mercer and Washington, and both men went on to win by sizable margins.[49] Roughly one hundred years later, as a recent analysis of voting patterns in Washington County, Oregon, demonstrates, a similar practice was still in vogue. Poll books, listing the order of names recorded under the viva voce method, indicate that the leading local politicians often arrived at polling places together with large groups of friends and supporters. As the authors of the Oregon study state, "In case after case, the visibles [powerful men in the community] led their cohorts to the polls, sometimes in perfect symmetry with the count of votes itself so that results swung back and forth as each platoon turned up until the [final] result was determined by the appearance of a handful of the majority group."[50] Secret balloting would eventually put an end to such arrangements.

As for the hours when ballots are cast, most voting in the modern era has taken place toward the middle part of the day, rather than the first or last hours that the polls are open. Indeed, approximately three-quarters of the voters have turned out between 8:00 A.M. and 6:00 P.M. A national study analyzing the time pattern of the 1972 general election found only 11.4 percent voting before 8:00 A.M. and 14.1 percent after 6:00 P.M.; 31.9 percent voted between 8:00 A.M. and noon, 21.4 percent between noon and 4:00 P.M., and 21.2 percent between 4:00 P.M. and 6:00 P.M. (A previous study calculating time of participation in the California gubernatorial race in Alameda County in 1966 indicated a generally similar distribution.) The 1972 analysis also showed farmers as being the least likely to vote before 8:00 A.M. or after 4:00 P.M., whereas blue-collar workers were most likely to vote after 4:00 P.M.[51]

In contrast to this fairly balanced pattern, voters before 1900, when the polling period lasted from approximately 6:00 A.M. to 6:00 P.M., cast ballots mostly at the beginning of the day, prior to going to work or attending to other tasks. In fact, three-fourths of the vote in many communities was recorded before noon, and sometimes before 10:00 A.M. In the late nineteenth century, men were pressed to vote early to prevent being stuck outside the voting booth late in the day and possibly denied a ballot. A notice in a San Francisco newspaper in 1880 warned, "Do not wait until late in the afternoon, and be compelled to form one of a long line, and perhaps have your vote excluded by the closing of the polls at the legal hour." Similarly, a Republican handbill in Chicago in 1892, referring to the Democrats' alleged use of deceitful tactics late in the day, urged GOP voters to come to the polls the first thing in the morning, regardless of whether they had eaten. "Every Republican should go to the polls and deposit his ballot as early as possible today. The voting-places will be open at 6:00 A.M. If breakfast is not ready at that hour vote before eating and in any case before going to work. [It is] important because Democrats in Republican wards will hold back enough votes in each precinct until the last hour . . . to be able to obstruct and delay." In addition, the notice said, Republican voters should assist their local campaign committee by getting their neighbors out to the polls early.[52]

Regardless of the era, once the polls closed there came the crucial task of counting the votes. Before the modern age, it was a much more difficult and time-consuming operation than it is now; election officials had to go through every ballot box and mark down each vote, then add up the totals manually. When several offices were being filled, it frequently meant the same ballots had to be looked at again and again. Each precinct then reported the local figures to some central authority—town, county, or state—which compiled the overall total. The process might take several days. As voting machines started to be introduced, counting became far easier, as most machines kept running tallies, which could be immediately known once the voting ended. Of course, even today some ballots, especially absentee ballots and those from rural precincts, are still counted by hand. Whatever method of counting has been employed, major problems have invariably occurred. For example, many ballots have been spoiled by voters who either tore or mutilated them, or designated more than one person for the same office. Sometimes mistakes have been made in the counting, despite the use of machines. In the presidential election of 2000, many machines in Florida failed to provide accurate counts. Even before that occasion, officials estimate, over 2 percent of ballots nationwide have been routinely lost or damaged. In one-sided contests, such abnormalities are minor and do not affect the outcome, but in close races they can bring the entire result into question.[53]

What will Election Day be like in the future? Will there be a resurgence of interest in voting and a renewed desire to create a holiday-like atmosphere? Or will the gradual reduction of public involvement in the latter decades of the twentieth century continue into the twenty-first? The answers are unclear. On the one hand, indifference to voting shows little sign of diminishing. Many people have become disillusioned with government and the political chicanery that goes on in campaigns and want nothing to do with the election process. In addition, individuals, as their lives have gotten busier, try to avoid time-consuming activities like standing in line to vote. Even when faced with a close race in the presidential election of 2000, nearly half the electorate did not bother to go to the polls. Hence, such alternatives as absentee ballots, mail-in ballots, and other forms of early voting appear to be catching on. The possibility of casting a vote on the Internet also seems appealing. On the other hand, the Election Day tradition and our democratic ideals still have great meaning to many citizens. After all, not everyone has disappeared from the polling place. Perhaps after the revelations surrounding the balloting process in 2000 and the recent terrorist attacks, Americans will take their civic responsibilities more seriously. In the future, if voting can be moved to the weekend and linked with some form of celebration, a greater number of people may seek to take part again in the regular election proceedings at the polls and make Election Day a major community event once more.[54]

NOTES

1. *Chicago Tribune*, November 7, 1916, 3. A short summary of betting in presidential races from the 1880s to the early 1930s appears in ibid., November 10, 1932. See also Henry B. Fearon, *Sketches of America* (London, 1818; reprint New York: B. Blom, 1969), 140–41, 147; Bayard Tuckerman, ed., *The Diary of Philip Hone, 1828–1851* (New York, 1889), 2:48. References to "Republican and Democratic weather" can be found in the *Chicago Tribune*, November 4, 1924, and *New York Times*, November 3, 1936, 14.

2. For national voting figures from the early nineteenth to the late twentieth centuries, see Ruy A. Teixeira, *The Disappearing American Voter* (Washington, D.C.: Brookings Institution, 1992), 9. For statements about traveling salesmen returning home and the exodus from Washington, D.C., see *Chicago Tribune*, November 4, 1884, and November 6, 1900. To some degree, the differences are generational and sectional, as younger people today are less apt to vote than their elders, and southerners are less apt to vote than northerners.

3. Andreas Teuber, "Elections of Yore," *New York Times*, November 4, 1980, A19.

4. Sir Charles Lyell, *Travels in North America in the Years 1841–1842* (New York, 1845), 1:83–84.

5. For Independence Day celebrations, see Len Travers, *Celebrating the Fourth: Independence Day and the Rites of Nationalism in the Early Republic* (Amherst: University of Massachusetts Press, 1997). For a description of mid-nineteenth-century election festivities in Baltimore, see Jean H. Baker, *Affairs of Party* (Ithaca, N.Y.:

Cornell University Press, 1983), chap. 7. The quotations are taken from the *New York Times*, November 3, 6, 1852.

6. Georges Lechartier, "Election Week in New York," *Living Age* 308 (January 22, 1921): 194. It was an official holiday only in some states and only for short periods.

7. For descriptions of election night revelry, see *Chicago Tribune*, November 7, 1900, 6; November 6, 1912, 11; November 8, 1916, 4; November 3, 1920, 5. Also *Atlanta Constitution*, November 6, 1912, 5; *New York Times*, November 3, 1920, 5.

8. *New York Times*, November 3, 1936, 2. Macy's at that time generally opened at noon so as to allow employees and prospective customers to vote.

9. Al Smith, *Up to Now* (New York: Viking Press, 1929), 52–54.

10. Lewis E. Atherton, *Main Street on the Middle Border* (Bloomington: Indiana University Press, 1954), 307.

11. *San Francisco Chronicle*, November 7, 1928, 7, 8.

12. Erik Barnouw, *A History of Broadcasting in the United States* (New York: Oxford University Press, 1966–70), 1:152–53; *San Rafael Independent*, November 3, 1948, 3.

13. The process was encouraged by the introduction of exit polling. This meant getting detailed information from people who had just voted about the choices they made so as to enable analysts to project the outcome more quickly.

14. On TV coverage, see Document 53. See also Reuven Frank, "Election Night," *New Leader* (October 5–12, 1992), 19, 21.

15. Henry Thoreau, "Civil Disobedience," in *The Selected Works of Thoreau*, ed. Walter Harding (Boston: Houghton Mifflin, 1975), 794.

16. Emma Goldman, "Woman Suffrage," in *Anarchism and Other Essays*, rev. ed. (New York: Mother Earth, 1911), 201–17; Elliott J. Gorn, *Mother Jones: The Most Dangerous Woman in America* (New York: Hill and Wang, 2000), 230, 232.

17. [Sarah Kemble Knight], *The Journal of Madam Knight* (Boston: D. R. Godine, 1972), 24.

18. Henry Melchior Muhlenburg, *The Journals of Henry Melchior Muhlenburg*, trans. Theodore G. Tappert and John W. Doberstein (Philadelphia: Fortress Press, 1945), 2:517.

19. Charles S. Sydnor, *Gentlemen Freeholders* (Chapel Hill: University of North Carolina Press, 1952), 51–59.

20. E.A. Powell, "Fifty-Five Years in West Alabama," *Alabama Historical Quarterly* 4 (Winter 1942): 469–70.

21. Quoted in Henry G. Crowgey, *Kentucky Bourbon: The Early Years of Whiskeymaking* (Lexington: University of Kentucky Press, 1971), 68.

22. Edmund S. Morgan, *Inventing the People: The Rise of Popular Sovereignty in England and America* (New York: Norton, 1988), 201–2.

23. For examples of nineteenth-century election riots beyond those presented later in this volume, see Richard Hofstadter and Michael Wallace, *American Violence: A Documentary History* (New York: Alfred A. Knopf, 1970), 82–84, 93–96.

24. Steven F. Lawson, *Black Ballots: Voting Rights in the South, 1944–1969* (New York: Columbia University Press, 1976).

25. Alexander Mackay, *The Western World, or Travels in the United States in 1846–1847* (London, 1849; reprint New York: Negro Universities Press, 1968), 13–

14. See also Joseph J. Gurney, *A Journey in North America* (Norwich, Eng., 1841; reprint New York: DaCapo Press, 1973), 359.

26. Harold Zink, *Government and Politics in the United States*, 3rd ed. (New York: Macmillan, 1951), 216–17; Harold Zink, *City Bosses in the United States* (Durham, N.C.: Duke University Press, 1930).

27. Larry J. Sabato and Glenn R. Simpson, *Dirty Little Secrets: The Persistence of Corruption in American Politics* (New York: Times Books, 1996), esp. chap. 10.

28. *Chicago Tribune*, November 8, 1916, 4. The headline on page 6, November 7, 1900, read "Rowdyism on State Street Results in Riot at Midnight."

29. Americans are twice as likely to feel satisfaction in voting than Europeans. See Gabriel A. Almond and Sidney Verba, *The Civic Culture: Political Attitudes and Democracy in Five Nations* (Newbury Park, Calif.: Sage Publications, 1989), 108.

30. Charles H. Lincoln, *The Correspondence of William Shirley* (New York: Macmillan, 1912), 1:418. See also James K. Hosmer, *The Life of Thomas Hutchinson* (Boston, 1896), 206, 231.

31. See Carl D. Arfwedson, *The United States and Canada in 1832, 1833, and 1834* (London, 1834; reprint New York: Johnson Reprint Corp., 1969), 286; Gurney, *Journey in North America*, 359.

32. *Atlanta Constitution*, November 9, 1892, 5.

33. On the question of voting rights, see Chilton Williamson, *American Suffrage from Property to Democracy, 1760–1860* (Princeton, N.J.: Princeton University Press, 1960); J. Morgan Kousser, *The Shaping of Southern Politics: Suffrage Restriction and the Establishment of the One-Party South* (New Haven, Conn.: Yale University Press, 1974); Eleanor Flexner, *Century of Struggle*, rev. ed. (Cambridge, Mass.: Harvard University Press, 1975); Lawson, *Black Ballots*.

34. Peter H. Argersinger, "Electoral Processes," in *Encyclopedia of American Political History*, ed. Jack Greene (New York: Scribners, 1984), 2:490–91.

35. See the provisions of the various state constitutions in Francis N. Thorpe, ed., *The Federal and State Constitutions, Colonial Charters, and Other Organic Laws*, 9 vols. (Washington, D.C.: Government Printing Office, 1909).

36. Robert J. Dinkin, *Voting in Revolutionary America: A Study of Elections in the Original Thirteen States, 1776–1789* (Westport, Conn.: Greenwood, 1982), 98.

37. Ibid., 97–98; Argersinger, "Electoral Processes," 495.

38. Argersinger, "Electoral Processes," 496.

39. Ibid.

40. Ibid., 498–500; *San Francisco Chronicle*, November 2, 1880, 2.

41. Jerrold Rusk, *Dictionary of American History*, rev. ed. (New York: Scribners, 1976), s.v. "Ballot." See also Jerrold Rusk, "The Effect of the Australian Ballot Reform on Split-Ticket Voting, 1876–1908," *American Political Science Review* 64 (1970).

42. On voting machines, see *Dictionary of American History*, 7:210–11; *Chicago Tribune*, November 6, 1912,11; "Half the Voters Vote by Machine," *American City* (September 1956): 152; "Automatic Counting Updates the Election Process," *American City* (August 1964): 86–88; "Big Business in Ballots," *Atlantic* 254 (November 1984): 22.

43. *Newsweek*, November 27, 2000, 38.

44. Dinkin, *Voting in Revolutionary America*, 100; Argersinger, "Electoral Processes" 497.

45. *Albany Evening Journal*, November 5, 1860, cited in Reinhard H. Luthin, *The First Lincoln Campaign* (Cambridge, Mass.: Harvard University Press, 1944), 218.

46. Abraham Ribicoff and Jon O. Newman, *Politics: The American Way* (Boston: Allyn and Bacon, 1967), 130–31.

47. See, for example, Documents 16 and 21. For the late nineteenth century, see Theodore Roosevelt, "Machine Politics in New York City," in *The Works of Theodore Roosevelt* (New York: Scribners, 1926), 13:76–98.

48. Ribicoff and Newman, *Politics*, 139; Barbara Trafton, *Women Winning* (Boston: Harvard Common Press, 1984), 136–38.

49. Cited in Robert J. Dinkin, *Voting in Provincial America: A Study of Elections in the Thirteen Colonies, 1689–1776* (Westport, Conn.: Greenwood, 1977), 118.

50. Paul Bourke and Donald DeBats, *Washington County: Politics and Community in Antebellum America* (Baltimore: Johns Hopkins University Press, 1995), 166.

51. Ricardo Klorman, "What Time Do People Vote?" *Public Opinion Quarterly* 40 (1976): 182–93; Douglas A. Fuchs and Jules Becker, "A Brief Report on the Time of Day When People Vote," *Public Opinion Quarterly* 32 (1968): 437–40.

52. *Chicago Tribune*, November 5, 1884, 9; November 8, 1892, 1. See also *San Francisco Chronicle*, November 2, 1880, 2.

53. Ribicoff and Newman, *Politics*, 140–42; Martin Merzer et al., *The Miami Herald Report: Democracy Held Hostage* (New York: St. Martin's Press, 2001), 5.

54. For early voting, see Edwina Rogers, "Election Daze: Is Early Voting Coming to a State Near You?" *Campaigns & Elections* (September 1994): 36–37; Robert M. Stein, "Early Voting," *Public Opinion Quarterly* 62 (1998): 57–69. A call for revitalization of Election Day can be found in Anna Quindlen, "The Delirium of Democracy," *Newsweek*, May 8, 2000, 88. See also Ron Hirschbein, *Voting Rites: The Devolution of American Politics* (Westport, Conn.: Greenwood, 1999).

The Colonial and Revolutionary Periods

Election Day in colonial America started out in a rather low-key manner. Not many colonies had competitive elections in the seventeenth century, and public interest in them was minimal. Turnout at the polls was probably small, and postelection celebration was likely limited as well. In fact, not much evidence from those early elections has been preserved. All that has come down to us are a few brief statements affirming that the balloting in a particular place had occurred and that certain individuals had been elected. But by the middle decades of the eighteenth century the atmosphere had changed, and elections in several colonies had become more competitive. As the homogeneity of the early settlements broke down, clashing interests—political, religious, and economic—began to emerge, and factions formed. Even where factional struggles were less apparent, individuals aspiring for wealth and prestige saw places on the local governing board or provincial legislature as desirable and increasingly strived for such positions. Heightened competition led to bigger turnouts, reaching 40 percent of the adult white male population in colonies like Virginia. Excitement over Election Day made it a time not only of casting ballots but also of celebration, as distant neighbors got together for fun and fellowship. A holiday atmosphere was most evident in the middle and southern colonies, where people's behavior resembled life in merry old England more than it did in Puritan New England. Yet everywhere it was a day of special interest, one with more than just political meaning for the participants.

(1) John Adams's First Election to Office—Braintree, Massachusetts, 1766

In New England, elections took place at the regular town meeting. Town meetings were held several times a year to conduct a variety of business, though the major election meetings were in March (for the designation of local officials) and April or May (for colonywide officers). The town meetings were very democratic institutions for their time. As affirmed by the eighteenth-century chronicler William Gordon, "Every freeman or freeholder gives his vote or not, and for or against, as he pleases; and each vote weighs equally, whether that of the highest or lowest inhabitant."

At the town meeting, the voting to fill various public offices was usually done by ballot rather than by a show of hands or voice vote. New Englanders strongly sought consensus and believed secret voting a better method of achieving it than open voting. When the selection process began, the eligible voters were generally asked to place written tickets into a hat or ballot box. One or more of these depositories would be set down at the front of the meetinghouse near or on a table at which the town officials sat. During the balloting, each elector's name would be checked against a tax list to ensure that only qualified persons handed in tickets and that no man dropped more than one paper into the container.

Although there may have been a few voting irregularities, New Englanders experienced almost none of the violence and disorderly conduct that at times accompanied elections farther south. Yet the atmosphere on Election Day in some of the larger towns must not always have been so calm, if one item in the Salem town records is any indication—shortly before the annual May election meeting in 1728, the town leaders hired six extra men to stand watch that day "to prevent & Suppress all disorders & Tumults that may arise from so great a Concourse of people, as usually there are on such public occasions."

In most New England towns, the desire to achieve consensus meant that little or no electioneering occurred even prior to Election Day, let alone on it. Frequently an agreed-upon ticket for all local offices was worked out in advance by the town leaders, and so no real contest took place. However, unresolved problems in certain communities could at times give rise to competing slates. Also, in the first stages of the revolutionary movement, some townsmen sought to elect firm patriots and remove incumbents who might be British sympathizers. A good example of this phenomenon can be found in Braintree, Massachusetts, in the year 1766. Here the thirty-one-year-old lawyer (and later U.S. president) John Adams started his political career, having been chosen as a selectman to replace Ebenezer Miller, an Anglican "inclined to the government." Adams did not actually "run" for the office; rather, his brother and some friends arranged matters behind the scenes, as was the custom. As was also the custom, ballots that included his name were circulated in the town meeting before the voting took place. A lengthy description of what transpired on that occasion more than two centuries ago appears in Adams's diary, excerpted below.

My Brother Peter, Mr. Etter and Mr. Field, having a Number of Votes prepared for Mr. Quincy and me, set themselves to scatter them in Town Meeting. The Town had been very silent and still, my Name had never been mentioned nor had our Friends ever talked of any new Select Men att all, excepting in the south Precinct. But as soon as they found their was an Attempt to be made, they fell in and assisted, and, altho there were 6 different Hatts, with Votes for as many different Persons, besides a considerable Number of Scattering Votes, I had the Major Vote of the Assembly, the first Time. Mr. Quincy had more than 160 Votes. I had but one Vote more than half. Some of the Church People, Mr. Jo. Cleverly, his Brother Ben. and Son &c. and Mr. Ben. Vesey of the Middle Precinct, Mr. James Faxon &c. I found were grieved and chagrined for the Loss of their dear Major Miller.

Etter and my Brother took a skillful Method. They let a Number of young Fellows into the Design. John Ruggles, Peter Newcomb, &c. who were very well pleased with the Employment and put about a great many Votes. Many Persons, I hear acted slyly and deceitfully. This is always the Case.

I own it gave me much Pleasure to find I had so many Friends, and that my Conduct in Town, has been not disapproved. The Choice was quite unexpected to me. I thought the Project was so new and sudden that the People had not digested it, and would generally suppose, the Town would not like it, and so would not vote for it. But my Brothers answer was, that it had been talked of, last year, and some Years before, and that the Thought was familiar to the People in general, and was more agreable than any Thing of the Kind, that could be proposed to many. And for these Reasons his Hopes were strong.

But the Tryumph of the Party was very considerable, tho not compleat. For Thayer and Miller, and the late Lessees of the North Commons, and

many of the Church People and many others, had determined to get out
Deacon Penniman. But instead of that, their favourite was dropped, and
I, more obnoxious to that Party than even Deacon Penniman, or any
other Man, was chosen in his Room, and Deacon Penniman was saved
with more than 130 Votes, a more reputable Election than even Thayer
himself had.

Source: Reprinted by permission of the publisher from THE ADAMS PAPERS:
DIARY AND AUTOBIOGRAPHY OF JOHN ADAMS, VOLUME 1, DIARY 1755–
1770, edited by L. H. Butterfield, Cambridge, Mass.: The Belknap Press of Harvard University Press, Copyright © 1961 by the Massachusetts Historical Society.

---

(2) An Election of Gentlemen in Colonial Virginia, c. 1770

Elections in the Chesapeake colonies of Virginia and Maryland
were generally livelier and more exciting than those in New
England. They often took place in a festive atmosphere, with
food and drink liberally dispensed to the participants. Also, outcomes were less predictable, as several gentlemen in each
county vigorously competed for places in the legislature. In
these two colonies, as well as in most of the South, elections
were held at the county seat. The voting normally went on in
the courthouse, though in good weather it might be moved outside to the courthouse green. Voters would come up one at a
time to a large table, where the sheriff and his clerks were
seated. There, within the hearing of those officials and all interested spectators, each man would state his name and in a loud
voice announce his preferences. The candidates were frequently
present and publicly thanked those who had just voted for them.
One of the clerks would record each choice on a large poll
sheet. The excitement of a close contest was magnified by the
practice of oral voting. Anyone present could usually tell how
the race stood, simply by obtaining the latest count from the
clerks at the table. Sometimes loud cheers could be heard as
one candidate pulled ahead of another. The proceedings would
continue in this manner until it appeared that all the votes were
in. Ultimately, the sheriff would call out, "Gentlemen Freeholders, come into court, and give your votes, or the poll will be
closed." Following any last-minute entries, the final tally would
be made and the winners declared.

    Robert Munford's early comedy about eighteenth-century Virginia elections, The Candidates (1770), provides a great deal of insight into the politics of the time and what transpired on Election Day. The plot is rather simple. Wou'dbe, an honorable gentleman, seeks to be reelected to a seat in the House of Burgesses. In past sessions of the legislature, he and another impeccable figure, named Worthy, have represented the county, but now Worthy has chosen not to run again. With this decision, three individuals of questionable character enter the race. These are Sir John Toddy, "a convivial sot"; Strutabout, "a conceited shallow coxcomb"; and Smallhopes, "a gentleman chiefly distinguished for his devotion to horsemanship." The play's action revolves about the strivings of these last three men for success at the polls. As in many Virginia elections in this era, there are no outstanding issues, though that did not stop one campaigner from making outrageous statements in hopes of gaining public support. Of Strutabout it was said, "He'll promise to move mountains. He'll make the rivers navigable, and bring the tide over the tops of the hills for votes."

The contest was fought primarily on the basis of the candidates' personal traits and of the prestigious alliance formed by two of the men running. This point is made clear by the climax of the play, when Wou'dbe is offered a dishonorable alliance, spurns it, and seems destined to lose; Worthy, observing the outrageous tactics of the other candidates, reconsiders his decision to retire and rejoins the fray. In the end virtue triumphs. With Worthy and Wou'dbe standing together again, their less than upstanding opponents are sent down to ignominious defeat. Indeed, Worthy and Wou'dbe are elected by acclamation. and their victory is celebrated by their supporters in the last scene, which is presented below.

SCENE IV. *The Court-house yard.*
The door open, and a number of freeholders seen crouding within

1st Freeholder. (*to a freeholder coming out of the house*) How do votes go, neighbour? for Wou'dbe and Worthy?

2d Freeholder. Aye, aye, they're just come, and sit upon the bench, and yet all the votes are for them. 'Tis quite a hollow thing. The poll will soon be over. The people croud so much, and vote so fast, you can hardly turn around.

1st *Freeholder.* How do Strutabout and Smallhopes look? very doleful, I reckon.

2d *Freeholder.* Like a thief under the gallows.

3d *Freeholder.* There you must be mistaken, neighbour; for two can't be like one.

1ˢᵗ & 2d Freeholders. Ha, ha, ha,—a good joke, a good joke.

3d Freeholder. Not so good neither, when the subject made it so easy.

1ˢᵗ & 2d Freeholders. Better and better, ha, ha, ha. Huzza for Worthy and Wou'dbe! and confusion to Strutabout and Smallhopes.

   Enter Guzzle.

Guzzle. Huzza for Wou'dbe and Worthy! and huzza for Sir John Toddy! tho' he reclines.

1ˢᵗ Freeholder. So Guzzle, your friend Sir John reclines, does he? I think he does right.

Guzzle. You think he does right! pray sir, what right have you to think about it? nobody but a fool would kick a fallen man lower.

1ˢᵗ Freeholder. Sir, I won't be called a fool by any man, I'll have you to know, sir.

Guzzle. Then you ought'nt to be one; but here's at ye, adrat ye, if ye're for a quarrel. Sir John Toddy would have stood a good chance, and I'll maintain it, come on, damn ye.

1ˢᵗ Freeholder. Oh! as for fighting, there I'm your servant; a drunkard is as bad to fight as a madman. *(runs off.)*

Guzzle. Houroa, houroa, you see no body so good at a battle as a staunch toper. The milksops are afraid of them to a man.

3d Freeholder. You knew he was a coward before you thought proper to attack him; if you think yourself so brave, try your hand upon me, and you'll find you're mistaken.

Guzzle. For the matter of that, I'm the best judge myself; good day, my dear, good day. Huzza, for Sir John Toddy. [*Exit.*]

3d Freeholder. How weak must Sir John be to be governed by such a wretch as Guzzle!

   The Sheriff comes to the door, and says,

Gentlemen freeholders, come into court, and give your votes, or the poll will be closed.

Freeholders. We've all voted.

Sheriff. The poll's closed. Mr. Wou'dbe and Mr. Worthy are elected.

Freeholders without and within. Huzza—huzza! Wou'dbe and Worthy for ever, boys, bring 'em on, bring 'em on, Wou'dbe and Worthy for ever!

   Enter Wou'dbe and Worthy, in two chairs, raised aloft by the freeholders.

Freeholders all.—Huzza, for Wou'dbe and Worthy—Huzza for Wou'dbe and Worthy—huzza, for Wou'dbe and Worthy!—*(they traverse the stage, and then set them down.)*

Worthy. Gentlemen, I'm much obliged to you for the signal proof you have given me to-day of your regard. You may depend upon it, that I shall endeavour faithfully to discharge the trust you have reposed in me.

Wou'dbe. I have not only, gentlemen, to return my hearty thanks for the favours you have conferred upon me, but I beg leave also to thank you for shewing such regard to the merit of my friend. You have in that, shewn your judgment, and a spirit of independence becoming Virginians.

Capt. P. So we have Mr. Wou'dbe, we have done as we ought, we have elected the ablest, according to the writ.

> Henceforth, let those who pray for wholesome laws,
> And all well-wishers to their country's cause,
> Like us refuse a coxcomb—choose a man—
> Then let our senate blunder if it can.

[*Exit omnes.*]

END OF THE CANDIDATES.

Source: Robert Munford, *The Candidates* (Williamsburg, Va., 1770).

---

(3) Pageantry and Partisanship—Westchester County, New York, 1733

The middle colonies, such as New York, witnessed a much greater amount of partisan conflict than did other regions. Clashes between imperial and local interests, conflicts between various merchant and landed groups, plus ethnic and religious differences—English and Dutch, Anglican and Dissenter—made New York a veritable battleground for the opposing sides at election time. One of the hardest-fought elections in the colony's history occurred in Westchester County in October 1733, during the administration of royal governor William Cosby. Governor Cosby's corrupt and arbitrary policies had alienated many local interests; in particular, a great deal of bitterness had arisen over his ouster of "country party" leader Lewis Morris as chief justice of the province. Morris sought vindication by running for a seat in the legislature against Cosby ally William Forster. As can be seen in the accompanying narrative, Forster, despite the backing of the "court" faction in Westchester, proved no match for Morris and his "country" followers, receiving only 36 percent of the vote. Besides illustrating the factional rivalry that existed in New

York, this event furnishes us with an example of the extensive pageantry that sometimes became part of colonial elections. What is described has some similarity to the colorful spectacles that characterized political contests in England at this time, and it foreshadows the kind of ritual display that increasingly took place in America in the next century.

Westchester, October 29th, 1733.

On this Day, *Lewis Morris*, Esq., late Chief Justice of this Province, was by a great Majority of Voices, elected a Representative for the County of *Westchester*.

This being an Election of great Expectation, and where in the Court and Country's Interest was exerted (as is said) to the Utmost: I shall give my Readers, a particular Account of it, as I had from a Person that was present at it.

Nicholas Cooper, Esq., High Sheriff of the said County, having by Papers affixed to the Church of *East-Chester*, and other Publick Places, given Notice of the Day and Place of Election, without mentioning any Time of the Day, when it was to be done; which made the Electors on the Side of the late Judge, verry Suspitious that some Fraud was intended: To prevent which about 50 of them kept Watch upon and about, the Green at *Eastchester*, (the Place of Election,) from 12 o'Clock the Night before, 'til the Morning of that Day: The other Electors begining to move on Sunday Afternoon and Evening, so as to be at *New-Rochell*, by Midnight, their Way lay through *Harrison's* Purchase, the Inhabitants of which provided for their Entertainment, as they pass'd each House in their Way, having a Table plentifully covered for that Purpose; about Midnight they all met at the House of *William Lecount*, at *New-Rochell*, whose House not being large enough to entertain so great a Number, a large Fire was made in the Street, by which they sat 'til Day-Light, at which Time they began to move; they were joynd on the Hill at the East end of the Town, by about 70 Horse of the Electors of the lower Part of the County, and then proceeded towards the Place of Election in the following Order, *viz*. First rode two Trumpeters and 3 Violines; next 4 of the principal Freeholders, one of which carried a Banner, on one Side of which was affixed in gold Capitals KING GEORGE, and on the Other, in like golden Capitals LIBERTY & LAW; next followed the Candidate *Lewis Morris* Esq., late Chief Justice of this Province; then two Colours; and at Sun rising they entered upon the Green of *Eastchester* the Place of Election, follow'd by above 300 Horse of the principal Freeholders of the County, (a greater Number than had ever appear'd for one Man since the Settlement of that County:) After having rode three Times round the Green, they went to the Houses of *Joseph Fowler* and——*Child*, who were well prepared for their Reception, and the late Chief Justice, on his allighting by several Gentleman, who came there to give their Votes for him.

About Eleven of the Clock appeared the Candidate of the other Side, *William Forster* Esq., School Master, appointed by the Society for Propagation of the Gospel, and lately made by Commission from his Excellency (the present Governour,) Clerk of the Peace and common Pleas, in that County; which Commission it is said, he purchased for the valuable Consideration of One Hundred Pistoles given the Governor; next him, came two Ensignes, born by two of the Freeholders; then followed the Honourable *James Delancey*, Esq., Chief Justice of the Province of New-York, and the honourable *Frederick Philipse*, Esq., second Judge of the said Province, and Baron of the EXCHEQUER, attended by about 170 Horse of the Freeholders and Friends of the said *Forster*; and the two Judges they entred the Green on the *East* side, and riding twice round it, their Word was *No Land-Tax*, as they passed, the second Judge very civilly saluted the Chief Justice by taking off his Hat, which the late Judge returned in the same Manner: Some of the late Judges Party crying out no *Excise*, and one of them was heard to say (tho not by the Judge) no Pretender, upon which, *Forster*, the Candidate, reply'd, *I will take Notice of you*, they after that, retired to the House of——*Baker*, which was prepared to receive and entertain them. About an Hour after, the High Sheriff came to Town finely mounted, the Housings and Holster-Caps being Scarlet, richly laced with Silver belonging to——: Upon his approach the Electors on both Sides went into the Green, where they were to Elect, and after having read his Majesty's Writ, bid the Electors to proceed to the Choice which they did; and a great Majority appeared for Mr. *Morris*, the late Judge: Upon which a Poll was demanded, but by whom is not known to the Relator, tho' it was said by many, to be done by the Sheriff himself. *Morris*, the Candidate several Times asked the Sheriff upon whose Side the Majority appeard, but could get no other reply, but that a Poll must be had, and accordingly after about two Hours delay, in geting Benches, Chairs, and Tables they began to Poll: Soon after one of those called Quakers, a Man of known Worth and Estate, came to give his Vote for the late Judge, upon this *Forster* and the two *Fowlers, Moses and William*, chosen by him to be Inspectors questioned his having an Estate, and required of the Sheriff to tender him the Book to Swear, in due Form of Law, which he refused to do, but offered to take his solemn Affirmation; which noth [noted] by the Laws of England and the Laws of this Province was indulged to the People called Quakers, and had always been practised from the first Election of Representatives, in this Province to this Time, and never refused; but the Sheriff was deaf to all that could be alledged on that Side; and notwithstanding, that he was told both by the late Chief Justice, and *James Alexander*, Esq; One of His Majesty's Council, and Councellor at Law, and by *William Smith*, Esq; Councellor

at Law, That such a Procedure was contrary to Law, and a violent Attempt of the Liberties of the People: He still persisted in refusing the
said Quaker to Vote; and in like Manner did refuse Seven and Thirty
Quakers more, Men of known and visible Estates.

This *Cooper*, now High-Sheriff of the said County, is said, not only to
be a Stranger in that County, not having a Foot of Land, or other visible
Estate in it, unless very lately granted; and it is believ'd, he has not where
with all to purchase any.

The Polling had not been long continued, before Mr. *Edward Stephens*,
a Man of a very considerable Estate in the said County, did openly in
the Hearing of all the Freeholders there assembled, charge *William Forster*, Esq; the Candidate on the other Side, with being a *Jacobite*, and in
the Interest of the *Pretender*; and that he should say to Mr. *William Willet*,
(a Person of good Estate, and known Integrity, who was at the Time
present, and ready to make Oath to the Truth of what was said) that
true it was, he had taken the Oaths to his Majesty King GEORGE, and
enjoy'd a Place in the Government under Him, which gave him Bread:
Yet notwithstanding That, should—*James* come into *England*, he should
think himself oblig'd to go there and Fight for him. This was loudly and
strongly urged to *Forster's* Face, who denied it to be true; and no more
was said of it at that Time.

About Eleven o'Clock that Night the Poll was clos'd. And it stood thus:

> For the late Chief Justice, ... 231
> Quakers, ... 38
> In all. 269
>
> For William Forster, Esq; 151
> The Difference 118
>   269

So that the late Chief Justice carried it by a great Majority, without the
Quakers. Upon closing the Poll, the other Candidate, *Forster*, and the
Sheriff, wish'd the late Chief Justice much Joy. *Forster*, said, he hop'd the
late Judge would not think the worse of him for setting up against him,
to which the Judge reply'd, he *believed that he was put upon it against his
Inclination; but that he was highly blamable, and who did or should know better
for putting the Sheriff, who was a Stranger and ignorant in such Matters, upon
making so violent an Attempt upon the Liberties of the People; which, would
expose him to Ruin, if he were worth £10,000 if the People agriev'd should
commence Suit against him.* The People made a loud Huzza, which the
late Chief Judge blam'd very much, as what he tho't not right: *Forster*
reply'd, *He took no Notice of what the common People did, since Mr. Morris
did not put them upon the doing of it.*

The Indentures being seal'd, the whole Body of Electors, waited on
their new Representative to his Lod[g]ings, with Trumpets sounding,

and Violines playing; and in a little Time took their Leave of him: And thus ended the *Westchester* Election, to the general Satisfaction.

Source: New York Weekly Journal, November 5, 1733.

---

(4) Benjamin Franklin's Side Defeated by Proprietary Faction—Philadelphia, 1764

Probably the most tumultuous elections anywhere in the American colonies took place in Pennsylvania during the mid-1760s. Partisan conflict in this province was aggravated by the existence of strong ethnic rivalries, as well as by the fact that the government of the colony was overseen by the Penn family, which refused to allow its extensive landholdings to be taxed for the common good. The opposition, led by Benjamin Franklin and backed by the Quakers, tried to build enough support to make Pennsylvania a royal colony, but the Proprietary party, or "New ticket," as it was sometimes called, worked successfully to block this move. The voters were perhaps unwilling to risk being taken over by the Crown at this juncture and therefore rejected Franklin's party at the polls, especially in the city of Philadelphia, where Franklin himself suffered a major defeat. (There were two separate slates chosen in Philadelphia, one for the city and another for the county.) The description of the Assembly contest given below indicates that in cases like this, where feelings ran high and many thousands took part, strict procedure was set aside, and individuals who may not have been qualified were herded to the ballot box and allowed to cast votes. No mention is made in the document of any festive aspect to this Election Day, but it is probable that some form of celebration occurred once the polls had closed.

I don't remember that I have told you anything about our late election, which was really a hard fought one and managed with more decency and good manners than would have been expected from such irritated partisans as appeared as the champions on each side. The most active, or rather at the head of the active on the old side, appeared Abel James and Thomas Wharton; and on the new side John Lawrence seemed to lead the van. The Dutch Calvinists and the Presbyterians of both houses, I believe to a man, assisted the new ticket. The church were divided and so were the Dutch Lutherans. The Moravians and most of the Quakers were the grand supporters of the old; the McClenaghanites were divided, though chiefly of the old side.

The poll was opened about nine in the morning, the first of October, and the steps so crowded, till between eleven and twelve at night, that at no time a person could get up in less than a quarter of an hour from his entrance at the bottom, for they could go no faster than the whole column moved. About three in the morning, the advocates for the new ticket moved for a close, but (Oh! fatal mistake!) the old hands kept it open, as they had a reserve of the aged and lame, which could not come in the crowd and were called up and brought out in chairs and litters, etc., and some who needed no help, between three and six o'clock, about two hundred voters. As both sides took care to have spies all night, the alarm was given to the new ticket men. Horsemen and footmen were immediately dispatched to Germantown, etc., and by nine or ten o'clock they began to pour in, so that after the move for a close, seven or eight hundred votes were procured; about five hundred, or near it, of which were for the new ticket and they did not close till three in the afternoon, and it took them till one next day to count them off.

The new ticket carried all but Harrison and Antis, and Fox and Hughes came in their room [place]; but it is surprising that from upward of 3,900 votes they should be so near each other. Mr. Willing and Mr. Bryan were elected burgesses by a majority of upward of one hundred votes, though the whole number was but about 1,300. Mr. Franklin died like a philosopher. But Mr. Galloway *agonized in death* like a mortal deist who has no hopes of a future existence.

The other counties returned nearly the same members who had served them before, so that the old faction have still considerable majority in the house. Mr. Norris was as usual elected speaker, but finding the same factious disposition remained, and a resolution to pursue the scheme for a change of the government, he declined the chair and withdrew himself from the house, whereupon Joseph Fox, Esq., was chosen speaker. But the governor being absent (attending his lower county assembly), they dispensed with the form of presenting him for approbation and went upon business. The first, or one of the first, resolves they made was to send Mr. Franklin to London in the capacity of agent for the province, to assist Mr. Jackson.

Source: William B. Reed, *Life and Correspondence of Joseph Reed* (Philadelphia, 1847), 1:36–37.

(5) Ritual Elections of Negro "Governors" in New England, c.1750–1830

Throughout the colonial era, African Americans were generally excluded from the electoral process. Although free Negroes appear to have cast ballots in a few places in the late seventeenth and early eighteenth centuries, subsequent legislation eventually barred almost all persons of color from voting. Black slaves, of course, never had any political rights from the outset. Nevertheless, the slaves in some New England towns seem to have created their own ritual election contests and to have celebrated the annual choice of their own Negro "governors." Such events usually coincided with the general election in the particular colony, when the actual (white) governor and other officials were being chosen. (The Negro governor was primarily a symbolic figure without any real authority, though the person selected often had achieved a certain level of respect within the local black community.) "Lection Day," as it was popularly known, was normally part of a holiday period for blacks and accompanied by a considerable amount of high-spirited fun and revelry. Indeed, there was probably more revelry associated with these unofficial gatherings of blacks than with the regular New England elections, where whites of Puritan background were the chief participants. There is no evidence of such events involving blacks taking place elsewhere in the American colonies. Perhaps the greater amount of liberty accorded slaves in New England enabled them to engage in behavior that would not have been permissible farther south. In any case, this ceremonial custom continued to be followed in a number of northern states down through the early decades of the nineteenth century. At that point, blacks began seeking actual political rights.

One form of diversion seems to have been peculiar to the New England slaves: the celebrated "election" of Negro "governors," which was followed by an elaborate inauguration ceremony terminating in feasting and games. Evidences of the "election" of Negro "Governors," which seems to have begun about the middle of the eighteenth century, have been found in all of the New England colonies. The "elections" varied as to time in the different colonies: in Massachusetts the slaves were allowed a vacation from the last Wednesday in May to the close of the week; in Rhode Island, election day fell on the third Saturday of June, while in Connecticut the slaves held "local elections" on the Saturday following the general election, and sent the results to Hartford. Whether "kings" were elected as in New Hampshire, or "Governors," as in the other colonies, it is probable that the master class supervised these celebrations.

On "Lection Day," as they called it, the slaves were fitted out in their best clothing and, since the dress of the slave was held to reflect the opulence of his master, owners are said to have vied with one another to see whose slave would be the best attired. As a result, many negroes were arrayed in all sorts of cast-off finery, even including pomaded wigs, and on this occasion some of them rode their masters' horses or even borrowed their owners' carriages. Following an elaborate reception, the election began about ten in the morning. Friends of each candidate then arranged themselves on either side of a line, with their favorite at the head, while votes for the rivals were cast. After a stated time all movement from one side of the line to the other was stopped, silence was enjoined, and the votes were counted by the chief marshal, who later announced the winner. The inauguration then followed; and the defeated candidate, after his introduction by the chief marshal, drank the first toast to his successful opponent. In the conviviality of the inaugural banquet all animosities were forgotten. With the newly elected "governor" presiding, his lady on his left and the losing candidate on his right, the day ended merrily with dancing, games of quoits and other sports.

Source: Lorenzo Greene, *The Negro in Colonial New England* (New York: Columbia University Press, 1942), 249–51.

---

(6) Partisan Division in Postrevolutionary Pennsylvania— Philadelphia, 1785

The competitiveness of elections fell off in the majority of colonies in the 1770s. As Americans closed ranks in response to the crisis with the mother country, the amount of internal rivalry at the polls declined. With the outbreak of war in 1775–76, voting often had to be curtailed and in some cases completely suspended. However, once victory over England was obtained and peace established in the early 1780s, the new state governments went into full operation, and the number of contested elections picked up considerably. Election Day now became a more politically meaningful event. The system was no longer under royal control, and many officials that had been appointed by the Crown were now popularly elected. In addition, the common people began to play bigger roles in the electoral process. Many in the past who had been just casual spectators were now full participants. Their experiences in the war had made them more conscious of their rights and better informed about current issues. When Election Day neared, remarked one contemporary, "the curiosity and interest of the inhabitants were aroused." Nevertheless, the world was not entirely turned upside down, especially in terms of the outcome. One astute foreign visitor, Count Francesco Dal Verme of Milan, after watching the election proceedings in Philadelphia in 1783, noted that despite the greater involvement of the lower classes, "the rich," there as elsewhere, were still "more influential than others."

The city of Philadelphia, and in fact the whole state of Pennsylvania, probably experienced the most competitive elections anywhere in America. The intense factionalism of the war never died down, as two highly organized political groups constantly vied for voter support. On one side were the "Constitutionalists," vigorous defenders of the state's new democratic constitution, advocates of paper money as an economic panacea, and fierce anti-Loyalists. On the other side were the "Republicans," representing the commercial elite, who disliked the state constitution, condemned the issuance of paper money, and opposed the stringent "test laws" that were still being applied to wartime Loyalists. Although they eventually fell into disfavor, the Constitutionalists, with strong support from small farmers and artisans (especially among Presbyterians), managed to remain in power till the mid 1780s, denouncing their well-to-do, conservative opponents as aristocrats and Tories. The following article conveys the intensity of the postrevolutionary election contests in the "city of brotherly love," particularly in its description of the vote-getting efforts made by the two camps on the day the polls opened. The author even gives a sense of the actual words used by those taking part in the electioneering as the voters approached the ballot box. In the end, he takes a rather dim view of the partisan attempts to influence the voters in their choices, believing that such actions undermined the idea of "free and voluntary" elections.

Yesterday, being the day appointed for holding the general election for this commonwealth, the inhabitants of this city, composed of a mixed assemblage of various nations, ranks, degrees, ages, fixes, and complexions, proceeded to the state-house, to exercise the sacred right of investing with legislative and executive powers, such of their fellow-citizens

as a majority of them might deem most worthy of the important trust.
What a noble idea must we not have of that constitution, which annually
strips the garments of office from its servants, awakes them from the
intoxicating delirium of power, and plunges them into the mass of the
people! May PENNSYLVANIA never cease to prize this inestimable privilege proportionably to its value! May her sons, till time shall be no more,
esteem life, when compared with it, as beneath the smallest regard!

The exalted reflections that must arise in every philosophic mind, on
beholding such a scene, were considerably allayed by the barefaced exertions made in the streets by the scouting advanced partizans of both
republicans and constitutionalists, to influence the electors in the choice
of their ticket.

"Well, Tom, going to vote?—Say?"—Yes—surely—"My dear fellow,
here's the staunch supporters of the constitution—your approved
friends—men who have taken care of the mechanic's interest—huzza!—
they are for the paper-money—Damn the bank—down with the bank
for ever!—We'll have no nabobs—no great men—no *aristocrats*—huzza,
boys!—Success to the constitution for ever!"——"My dear friends!—
Happy to see you!—How are you, Jack?—How's all your family, Bill?—
What's the matter with you, Ned?—How do, Harry?—Welcome to Philadelphia, once more, Dick.—Are you going to vote?—Here's the ticket—
friends of equal liberty—men who understand trade and commerce—
not the damned prospeteran [Presbyterian] crew, who ride rough-shod
over the people, like Oliver Cromwell—huzza!—Three cheers!—Commerce and equal liberty for ever!—Come on, my lads, come on!"

[The ballots are counted, and the Republicans carry both the city and
county of Philadelphia "by a considerable majority." The article then lists
the names of the winners.]

It is a long established maxim, that the existence of liberty depends on
the purity of representation, which equally depends on the freedom of
election. Every friend of this country must, then, have beheld with in-
dignation the undue steps taken to influence the votes of the electors of
this city . . . by both parties. Can the election be "free and voluntary," as
the constitution declares it "shall be," when persons go from house to
house, ransacking every story from cellar to garret, begging, praying and
insisting on votes—and exhorting promises of them?—Certainly not. The
constitution expressly forbids any candidate "directly or indirectly to
give, promise, or bestow any rewards" for the purpose of procuring his
election.—This is a nugatory proviso, if agents are permitted to bias the
votes of electors.

Source: Pennsylvania Evening Herald, October 12, 1785.

(7) Violence and Bloodshed in Postrevolutionary Delaware—Sussex County, 1787

After Pennsylvania, the neighboring state of Delaware experienced some of the most aggressively fought elections in the postwar period. Indeed, the annual battles for seats in the small state legislature were often so bitter that the protagonists on both sides turned to violence or the threat of it to influence the outcomes. In many cases armed men prevented prospective voters from casting ballots. The Whig-Tory divisions that had existed here before and during the war showed no sign of abating even after the peace treaty was signed. During the 1780s power shifted back and forth between the two adversaries. First the Whigs gained control of a majority of seats, then the Tory faction took over. The climax came in 1787, when militia bands in Sussex County caused a great deal of bloodshed among both voters and spectators near the polling site. Moreover, the results of the balloting were so sharply disputed that a second election had to be called. Irregularities marred this contest too, but the Tory legislative majority, eager to end the whole controversy, rejected the Whig protests and accepted the winning Tory ticket as valid. In the following selection, a member of the Whig opposition describes this second, highly irregular Sussex election in 1787, in which, he charges, military-style intimidation was used to prevent a fair and honest outcome.

In Sussex, they were to elect representatives, as well as delegates to the state convention. The tory candidates had gone home from the last meeting of the legislature minutely instructed as to a plan, by which they might defend the freedom of election for their refugees and black campers. The constitution of the state requires, that no military force shall be within a mile of the place of election. They were therefore instructed to raise what force they pleased, only to keep it a mile off to serve in case of exigency. Secure in the favour and protection of the legislature, the tories made large provision of arms and ammunition; marked out a camp, at a proper distance, before hand; and on the day of election, marched in companies, with drums and fifes, to the appointed field of encampment. From this place of arms, where a guard of several hundred men stood constantly paraded, they marched in companies to the place of election, and carried their whole ticket of representatives and convention-men, without opposition. For certain leading characters

among the Whigs, employed all their assiduity and address, to prevent
the Whigs from going to the election. They foresaw that bloodshed
would be the inevitable consequence of a meeting of the parties in arms;
and they could not imagine any possible event of the election to be
equivalent to such a misfortune. With much difficulty the whigs were
restrained and encouraged to hope for a constitutional redress of their
grievances. . . .

At a meeting of the legislature, in January, petitions were received
from 504 inhabitants of Sussex, praying to be heard by council, as to a
variety of facts stated in their petitions, showing the late election for
representatives to be illegal. . . .

It was proved and admitted on all hands, that with the cognizance
and concurrence of the members elected, companies of armed men with
drums and fifes, moved on from all quarters of the county, and joined
in full force at an open field, about a mile from the place of election; that
they there formed in military array, under superior and inferior officers;
that their commander in chief was a member of Congress, and their
second in command a refugee; that their ostensible purpose was to protect the privileges of election; and their chief conversation consisted of
cursing Presbyterians and Irish-men; that sundry of the whigs were
taken prisoners by this armed body, and could no otherwise be released,
but by order of the Commander in Chief; that the body of the whigs of
the county did not attend the election, on account of this armed force;
that from the field they marched in companies and voted, while a guard
of several hundred remained constantly under arms. . . . Many witnesses
declared, that a number of persons were armed at the place of election,
as well as in the field; and one witness deposed, that he believed half
the people at the house of election were armed with clubs and other
weapons. It was also given in evidence, that sundry persons were in-
sulted and violently assaulted, professedly because they were whigs,
Presbyterians, or Irish-men; that one fellow in particular, after assaulting
a whig with several blows, swore his tooth had grown an inch on that
day, that he might eat Presbyterians and Irish-men; that some huzzaed
for the King, and others expressed a hope, that they might again come
under the old government. It was agreed by all, and acknowledged by
the sheriff, that, before the election was closed, he had called in 40 or 50
armed men from the field, as a guard round the house where the election
was held.

The council for the petitioners respectfully set forth, the dangers of
infringing the freedom of election; that from the testimony adduced, the
whigs and best citizens of the county of Sussex, were manifestly restrained from attending, and the freedom of election infringed; lastly,
that calling in the aid of an armed force, to protect an election in a
military manner, must vitiate such election. Besides the constitution and

the laws of the state, many learned authorities were quoted, to shew the great abhorrence the freedom of election had to every kind of military force. He therefore hoped and expected the honorable house of assembly would widely determine the late election of Sussex to be illegal and void.

Source: Timoleon, pseud., *The Biographical History of Dionysius* (Philadelphia, 1788), 74–77.

The Early National Period, 1789–1828

Voting for members of the new national government established under the new federal Constitution soon brought a new level of excitement to Election Day. Elections became more competitive than before, especially in those states south of New England where partisan activity had long existed. As campaigns were still relatively brief, Election Day itself was still a time of much electioneering, heavy drinking, and sometimes tumults and riots. A Frenchman traveling through Virginia and Maryland in the early 1790s declared that "election days are days of reveling, of brawls; and the candidates offer drunkenness openly to anyone who is willing to give them his vote. The taverns are occupied by the parties. The citizens flock to the standards of the candidates; and the voting place is often surrounded by men armed with clubs, who drive back and intimidate the citizens of the other party.... The inhabitants of the rural sections go on horseback, and in groups, filing by in pairs. Drummers, followed by bribed persons, and crying loudly, huzza, complete the warlike confusion of an election day. Women go about canvassing, running from shop to shop; they beg for votes."(Ferdinand Bayard, *Travels of a Frenchman in Maryland and Virginia*, p. 66.) Even if what Bayard recorded was not typical everywhere, clearly the activities described were increasingly common by this time. As contending interests in many states established political parties over the next few years, competitive elections between Federalists, who sympathized with the probusiness and "strong government" ideas of Alexander Hamilton, and Republicans, who sympathized with the pro-agrarian and "limited government" ideas of Thomas Jefferson, were becoming the norm. This intensified "the warlike confusion of an election day" even further.

---

(8) John Marshall's Election to Congress—Richmond, Virginia, 1799

Partisan strife, which began on a small scale in the early 1790s, grew more heated as the decade wore on. After the first contested presidential election in 1796, in which John Adams and the Federalist ticket narrowly defeated Thomas Jefferson and the Republican side, tensions increased further during the next couple of years. For the United States it was a time of deepening conflict with France and rising division at home, particularly over passage by Federalists in Congress of the Alien and Sedition Acts (1798), which sought to silence critics of the government. Fierce battles occurred in several districts during the next round of congressional elections (1798–99), one of which attracted a considerable amount of national attention. It pitted arch-Federalist and future Supreme Court chief justice John Marshall against a feisty Republican opponent, John Clopton, each seeking to represent the area around Richmond, Virginia. Prior to the election, Clopton and his supporters accused Marshall of hiding his extreme Federalist views from the public and condemned his extravagances as a campaigner. One editor ridiculed Marshall as "the pay-master of strong liquors, the barbecue representative of Richmond." The proceedings at the polling place, as reconstructed below by Marshall's later biographer, Albert J. Beveridge, show that some of the traditions followed in the previous era—voice voting and contestants thanking electors—still prevailed. Yet the seriousness and intense partisanship of the race made it a far different experience than the kind of gentlemanly rivalry depicted in Robert Munford's *The Candidates.*

Late in April the election was held. A witness of that event in Richmond tells of the incidents of the voting which were stirring even for that period of turbulent politics. A long, broad table or bench was placed on the Court-House Green, and upon it the local magistrates, acting as election judges, took their seats, their clerks before them. By the side of the judges sat the two candidates for Congress; and when an elector declared his preference for either, the favored one rose, bowing, and thanked his supporter.

Nobody but freeholders could then exercise the suffrage in Virginia. Any one owning one hundred acres of land or more in any county could vote, and this landowner could declare his choice in every county in which he possessed the necessary real estate. The voter did not cast a printed or written ballot, but merely stated, in the presence of the two candidates, the election officials, and the assembled gathering, the name of the candidate of his preference. There was no specified form for this announcement.

"I vote for John Marshall."

"Thank you, sir," said the lank, easy-mannered Federalist candidate.

"Hurrah for Marshall!" shouted the compact band of Federalists.

"And I vote for Clopton," cried another freeholder.

"May you live a thousand years, my friend," said Marshall's competitor.

"Three cheers for Clopton!" roared the crowd of Republican enthusiasts.

Both Republican and Federalist leaders had seen to it that nothing was left undone which might bring victory to their respective candidates. The two political parties had been carefully "drilled to move together in a body." Each party had a business committee which attended to every practical detail of the election. Not a voter was overlooked. "Sick men were taken in their beds to the polls; the halt, the lame, and the blind were hunted up and every mode of conveyance was mustered into service." Time and again the vote was a tie. No sooner did one freeholder announce his preference for Marshall than another gave his suffrage to Clopton.

"A barrel of whisky with the head knocked in," free for everybody, stood beneath a tree; and "the majority took it straight," runs a narrative of a witness of the scene. So hot became the contest that fist-fights were frequent. During the afternoon, knock-down and drag-out affrays became so general that the county justices had hard work to quell the raging partisans. Throughout the day the shouting and huzzaing rose in volume as the whiskey sank in the barrel. At times the uproar was "perfectly deafening; men were shaking fists at each other, rolling up their sleeves, cursing and swearing. . . . Some became wild with agitation." When a tie was broken by a new voter shouting that he was for Marshall or for Clopton, insults were hurled at his devoted head.

"You, sir, ought to have your mouth smashed," cried an enraged Republican when Thomas Rutherford voted for Marshall; and smashing of mouths, blacking of eyes, and breaking of heads there were in plenty. "The crowd rolled to and fro like a surging wave." Never before and seldom, if ever, since, in the history of Virginia, was any election so fiercely contested. When this "democratic" struggle was over, it was found that Marshall had been elected by the slender majority of 108.

Washington was overjoyed at the Federalist success. He had ridden ten miles to vote for General [Henry] Lee, who was elected; but he took a special delight in Marshall's victory. He hastened to write his political protege: "With infinite pleasure I received the news of your Election. For the honor of the District I wish the majority had been greater; but let us be content, and hope, as the tide is turning, the current will soon run strong in your favor."

Source: Albert J. Beveridge, *The Life of John Marshall* (Boston: Houghton Mifflin Company, 1916), 1:413–16.

---

(9) Aaron Burr Leads Republicans to Victory—New York, 1800

The election of 1800, with Republican leader Thomas Jefferson once again challenging Federalist stalwart John Adams for the presidency, was by far the largest and most heated encounter in the early years of the republic. The magnitude of electioneering would not be surpassed for almost a quarter of a century. More people were involved, more literature was distributed, and more canvassing went on than in any major race before the Jacksonian era. Yet for all the activity involved it was by no means a national campaign. No national organizations existed on either side, and no attempt was made to oversee the entire operation. State parties may have received advice from the national leaders, but each acted more or less independently. Moreover, the election system still lacked any semblance of uniformity. Voting in the sixteen states occurred at different times under different laws, and in some cases the electoral results hinged upon local legislative contests. Only five states permitted the designation of presidential electors by direct popular vote.

The biggest state contest occurred in New York, beginning on the last day of April. New York possessed twelve crucial electoral votes, which were to be designated by the newly chosen state legislature. Because the overconfident Federalists refused to adopt the district system, the election became a winner-take-all situation for the party that obtained a majority. Thus, Aaron Burr, Jefferson's running mate and the man in charge of the state's Republican campaign, needed to achieve a clear-cut victory. New York City held the key, and to entice straddlers Burr put together an attractive ticket, persuading such notables as former governor George Clinton and Revolutionary War general Horatio Gates to appear on the slate. Leaving little to chance, he also built an innovative local machine—creating a finance committee, setting up ward and precinct meetings, compiling a list of past voter preferences. On the morning the balloting began, the Burr-led Republicans had numerous "carriages, chairs, and waggons" ready to transport their party's supporters to the various voting sites. In addition, guards were hired in each ward to make sure that no fraud was committed during the counting process. Alexander Hamilton, in command of the Federalist forces, sought to counter Burr's actions through his own burst of electioneering activity, but his effort was in vain. The Republicans triumphed by a wide margin, enabling the party to capture the state's twelve electoral votes. Matthew L. Davis, the editor of Burr's memoirs, presents a brief description of what happened in New York City over the three-day voting period and its aftermath, including a subsequent attempt by Federalist extremists to nullify the results.

Those who possess a knowledge of the character of Colonel Burr know what were his qualifications for execution. The plan of the campaign having been opened, it only remained to be executed. In the performance of this duty, all Mr. Burr's industry, perseverance, and energy were called into operation. Nor were the federal party idle or inactive. They possessed wealth and patronage. Led on to the contest by their talented chieftain, General Hamilton, whose influence in their ranks was unbounded, they made a desperate but ineffectual resistance to the assaults upon their political citadel. If defeated here, their power was gone, and the administration of the government lost. Both General Hamilton and Colonel Burr exerted themselves personally at the polls during the three days of election. They repeatedly addressed the people, and did all that men could do. They frequently met at the same polls, and argued, in the presence of large assemblages, the debatable questions. Their deportment towards each other and towards their opponents was such as comported with the dignity of two of the most accomplished and courtly gentlemen of the age in which they lived.

The polls of the elections opened on the morning of the 29th of April, and finally closed at sunset on the 1st of May. Immediately after, the inspectors commenced counting and canvassing the ballots. Sufficient progress was made during the night to render it, in a great measure, certain that the republican ticket had succeeded; and on the 2d of May this result was announced, the average majority being about 490. All doubts as to the presidential vote of the state of New York was now removed, unless the federal party, in their expiring agonies could devise some plan by which the will of the people, thus clearly expressed, should be defeated. Such apprehensions were entertained, and, it was soon discovered, not entertained without good reason.

In both branches of the legislature elected in 1799 the federalists had a majority. The time of service of the members would expire on the 1st of July, 1800. After the nomination of the republican assembly ticket, but previous to the election in April, 1800, it was suspected that certain federalists had in contemplation a project to render the city election null and void if the republicans succeeded. When the polls were closed, therefore, discreet and intelligent men were placed at them to guard, if it should be found necessary, the inspectors from committing, inadvertently, any errors, either in canvassing or making their returns. Every movement, subsequently, of leading federal gentlemen was narrowly and cautiously watched. The result of the election was announced on the 2d of May. On the 3d of May, in the evening, a select and confidential federal caucus was held. On the 4th a letter was written to William Duane, editor of the Aurora, stating that such a caucus had been held the preceding night, and that it was determined by the caucus to solicit Governor Jay to convene the existing legislature forthwith, for the purpose of changing the mode of choosing the electors for president, and placing it in the hands of the people by districts. The effect of such a measure would have been to neutralize the State of New York, and, as the result finally proved, would have secured to the federal party their president and vice-president.... [The author then tells how Governor John Jay found the suggestion distasteful and refused to go along with the Federalist proposal, which meant that the Republican victory was confirmed.]

Source: Matthew L. Davis, ed., *Memoirs of Aaron Burr, with Miscellaneous Selections from His Correspondence* (New York, 1836; reprint, Freeport, N.Y.: Books for Libraries Press, 1970), 2:60–61.

(10) Women Vote in Tainted Election—Essex County, New Jersey, 1807

As mentioned in the introduction, Election Day in the early years of the republic was still essentially an all-male experience. Although in certain locales some women might attend the proceedings as onlookers, almost none ever participated as voters. The one major exception to this standard was in the state of New Jersey. Either by design or by chance, the framers of that state's constitution in 1776 had permitted property-holding single women to exercise the right of suffrage, and a number of them would ultimately do so. Indeed, in 1790, such voting was reaffirmed by statute, and female turnout gradually increased over the next decade and a half. Both parties actively campaigned for women's votes at the turn of the nineteenth century, when the Federalist-Republican struggle reached its highest levels. The participation of women, however, eventually came under attack; it was charged that they were herded to the polls by partisan leaders and that they deposited multiple tickets in the ballot box. It was also claimed that some of the alleged female perpetrators were not even eligible voters. The biggest instance of such improper behavior is said to have occurred at an Essex County election in 1807, which was to decide where to build the new county courthouse, in Newark or at Day's Hill, near Elizabethtown. The election was deemed so fraudulent that it was later nullified. As the following description indicates, men were probably as much if not more at fault than the women. Regardless of that fact, the undeniable female complicity in the wrongdoing was subsequently used by members of the all-male legislature as a pretext to disenfranchise permanently all women in the state. The controversial Essex County election therefore was the last one in which New Jersey women participated on an equal basis for over a century.

It was agreed to submit the matter of the court-house location to a vote of the people, for which authority was obtained through a special act of the Legislature. In this election all single women and widows were allowed to vote, "only wives . . . being placed on a political level with infants and idiots." Neither was there any restriction in regard to color. Seven localities were placed in nomination for the site. These were distributed in Newark, Elizabethtown and Day's Hill, and the contest was ostensibly between the first and the last, Elizabethtown's choice being the latter, which was within its bounds. Great excitement attended the canvass, the election and the count succeeding it. Mass-meetings were held in all parts of the county, and the claims of the different localities were urged by a score of orators with a vigor and virulence not transcended even in the hottest of modern political contests. Everybody was enlisted in the war. Such animosity was engendered that it was not safe for Newark people to visit Elizabethtown or those who were active champions of the latter town's claim to enter the boundaries of Newark.

The election, which lasted three days, began at Day's Hill, Feb. 10, 1807. During the forenoon the election was believed to be fairly conducted, but in the afternoon illegal voting was commenced, and carried on with the utmost boldness until the close of the polls. Next day the struggle was transferred to the Elizabethtown polls, and there greater dishonesty prevailed than at Day's Hill. Next came Newark's chance, and here the corruption was more open and shameless than at either of the other places. As early as one o'clock in the morning of the day, big with the fate of Newark, the polls were opened at the old courthouse, and the third and conclusive day of the battle was begun. Aaron Munn was judge of the election. The voting had not long been in progress when fraud was resorted to, and carried on in every way known to the "ballot-box stuffers" of the times. "Repeating" was resorted to, by many who would in any other cause have scorned such action. Men usually honest seemed lost to all sense of honor, so completely were they carried away by the heat of the strife. Women vied with the men, and in some instances surpassed them, in illegal voting. Only a few years ago there were living in Newark two ladies, who, at the time of the election in their 'teens, voted six times each. Married women, too, indignant, perhaps, at being placed on the same political level as children and idiots, in defiance of the law, cast their ballots. Governor Pennington is said to have escorted to the polls "a strapping negress." Men and boys disguised themselves in women's attire, and crowded about the polls to assist in winning the day for Newark. Challenging seems not to have been resorted to. Vehicles of all kinds were pressed into service to transport the voters from one polling-place to another, voting at several being as common as voting "early and often" at one. Spies were sent to Elizabethtown at intervals to see how many more votes were wanted to keep ahead. Men were brought down the river in large gangs to cast their ballots when it was feared that the fight would be lost. The whole transaction was the broadest kind of a burlesque and the most flagrant outrage. At the close of the polls victory perched upon the Newark banners, but women suffrage was at an end in New Jersey, for the Legislature at its next session passed an act limiting the right to vote "to free white male citizens."

"The election," says the Newark *Centinel,* "was the most warm and spirited ever held in the county of Essex, and probably ever witnessed in the State. For weeks preceding the election the most indefatigable labor had been spent by each in organizing for the election. When the 10th of February arrived, every man stood ready at his post prepared for the combat; every town and village was divided into districts, and men specially appointed to see the electors to the polls. Every nerve was strained by each party to ensure success.

"On Saturday, when the county clerk proclaimed the majority in favor of Newark, the old court-house resounded with the loud and repeated huzzas of an assembled multitude; every heart beat with joy, every countenance beamed satisfaction, and such mutual congratulations, we doubt, were ever witnessed before. Cannon announced the triumph of Newark and her friends, and in the evening the court-house, as well as the town in general, was brilliantly illuminated."

Source: William H. Shaw, *History of Essex and Hudson Counties, New Jersey* (Philadelphia, 1884), 1:212–13.

(11) Federalists Seek to Survive against Republican Rivals— New England, 1801–1815

In the aftermath of their defeat in the election of 1800, certain Federalist leaders realized that if they wished their party to compete successfully with the Jeffersonian Republicans, it needed to change. In order to win at the ballot box they were going to have to adopt some of the intensive vote-getting methods used by their opponents. Over the next several years in many of the New England states, the Federalists inaugurated a number of reforms toward that end. Most important was the creation of an intricate committee system, one of whose tasks was to identify prospective Federalist voters and get them to the polls on a regular basis. Nothing was so crucial not only for the survival of the party but for the future of the new nation, their leaders agreed. "Let every Federalist on election day quit his shop, his farm, his office, or his counting house, and make everything subservient to the great duty he owes his country," exclaimed an editorial in the partisan Newburyport, Massachusetts, newspaper shortly before the balloting in 1804. Evidently their mobilization efforts worked, for the state of Massachusetts was able to resist Jeffersonian domination longer than any of its neighbors. No single contemporary source conveys the wide-ranging activities undertaken by Bay State Federalists prior to and on Election Day as the modern account presented here by historian James M. Banner, Jr.

Because of the multitude of offices to be filled by election in Massachusetts and because of the continuity of the town caucus which, unlike the county caucus, could easily assemble the Federalist townspeople, town caucuses and committees worked in close harmony. Here, as nowhere else in the Federalist system, public sentiment was transmitted immediately from the rank and file into the committee hierarchy. In many cases, town committeemen were members of the town caucus. What this meant was that the Central Committee was exposed to shifts in public opinion not only from the caucus above but, through the intermediation of the county committees, from the town committees below.

When functioning at its best, the committee system was a well-drilled electoral machine turning out as many Federalist votes as possible. All energies concentrated on achieving maximum Federalist voter partici- pation. "As we value our liberties," declared the Salem town committee, "it behoves us to see that every qualified voter in our town give in his vote." Circular after circular brought home the point that "your in- creased exertions may possibly procure one additional vote; and that single vote may save the Commonwealth." "You must embolden the confident, awaken the inert, encourage the desponding, *conciliate the doubtful*, and *support the feeble*," was a common admonition of party lit- erature.

Surviving voter lists show how committee members tallied up firm and doubtful Federalists and unregenerate Republicans before each elec- tion and then went after the apathetic, the undecided, the absent, and the infirm. Despite Central Committee urgings to adopt only "fair and honourable measures," methods which earlier would have appalled the "better" sort became commonplace. Federalist employers threatened with dismissal those employees who voted Republican. Food and wine were liberally dispensed before polling hours. Federalists attempted il- legally to enroll aliens and minors, took property vouchers from men who lived in distant towns, falsified vouchers for some who owned no property at all, and, in desperation, even summarily struck voters from the rolls and resorted to outright bribery. They loaned money to indi- gents to satisfy voting requirements, and, in order to learn who voted for whom, printed their tickets on special-colored paper. In the maritime towns, they stacked their vote-canvassing committees with shipmasters who exercised their renowned talents for persuasion at sailors' doors and aboard ship. During the 1808 congressional campaign in Beverly, fully one seventh of the town's vote, or one sixth of the Federalist electorate, was honored with appointment to vote-distributing committees, and in 1804 Salem's canvassing committee numbered 193.

The party often laid plans to enter the polling place en masse when it opened, take every seat in the room, then ballot as slowly as possible so that opponents could not get to the ballot box before the polls closed at an arbitrary hour. It was also customary among Federalists to hire car- riages for free transportation to the polls and to prepare workers for being called away from their labor if their votes were needed. "Not a single person is left unnoticed, not a single hamlet unexplored," noted one newspaper. "If they are sick they are conveyed to the meeting house almost upon their beds. . . . Property, loaned expressly for the occasion, is put in the hands of indigent brothers." In Boston, a special committee visited the wharves in 1812 and brought up all the qualified voters who could be found. "Carriage loads of seamen and others belonging to Plymouth and Salem," reported one observer, "were sent last night to those towns to vote, and to be brought back immediately to their vessels."

Source: James M. Banner, Jr., To the Hartford Convention (New York: Alfred A. Knopf, 1969), 255–57. Reprinted by permission of Random House, Inc.

(12) Factional Conflict in Era of Good Feelings— Philadelphia, 1817

The War of 1812 divided America and led to the complete demise of the Federalist party on the national level, especially when some of its leaders at a meeting known as the Hartford Convention talked about the possibility of secession by the northern states. During the presidential election of 1816, Federalist officials went through the motions of putting up a slate of candidates, but they did not really engage in active campaigning. In the final tally, James Monroe of Virginia, the Republican nominee, won the vast majority of electoral votes. On the state level as well, heated contests diminished at this time, and by 1817 the Republicans had come to dominate every state government, with the exception of Delaware and Massachusetts. In certain states such as Pennsylvania, the main rivalry now lay between competing factions of the Republican party (sometimes referred to as the Democrats and the Moderate Democrats). The Federalist ticket there attracted only a small minority of voters. However, in the postwar elections in the Keystone State, ideals and party issues did not appear to play significant roles. The author of the following selection notes that among Philadelphians casting ballots in the gubernatorial race between William Findlay and Daniel Hiester, "few, if any, appeared to care one straw about principle." Winning seems to have been the only thing that counted, to which end each side sought to control the balloting process in every district. Another item of interest to the modern reader is the reference to gambling on the outcome, something that became increasingly common throughout much of the nation in subsequent decades. After his somewhat critical account of the election, the author, an Englishman, makes some parting remarks about the quality of American democracy.

> While admitting there is "much to lament" over it, he concludes
> that "we must endure evils, in order to insure a preponderance
> of good."

The election being now closed, I can sit down and review it calmly as a
whole. It has been to me a highly interesting scene. . . .

The present candidates for the office of governor are each of them of
the democratic party. General Hiester is of the moderate faction, and is
also supported against his opponent by the federalists and quids [con-
servative Republicans]. Mr. Finlay has the powerful aid of the unyielding
democrats; and, though he is in a minority in the proportion of one to
three within the city of Philadelphia, little doubt is entertained of his
election's having been carried by a large majority throughout the State
at large. . . . The general election is preceded by an election in the different wards of officers called Inspectors, whose business it is to receive the
ballot ticket of voters; parties try their strength in this first step. I witnessed the mode of voting: the persons choosing inspectors attend at a
stated place in their own ward, and deliver in their ballot through a
window. The number assembled at any one time did not exceed twenty.
There was no noise, no confusion, in fact, not even conversation. I was
astonished to witness the anxiety felt by leading men, that *their* party
should be elected *inspectors*. The eventual choice at the general election
seemed, in fact, in their estimation, actually to rest upon having "Inspectors" of their own party. I remarked to them that it could be of no
consequence of what party these gentlemen were, as they were protected
from partial or corrupt conduct by the mode of voting being by ballot.
One of them informed me afterwards, that the fact of the inspectors being
on one side or the other had been calculated to make a difference of
upwards of 200 votes in a particular section!—arising from the reception
of improper, and the rejection of good votes. The means by which an
inspector can effect this, though the mode is by ballot, is said to be re-
markably exact. That there may be some truth in this statement, would
seem probable from a scene which I witnessed in the evening [prior to
the vote]. I called upon the gentleman before alluded to. His room was
completely crammed with the *managers* of the forth-coming election; and
here, instead of finding that the general anxiety was at all connected with
the advancement of correct political principles, I heard the following
conversation:

"I'll bet you fifty (dollars) on Hiester in Chesnut ward."

"What majority will you give him?"

"One-fourth."

"Give old Sour Kraut (Hiester) a hundred and thirty, and I'll take
you."

"Done."

"What will you give Finlay in Lower Delaware ward?"

"One hundred."

"And what to Hiester?"

"Three hundred."

"Give Bill three and a half, and I'll take you for five hundred."

"No: I'll give him three and a half for a pair of boots."

"Guess I'll take you for a pair and a hat.—What for Dock ward?"

"I won't bet on Dock: they're all a set of d——d Tories."

"Will you give Joe four hundred in South Mulberry?"

"I won't take Joe, I guess, in that ward."

"What will you give Billy in South Mulberry?"

"A couple of hundred."

"Done for five hundred."

The following morning I was early on the election ground. The place appointed to receive votes for the city (exclusive of Southwark and the northern liberties), was in the State-house—the same building in which that immortal document was passed—THE DECLARATION OF INDEPENDENCE! There were two inspectors for each ward of the city placed at separate windows. The electors delivered in their votes from the street. The ground was what is here called *manned*; that is, persons in the interest of the parties have written on their hat or breast, "Federal Ticket," or "Democratic Ticket," soliciting citizens as they approach the poll "to vote their ticket"; for which purpose they are prepared to furnish them with the printed balloting list of their party. The neighbouring public-houses were, of course, occupied by the electioneers. I resolved to devote to this as much of my time as possible, in obtaining an insight into the character and mind of this people, and to observe them acting in their political capacity. They were all betting upon the election; but I lament to say, that few, if any, appeared to care one straw about principle. Old General Barker (whom I had heard the previous evening make a most able speech in favour of Mr. Findlay, at a public meeting of the democrats) was travelling about to the several depots of leading characters. I could hardly credit my sight that he was the same person whom I had heard the previous evening. His chief employment during the day seemed drinking rum and gin, with any and everybody. I made some remarks to him concerning his speech: he pleasantly answered, "My good fellow, I did as well as I could, I guess: they made me open the ball." This old general was the companion in arms of Washington: he has been both sheriff and mayor: he has the character of possessing a good heart, and very improvident generosity.

The election terminated throughout the State in *one day*. The excitement of party and pecuniary feeling, by the universality of gambling upon the occasion, was very great; yet there was no confusion, no disturbance. Let it be borne in mind, that here was the right of voting to the utmost extent, and exercised by a people, concerning whom it is high praise to say, that they are not superior in intellect, in information, in honest zeal, and in temperate ideas of liberty, to the English nation; yet there is much to lament here. The original documents given in the preceding pages are too full upon this point: they, indeed, are far from complimentary to our nature; but at the same time we should recollect, that in the political, as in the moral and natural worlds, we must endure evils, in order to insure a preponderance of good. The extent of my approbation, then, upon this occasion, is a conviction of the compatibility of popular election with peace and good order; and, if possessed by the English people, I should presume, it would not be attended with so many abuses.

Source: Henry B. Fearon, *Sketches of America* (London, 1818; reprint, New York: B. Blom, 1969), 137–41, 146–48.

The Jacksonian Era, 1828–1849

Election contests in the early republic may have been vigorously fought on some occasions, but they were hardly of the same magnitude as those of the coming generation of the 1830s and 1840s. A similar statement can be made about what transpired on the day of voting itself. Election Day, in what we now refer to as the "Jacksonian era," became a grander event, touching many more people than in previous epochs. Not only did more individuals get involved, but those taking part were more active and committed to the political process than most of their forebears had been. During the second quarter of the nineteenth century, political parties of a more highly developed nature than their predecessors began to emerge. As a result, fiercely competitive elections between the party of Jackson (eventually known as the Democrats) and that of his opponents (called the National Republicans, and later the Whigs) grew increasingly commonplace. Campaigns lasted longer than they had and were accompanied by much more hoopla. Also, more offices had become elective. White manhood suffrage had been achieved in most of the states by this time, which meant that greater numbers of voters could go to the polls. Tumults and riots seemed larger and more frequent, as many of the gentlemanly aspects of contests in prior epochs receded from view. Post-election celebrations were now bigger and more festive than before. Yet certain facets of the election process—especially the way that voting was conducted—remained much the same.

(13) The Rituals of a Jacksonian Victory Parade Observed—
New York, 1832

The party of Andrew Jackson introduced many new rituals into
political campaigns and into postelection events as well. Victory
parades featuring numerous marchers carrying flags, banners,
and various symbolic items became well established in this era.
The new postelection pageantry is best captured in the description of a Democratic parade in New York City in 1832, celebrating the triumph of President Jackson over his National
Republican challenger, Henry Clay. The author, a perceptive
French visitor, Michael Chevalier, noticed the strong similarity
between the political procession he was observing in the United
States and solemn religious processions he had recently encountered in Mexico. "The American standard-bearers," he
pointed out, "were as grave as the Mexican Indians who bore
the sacred candles. The Democratic procession like the Catholic
procession, had its halting places; it stopped before the houses
of Jackson men to fill the air with cheers and halted at the doors
of the leaders of the Opposition to give three, six, or nine
groans." One might say that the Americans, who had few official
ceremonies, were inventing political rituals that corresponded to
the religious rituals found in other lands. While this event, taking
place after the election had ended, was somber in tone, it is
probable that what had transpired when the polls were open
was much less so, as will be seen in several of the subsequent
documents.

In the older States of the North there are political processions, pure party
demonstrations for the most part, but which are interesting in that the
democracy has a share in them; for it is the Democratic party that gets
up the most brilliant and animated. Besides the camp meetings, the political processions are the only things in this country which bear any
resemblance to festivals. The party dinners with their speeches and deluge of toasts are frigid, if not repulsive; for example, I have never seen
a more miserable affair than the dinner given by the Opposition, that is
to say, by the middle class, at Powelton, in the neighborhood of Philadelphia. But I stopped involuntarily at the sight of the gigantic hickory
poles which made their solemn entry on eight wheels for the purpose of
being planted by the democracy on the eve of the election. I remember
one of these poles, its top still crowned with green foliage, which came

on to the sound of fife and drums and was preceded by ranks of Democrats, bearing no other badge than a twig of the sacred tree in their hats. It was drawn by eight horses, decorated with ribbons and mottoes. Astride the tree itself were a dozen Jackson men of the first order, waving flags with an air of anticipated triumph and shouting, *Hurrah for Jackson!*

But this parade of the hickory tree was but a by-matter compared with the procession I witnessed in New York. It was the night after the closing of the polls when victory had gone to the Democratic party. The procession was nearly a mile long; the Democrats marched in good order to the glare of torches; the banners were more numerous than I had ever seen at any religious festival; all were transparencies on account of the darkness. On some were inscribed the names of the Democratic societies or sections; *Democratic young men of the ninth or eleventh ward*; others bore imprecations against the Bank of the United States; *Nick Biddle* and *Old Nick* [Nicholas Biddle, president of the Bank of the United States, 1823–36] were shown, more or less ingeniously, doing business together; it was their form of our banner with the prayer, "Deliver us from evil." Then came portraits of General Jackson afoot and on horseback; there was one in the uniform of a general and another in the person of the Tennessee farmer with the famous hickory cane in his hand. Portraits of Washington and Jefferson, surrounded with Democratic mottoes, were mingled with emblems in all designs and colors. Among these figured an eagle—not a painting, but a real live eagle—tied by the legs, surrounded by a wreath of leaves and hoisted upon a pole, after the manner of the Roman standards. The imperial bird was carried by a stout sailor, more pleased than was ever any city magistrate permitted to hold one of the cords of the canopy in a Catholic ceremony. Farther than the eye could reach the Democrats came marching on. I was struck with the resemblance of their air to the train that escorts the Eucharist in Mexico or Puebla. The American standard-bearers were as grave as the Mexican Indians who bore the sacred candles. The Democratic procession, also like the Catholic procession, had its halting places; it stopped before the houses of Jackson men to fill the air with cheers and before the doors of the leaders of the Opposition to give three, six, or nine groans. If these scenes were to find a painter, they would be admired at some distant day no less than the triumphs and sacrificial pomps which the ancients have left us in marble and brass. For this is something more than the grotesque fashion of scenes immortalized by Rembrandt; this belongs to history, it belongs to the sublime; these are episodes of a wondrous epic which will bequeath a lasting memory to posterity, the memory of the coming of democracy.

Source: Michael Chevalier, *Society, Manners, and Politics in the United States* (Boston, 1839), 306–8.

---

(14) Violent Party Battle in the "City of Brotherly Love"— Philadelphia, 1832

The heated atmosphere associated with Election Day during the Jacksonian era can be clearly seen in the contest described below. It comes from the pen of a foreign observer who witnessed the presidential election of 1832 in the city of Philadelphia. The author, Carl D. Arfwedson, takes note of the high level of interest in politics and the bitterness displayed on all sides. "Whichever way I turned, I heard the severest censure directed by one party against the other." He then writes about the immense efforts made on the day of election to influence the voters' choices. Each party had its organization of loyal supporters who would stop at nothing to help their side win—even resorting to the use of force to keep opponents from the ballot box. All this led to a great deal of violence and bloodshed. Several men who took part in these clashes were severely injured in the process and had to be "carried from the field of battle wounded" and disfigured. Interestingly, despite his dismay at what he had observed, the writer dwells on some of the positive aspects of the contest, especially the acceptance of the final verdict by the losing side. He asserts that when the polls were closed and the decision rendered, little bitterness could be seen among the losers; some even engaged in laughter. Nevertheless, Arfwedson, while praising many aspects of the American electoral system, expresses deep anxiety about the power of the masses at the ballot box. He concludes that "if ever the beautiful republican ship [the U.S. government] should strike on a shoal, it would be at the period of a Presidential election."

The President and Vice-President of the United States are, as it is well known, elected to their respective offices for the period of four years. In Pennsylvania, the election takes place in the following manner: four months before the duties of the office are entered upon, electors are chosen by the people, who afterwards vote. A similar day of election took place on the 2d of November in Philadelphia. The friends of the respective candidates, Jackson, Clay, and [William] Wirt [of the Anti-Masonic party], had, during the preceding week, used every exertion to influence voters to avail themselves of their privilege. No pains had been spared, and no inducement neglected. In England, where I have likewise attended popular elections, the zeal of the friends of the candidates is certainly very great; but in America it is carried to a still higher pitch. Both young and old, poor and rich, men and women, feel such an intense interest in the issue of the contest, that the least result which an impartial foreigner can possibly expect is, the dissolution of the Union, effusion of blood, and civil war. Whichever way I turned, I heard the severest censure directed by one party against the other. In one place, appeared a number of Clay-men attacking and tearing down the hickory trees. In another, a numerous and savage mob was seen dancing round similar trees erected in the streets, calling out—"Jackson for ever!" Not far off, a procession of anti-masons, to whose party the last-mentioned candidate belonged, was seen moving and laughing at their antagonists. In another group, were observed a number of the most influential politicians in the city, haranguing the people on the brilliant prospects of their cause, the certain defeat of their opponents, the matchless qualifications of their candidate, and the duplicity, vacillation, and deception, of the other two. It was evident, that the prevailing policy was to keep up party-spirit by holding forth encouragement, and to acquire new adherents, either by the propagation of false statements or by attempting to frighten the opponents.

The State of Pennsylvania is divided into certain districts, where elections take place on the same day. Philadelphia constitutes a district of itself. The city, however, is so extensive, that it is necessary to subdivide it into wards, to facilitate the elections. Commissioners from each ward assemble in the Statehouse at eight o'clock in the morning of the day appointed. Each of them had his own particular box placed near the avenue of trees fronting the house. The voters approached these boxes whenever they wished to give a vote, and delivered a printed card, on which the name of the electors was inscribed, and signed by the voter. It being understood that none except those who belong to the ward of which the box bears the name are allowed to vote, it may be supposed that the person who receives the vote must know the respective voters. But, if any doubt arises as to the eligibility of the party, the commissioner has the privilege of insisting upon his oath, and the production of receipts for paid taxes. Before the boxes thronged a number of people belonging to the three aspiring candidates, distinguished only by the different names on voting cards, and which were pasted on boards and carried about in the shape of flags. Some of these cards had the portraits of the candidates for the presidency; on others were written or printed eulogies of them. The conflict near the boxes was often attended with bloodshed, and several of the combatants were carried away from the field of battle wounded and disfigured. These fights continued the whole day uninterruptedly; and about ten o'clock at night the boxes were shut up, when a retreat was effected by the straggling party to other parts of the city. The uproar spread in every direction; yells and discordant sounds were heard in all parts; the arrival of an enemy, or of the plague, could not have caused a greater disturbance. I took a walk late in the evening to look at the different transparencies which each party had exhibited before their committee-rooms. An attack, perfectly organized, took place on one of these rooms, and the assault was only repulsed by the besieged after a most obstinate resistance, when about fifty wounded were left on the field of battle. These scenes did not end till morning.

On the following day, the inhabitants of the city were officially informed that the anti-Jackson party had a majority in Philadelphia of about one thousand nine hundred votes. Returns were also transmitted from different parts of the State in the course of this and the following day, showing the issue of the election; but, when all these were summed up at last, Jackson's party appeared to have the ascendancy, and his election in Pennsylvania was consequently secured. This result, quite contrary to the wishes of the majority in Philadelphia, did not, however, create any disturbance among the party who but a few evenings before had displayed an almost revolutionary zeal in the cause, and actually shed blood to secure victory over the Jackson men. On the contrary, they heard the announcement of their defeat with a composure worthy of imitation; I observed even some, who commanded at the late attack on the committee-room, laugh at the issue of the election. This singular circumstance was often adduced to me as the perfection of the electioneering system. A strong feature in its favor it undoubtedly is; but to say that the system is altogether perfect is an assertion by no means admitted by all enlightened citizens in America.

Source: Carl D. Arfwedson, *The United States and Canada in 1832, 1833, and 1834* (London, 1818; reprint New York: Johnson Reprint Corp., 1969), 1:280–85.

---

(15) Prominent Merchant Serves as Election Judge— Philadelphia, 1840

A somewhat more favorable view of election proceedings in Philadelphia during this period can be seen in the diary entries of Sidney George Fisher, a prominent businessman and Whig party supporter. Like the previous writer, Fisher was bothered by the harmful effects of recurring elections, which he saw as a "growing and serious evil," for the people "are kept in a constant state of agitation," leading to "drunkenness, mobs, & riots." Yet, despite his misgivings about what he had observed on former occasions, Fisher, in acting as election judge in one of the city wards for the Pennsylvania statewide contest in October 1840, found the experience "novel & interesting." Even though Fisher, as judge, had to be on hand for many, many hours with little to do, his overall response to having presided over the balloting process was a positive one. It was, he exclaimed, "a new page of life opened, and to see the mode in which the great main spring of democratic government is managed was worth the trouble that I had." The full statement of his impressions of being an election judge appears below.

On Tuesday, the election day, went to the State House at 7 o'clock in the morning to perform my duties as one of the judges. The polls were opened at 8 & the voting commenced. It continued at some of the wards 'till 12 o'clock at night, when the polls were closed. At my ward, Walnut, all the votes were given before 10 o'clock, so that the duties were comparatively slight. Still they were sufficiently irksome. I was there all day with almost nothing to do, as I had only to decide upon the qualifications of voters when the inspectors disagreed & was rarely appealed to, and after the voting ceased, was busy helping to count votes till 4 o'clock in the morning. The scene however was novel & interesting. The two large rooms of the State House, with the officers of the wards at the windows, receiving votes & discussing the claims of applicants, the shouts & hurrahs of the crowd outside, and the variety of character & demeanor of those in the house, gave the affair enough of excitement to me, who had never witnessed anything of the kind, to compensate for the labor, confinement and the vulgarity of my associates. It was a new page of life opened, and to see the mode in which the great main spring of democratic government is managed was worth the trouble that I had. Having counted the votes, sealed the ballot boxes and delivered them to a magistrate, I went home tired enough at 4 o'clock. Mine is one of the smallest wards in the city so that I got thro very soon. At some of the wards they were occupied in counting 'till 12 o'clock the next day. Went the next morning to sign the returns, which ended my duties till the Presidential election on the 30th. . . . [Fisher goes on to state that the result of the election in Philadelphia was not very favorable to the Whigs. In the county the Van Buren party had a large majority, while in the city the Whigs' margin of victory was smaller than on former occasions. The election, however, was very quiet and orderly, notwithstanding the great excitement—which, he says, was an improvement.]

Source: N. B. Wainwright, ed., A Philadelphia Perspective: The Diary of Sidney George Fisher Covering the Years 1834–1871 (Philadelphia: Historical Society of Pennsylvania, 1967), 104–5.

(16) Young Man Observes Riotous Election in the West—
St. Louis, 1838

Heated conflicts on Election Day in this era took place not only in Middle Atlantic states like New York and Pennsylvania; they also occurred in the South and West, especially in border states like Missouri. One example can be seen in the journal of a young man from St. Louis, Henry B. Miller, who in this excerpt describes the Missouri legislative contest in the spring of 1838, centering on the reelection of Thomas Hart Benton to the U.S. Senate. Benton, a leading Jacksonian, had fought against the Bank of the United States, high protective tariffs, and federally financed internal improvements; he was strongly opposed by Missouri Whigs, who wanted to elect a candidate that favored those measures. The turnout in St. Louis was so heavy on the first day of balloting that officials allowed the subsequent casting of votes at a few additional sites outside the city, such as Carondalet. It was here that young Miller delivered his first vote, giving it to Benton's side, as would the majority at the polls the next day. But the outcome was not so simple. The voting, as Miller describes it, was tainted with fraud and involved plenty of fighting and bloodshed. He shows that the Whig partisans were not as gentlemanly as they have often been portrayed but possessed "a goodly number of Blackguards in their ranks." On the second day at Carondalet, these men used excessive force to drive many of their Democratic opponents away from the polling area, giving the Whigs a sizable margin in the county. But despite the unfavorable result in the St. Louis area, the Democrats prevailed statewide, and Benton was reelected to the Senate.

There was a great time down at Carondalet (generally better known by the name of Vete Bush). I went down on Tuesday afternoon in order to vote and see the fashions. The steam Boat *St. Lawrance* took a load down in the afternoon; there was a band of music aboard playing up some lively airs, amongst the rest Yankee Doodle with great spirit; we had the Broad stripes & stars in the front of the Boat. The Whigs were down with a strong force and had possession of the Polls; when we came down there was a great excitement, the whigs collecting round the Polls & crying out, "Whigs, Stick to the Polls, don't let the damned Democrats vote." The Democrats formed a procession from the Boat to go up to the town with their banner and music in front. When we came up to the house where the Election was held, great hurraing and noise; the Democrats marched round to the Polls. The Whigs crowded up; great crying, Hurra for the Whigs, pull down the Banner, Lick them, drive them away, Keep the Polls, Hurra for Darby, Hurra for Sublette, Hurra for Benton and Democracy, Hurra for Clay, down with the damned Democrats, Hurra for Jackson, Hurra for Hell, see who'll get there first. By this time the noise and confusion had become so great as to be amusing to those who did not get much excited. Some Halloed one thing, some another; some imitated the Barking of Dogs, some the roaring of Bulls, all making as much noise as they could. It was the greatest medley Concert I ever heard. We planted our Banner at one of the gate ways and began to go in; the Democrats felt rather weak, consequently rather shy; considerable fighting [took place,] in which fair play was a scarce article and the Democrats [were] generally licked. I undertook to crowd up to the Polls quietly and without much noise. When I got near the window, there were several known Democrats there; the Whigs seeming to think that they were in a Free country, consequently they had a right to let vote who they pleased. There were some words between them and the first thing I knew I heard the Whigs Hurraing; those they had known they had thrown down off the porch (about 5 steps down) and came running in hunt of more. One came to me and asked me if I was a democrat; I said yes; no sooner said than three or four caught hold of me and the way I was sent down the 5 steps was rather faster than when I put on my hat & walk leisurely out of church. As soon as I could stop myself, I turned around to see where I had come from; I saw the Whigs Exulting in what they had done. I was very angry but felt much like a whipped dog. I made some remark on the liberty of suffrage, &c., &c.

I walked up to our Banner, where the Whigs were not quite so plenty. I stayed there awhile, and then with a number of others went up to the Polls where we voted without much difficulty. This was the first vote I ever gave in my life and which I gave for Thomas H. Benton; not that I was prejudiced to do so with a view to go with a party right or wrong, but because I liked his principles and the course he took and maintained in the U.S. senate. Let Posterity decide whether I acted wisely or not. After I had voted I with a number of other young men stood round our Banner to support it (there still being a strong cry to pull it down and drive the Democrats from the ground). I got up on the fence and there had a fair opportunity to see the greater part of the fighting that was going on for that time. I saw more of that than I ever saw before in life to put all together and some of the bloodiest too; derks [dirks], Bowie Knives, clubs, handkerchiefs with stones in, with all other kinds of tools that the occasion might require; some of the scenes were disagreeable and some very ludicrous. One I will name as it afforded me much sport at the time. There was a small fight took place between two men, both too drunk to hurt each other much; one a very large man that would weigh 250 or upwards, he whipped the other one; his party then raised great hurraing and undertook to carry him on their shoulders round the house; two or three men got him up and commenced carrying him along, but they did not get very far; they, it is true, done their part faithfully and carried with all their might, but they were too heavy freighted, and had to give it over as a bad job, or wrong calculation. This was the most amusing sight I saw this day and my inference was that this was the way the Whigs would succeed in carrying the state; they were taking it up here and carrying along right strong, but their strength has failed them and they have to set down their reform (as they have been crying all the time and by the way gave us a spesiman at Vete Bush), and leave things to take their course as formerly. We came up in the evening and marched round town to the court house where we were disbanded and came home, having seen some of the election. The next day I was told (and no one denied it) that the Whigs dreve the Democrats away entirely and had the Polls to themselves; the returns of that day substantiate the assertion or report truly. This is but a faint or brief account of the election in this place. The Whigs had about 800 of a majority in the city and County, but have lost the State by considerable, the bush counties comeing strong for Democracy. This Election learnt that there were many rowdies amongst the Whigs as well as the Democrats; the Whigs have so often took it on themselves to say that there were no bad characters amongst their ranks as among the Democrats, that the Democrats had a habit of taking possession of the Polls or Ballot Box, and throwing the others away, or beating them off, but their party were too much of *Gentlemen* to do such things. Their conduct down to Carondalet has proved that this story will not stand and all the arguments the Whigs can bring about their Gentlemenly party they cannot persuade me of otherwise than that they too have a goodly number of Blackguards in their ranks as well as the others. I for my part never would wish to be understood that I would intimate that this was their principals and was sanctioned by their leading men; not at all; any liberal minded freeman will detest such proceedings if he sees them in his own or any other party, and will raise his voice against it. This is the case with many of the Whigs and the most respectable of them at present, and has been so with the Democrats and is so still. The cry with the Whigs has been wherever the Democrats were the strongest they done so, and we may say the same of the other party.

Source: "The Journal of Henry B. Miller," *Missouri Historical Society Collections* 6 (1931): 261–65. Courtesy Missouri Historical Society, St. Louis.

(17) Prominent Whig Assesses Harrison–Van Buren Contest—New York, 1840

The presidential election of 1840, which pitted Whig standard-bearer "Old Tippecanoe" William Henry Harrison against Democratic incumbent Martin Van Buren, has long been known as one of the most exciting and hardest-fought contests in American political history. The "log cabin, hard cider" campaign was notable for bringing about the elevation to the presidency of a relatively unknown figure in politics—Harrison, a general in the War of 1812, had done little of note since that time—through the massive use of hoopla. Some political historians see it as the beginning of the modern age in American politics, when image started to become more important than reality. The partisan conflict, silent on issues but noisy otherwise, created a frantic atmosphere rarely seen at elections before or since. One can get some idea of the enthusiasm of the moment by looking at the published diary of Philip Hone, a leading Whig and one-time mayor of New York City. The day prior to the balloting there, Hone wrote, "The greatest excitement prevails; men's minds are wrought up to a pitch of frenzy, and, like tinder, a spark of opposition sets them on fire. . . . Both parties here claim the victory, and every hour the wheel turns each uppermost. Betting is going on at an enormous extent. Riot and violence stalk unchecked throughout the streets, and lying is no longer considered a crime." The author, a man of wealth and high position, is not exactly sympathetic to the expanding democracy of this era. Reflecting the xenophobic views of many Americans of his time, Hone is especially critical of enfranchising recent immigrants, who, he exclaims, oppose "everything good, honest, lawful and of good report." His comments on Election Day and its aftermath follow.

November 4.—The fire is out, the powder expended, and the smoke is passing away. The election throughout the State ended when the sun went down. Ours was held only to-day, and, thanks to the registry law, forty-three thousand men went to the polls, voted, and came away without confusion, and generally without riot or opposition. In some of the Loco-foco [Democratic] districts crowds of violent men assembled, but not to the extent formerly experienced. This beneficial change has been

produced by dividing the wards into election districts, so that not more
than about six hundred are taken in one place, and all in one day. Instead
of seventeen polls, as it used to be, there are now eighty odd, and the
elements of riot and disorder are weakened by being divided. The polls
are opened at sunrise and closed at sunset, and by ten o'clock two-thirds
of all the votes in the city were in. The number of votes registered in the
second district in the fifteenth ward, in which I reside, is six hundred
and seventy, of which six hundred and sixty-four voted.

I was selected by the general committee to act as chairman this evening, at Masonic Hall, where the mighty mass of Whigs assembled to
hear the reports. It is hard duty, and I am hoarse and sore, and jaded as
a horse in an omnibus. I took the chair at seven o'clock. The interval of
time before the reports came in was filled by speaking and singing Whig
songs. By and by messengers began to arrive with reports from the several wards, which soon satisfied us that we had lost the battle. Many of
our people had been sanguine enough to calculate upon our gaining the
city, and it was most desirable that we should have sent again to Congress a Whig delegation, particularly Grinnell, whose election would
have so severely rebuked the men who assailed him on the eve of the
election, and the State senator and members of Assembly would have
been a prodigious gain; but, although many of us hoped for such a result,
none acquainted with the state of the parties calculated upon it, and the
result is, in fact, a cause of triumph. The administration majority is not
over twelve hundred; they reckoned upon three thousand. We were
beaten a year ago by almost eighteen hundred; that was the majority
against me for the Senate. The State will go for Harrison, I think, without
a doubt; but his majority will not be so great as was expected. The contest
has been violent; every effort which a party, unscrupulous at all times
but desparate now, could make to sustain themselves in power, has been
resorted to; but it will not do. The sceptre has departed from Mr. Van
Buren.

Scenes of violence, disorder, and riot have taught us in this city that
universal suffrage will not do for large communities. It works better in
the country, where a large proportion of the voters are Americans, born
and brought up on the spot, and where, if a black sheep comes into the
flock, he is marked immediately. But in the heterogeneous mass of vile
humanity in our population of three hundred and ten thousand souls
the men who decide the elections are unknown; they have no local hab-
itation or name; they left their own country for ours, to better their condition, by opposing everything good, honest, lawful, and of good report,
and to effect this they have banded themselves into associations to put
down, at all hazards, the party in favour of order and good government.
A mighty army of these banditti paraded the streets last night under the
orders of the masters, who, no doubt, secretly directed their movements,

attacking every place where the Whigs met. National Hall, in Canal street, the conservative headquarters, was besieged by this army of Jack Jades, and its appearance this morning is a melancholy sample of the effects of unrestrained power in the hands of a mob of political desperadoes. All the windows of this large building are broken; bushels of brickbats cover the floors, and the doors show where the ruffians endeavoured to gain admission by setting fire to the house. This evening, thus far, has been quiet in my part of the city. I came home from Masonic Hall as soon as the result was known, and did not witness any disturbance. Having beaten us in one way, they don't think it worth while to do it in another.

November 5.—The same subject day after day; but this week settles all. At present it swallows up everything else. No business is done; the hammer is suspended on the anvil; the merchant neglects his counting-house, and the lawyer his office. Nobody invites a friend to dine, and no topic of conversation is permitted but election.

November 10.—The election returns come in from all quarters in favour of Harrison and the Whig cause.

Source: Bayard Tuckerman, ed., *The Diary of Philip Hone, 1828–1851* (New York: Dodd, Mead, 1889), 2:49–51.

---

(18) Peaceful County Elections—Springfield, Ohio, 1831, and Upstate New York, c. 1840

As mentioned above, Philip Hone, like many others of his background, always had great doubts about the workability of universal manhood suffrage, especially in big cities like New York, which contained large laboring classes and immigrant populations. He and his cohorts generally believed that the political process worked better in the countryside and small towns of the expanding nation, where the majority of voters were native-born. Perhaps this is why certain foreign observers who watched Election Day proceedings in rural settings had a much more positive assessment of our political system and democratic government in general. Also, when a contest involved the choice of county officials (in contrast to state and national officials), there tended to be less partisanship and therefore less of a likelihood of corruption and violence. This was the case in the election described here by Sandor Farkas, an Eastern European visitor to Springfield, Ohio, in 1831. The atmosphere around the polling place is depicted as idyllic—"No noise, no tempered squabblings, no violent clashes." The voters come forward and "calmly" cast their ballots, hardly creating a stir. Virtually the same response can be found in the writings of another foreign traveler, Joseph Gurney, an Englishman, who in the next document sees American elections as more "quietly conducted" and less corrupt than those in the British Isles.

From Erie we took a stagecoach to the state of Ohio, traveling in the direction of Fairview. We drove only a few hours when the coach's axle broke. We walked to the village of Springfield, busy with district elections, which coincided with county elections. On that day, the sheriff, auditor, commissioner, assemblyman, and trustees of Erie College were elected. Springfield comprises several villages. The voters gathered in groups before the assembly hall while their carriages lined the streets with horses tied to fence posts or other carriages. The whole scene was reminiscent of our county meetings and, in fact, we fully expected to see and hear the same thing as in our county elections. But here, despite three hours of watching and observing, things were completely different. No noise, no tempered squabblings, no violent clashes. When his turn came, the registered voter calmly entered the ballot room and calmly cast his vote into the ballot box. That was the end of the great thing. Yet the citizens have just fulfilled their fundamental duty in a republican government by electing administrative officials responsible for the county and state's happiness or unhappiness, until the next elections. . . .

Whenever a public office is lawfully vacated, all citizens participate in choosing the best candidate to fill it. To reduce the cost of traveling to assemble as electors and to speed up the election returns, the citizens assemble in towns, districts, and villages in wards. Everywhere the elections are held on the same day. Every district sends its ballot results to a designated place where they are tallied, and those who receive the majority vote are declared winners. To close the avenue to all human frailties, elections are based on secret ballot. Public offices not being hereditary but subject to annual elections, office-hunting is not so irritating. To gain public office by majority vote of one's fellow citizens is a distinct honor to every citizen.

Source: Sandor B. Farkas, *Journey in North America, 1831* (Santa Barbara, Calif.: ABC-Clio Press, 1978), 163–64.[lb]

It may not be unsuitable to take this opportunity of remarking that the *elections* in America—frequent as they are, and often marked by no small virulence of party spirit—are on the whole more quietly conducted, and are attended with much less of treating and bribery than are common in

Great Britain and Ireland. The population is so generally imbued with the feeling of personal independence, that bribery for the most part is out of the question; and this offence against the laws (for it is forbidden in most of the states, on pain of imprisonment and hard labour) is still further precluded by the large number of voters on the one hand, and the absence of a surplus of ready money on the other. The vote by ballot is found to be a convenient method, and undoubtedly contributes to the same end. Each voter inserts a card into the box, inscribed with the name of the candidate whom he supports; and the officers in attendance trouble him with no questions. While these remarks are amply borne out in a general point of view, I don't mean to say that the elections are by any means *free* either from dissipation or corruption; especially in large cities, where a loose and low population is too often included among the voters.

Source: Joseph J. Gurney, *A Journey in North America* (Norwich, Eng., 1841; reprint, New York: DaCapo Press, 1973), 358–59.

---

(19) John Q. Adams Reacts to Reelection to Congress— Quincy, Massachusetts, 1844

In the Election Day literature prior to the twentieth century, there are not many examples showing how candidates for office themselves reacted to the results of the balloting. At the close of the polls or at a celebration shortly thereafter, some individuals, following a tradition that went back to colonial times, made short statements to the voters, thanking them for their support and promising to serve with honor. But rarely did anyone commit any words to paper about the outcome and how he personally felt on the occasion. One of the few documents in that vein, presented here, came from the pen of the venerable statesman John Quincy Adams upon his reelection to Congress in 1844. Having been defeated by Andrew Jackson in the presidential election of 1828, the former president was chosen to sit in the House of Representatives from the Eighth District in Massachusetts, starting in 1830. Over the years he had become the leader of the antislavery forces in the House, a position not very popular even in the North. Although he won reelection several times, by 1844 Adams doubted that as a Whig he would be kept on in his post by the district's voters. Not only was the issue of slavery rearing its head, but the nation was turning toward aggressive expansionism, calling for the acquisition of Texas and

Oregon, even if it meant war—a policy which Adams opposed but which his Democratic adversary favored. During the campaign, he also faced the allegation that he had once deliberately snubbed former president Jackson, the great military hero, a charge he denied. The following selection from Adams's diary reveals his pre-election anxieties and then his feeling afterward of vindication upon having been reelected to Congress once again by a considerable margin.

Quincy, November 11. Thick fog in the morning, thunder and lightning with a sprinkling of rain in the afternoon. Evening, calm, moderate, damp, cloudy. It was the day of elections for Electors of President and Vice-President of the United States; for Governor, Lieutenant-Governor, Senators and Representatives of the Commonwealth of Massachusetts, and for members of the House of Representatives of the United States in the Twenty-Ninth Congress. For this last office I was the candidate nominated by the Whigs, with two opponent nominations—Isaac H. Wright, of Roxbury, by the Democrats, and Appleton Howe, of Weymouth, by the Liberty party. I passed the day under a scarcely doubting anticipation of the failure of my own election. Just before noon I went to the Town-House, where I tore off my own name from the Whig ticket, and deposited the remainder in the ballot-box. . . .

In the evening E. Price Greenleaf came in, with a report of the election returns from the adjoining towns of Braintree, Randolph, and Hingham—more favorable, on the whole, than I had expected, yet not enough so wholly to resolve my doubts.

November 12th. . . . The following is a copy of the Whig ticket voted for yesterday at Quincy, and for which I voted, after tearing from it my own name and pinning to the remnant of the paper the strip bearing the name of Samuel Curtis: [The entire Whig ticket is then listed]. The practice is for each voter to put into the ballot-box the whole printed ticket; but any individual strikes out or effaces any name for which he chooses not to vote, and substitutes another name in its place. Candidates usually strike out their own name but not always. There is no law authorizing the rejection of any man's vote for himself. The majority in the town of Quincy at the autumnal elections has been for several years Democratic, consisting of transient stone-cutters from New Hampshire. There were taken yesterday seven hundred and nineteen votes. Of the returns, I only know that there were three hundred and forty-five for me; not a majority of the whole. The Boston Atlas and Courier of this morning did not come by the regular mail, but I received a Courier under a blank cover. My son came out from Boston with the Atlas, which has the returns from the whole Commonwealth except six towns. The Whig ticket has been sweepingly successful. The vote in the Eighth Congressional District is eight thousand and forty-one for me; five thousand three hundred twenty-two for Wright; eight hundred and fifty for Howe and all others. A result which I dared not expect, and upon which I dare not attempt to express my feelings.

November 16th. . . . My constituents have answered, and nobly vindicated my character. In the same district where, in 1842, I only received five thousand nine hundred and ninety-six votes, I have now received eight thousand and ninety-one; and where I had a majority of less than five hundred, I have now a majority exceeding nineteen hundred. The voice of the world and of posterity has yet to be heard.

Source: Charles Francis Adams, ed., *Memoirs of John Quincy Adams* (Philadelphia: Lippincott, 1874–77), 12:104–6.

---

(20) President Polk Reacts to the Election of His Successor— Washington, D.C., 1848

The year of Adams's reelection to the House of Representatives (1844) also saw the ascendance of former congressman James K. Polk, a Jacksonian Democrat from Tennessee, to the presidency. Polk was one of the few nineteenth-century presidents who kept a diary of his years in the White House. Unfortunately, it does not begin until he took office in 1845 so the reader finds no personal response to his election the previous November. However, Polk, who declined to run again, does comment in his diary on the next presidential election in 1848, and has unpleasant things to say about his apparent successor, General Zachary Taylor, the candidate of the Whig party, which Polk negatively refers to as the Federal party. Unlike the present time, when the incumbent administration is often deeply immersed in the contest at hand, Polk and his cabinet seem not to be involved. On Election Day, it was business as usual with the president and his advisers listening to reports and discussing current issues.

TUESDAY, 7th November, 1848.—This is the day appointed by law for the election of President and Vice President of the U.S. Heretofore the people of the several states have by state laws fixed the period of holding the election in each state. Since the last Presidential election Congress for the first time exercised the power vested in them by the constitution, and fixed the same day for holding the election in all the states. There will probably not [be] less than three millions of votes polled in this election.

The Cabinet met at the usual hour, all the members present. There being no other pressing business, I read to the Cabinet portions of my next annual message which I had prepared, and invited the freest suggestions or criticism which any member of the Cabinet might think proper to make. The subjects mainly treated of in the paper which I read, were the veto power, a review of the system established shortly after the close of the war with Great Brittain in 1815, called the "American system" [comprising a national bank, tariffs, internal improvements, etc.], the physical strength of our country in war, the vast territorial acquisitions we had made, their great importance and value, and the urgent necessity of establishing Territorial Governments over them. In connection with the latter subject the slavery question was considered, and concession and compromise recommended. . . . The Cabinet adjourned about 3 o'clock P.M. I saw no company to-day. After the Cabinet adjourned I attended to business on my table.

Wednesday, 8th November, 1848.—Information received by the telegraph and published in the morning papers of this City and Baltimore indicate the election of Gen'l Taylor as President of the U.S. Should this be so, it is deeply to be regretted. Without political information and without experience in civil life, he is wholly unqualified for the station, and being elected by the Federal party and the various factions of dissatisfied persons who have from time to time broken off from the Democratic party, he must be in their hands and be under their absolute control. Having no opinions or judgment of his own upon any one public subject, foreign or domestic, he will be compelled to rely upon the designing men of the Federal party who will cluster around him, and will be made to reverse, so far as the Executive can reverse, the whole policy of my administration, and to substitute the Federal policy in its stead. The country will be the loose [loser] by his election, and on this account it is an event which I should deeply regret.

Source: *The Diary of James K. Polk during His Presidency, 1845 to 1849* (Chicago: McClurg, 1910), 4:181–85.

---

(21) The Strange Death of Edgar Allan Poe—Baltimore, 1849

One of the more bizarre developments connected with an American election in the middle of the nineteenth century (or any

period) was the allegedly brutal treatment of author Edgar Allan
Poe at the hands of political partisans in Baltimore, Maryland,
on October 3, 1849, resulting in his tragic death a few days
later. The story given below of what happened to Poe—his supposed kidnapping by party ruffians who then beat, drugged, and
subsequently transported him by wagon from ward to ward,
forcing him to vote for Whig candidates at each polling stop—
may or may not be accurate. There is little corroborating evidence. Indeed, a recent Poe biographer, Kenneth Silverman, re-
fuses to give the tale any credence whatsoever and attributes its
longevity to the public's need to place famous figures in dramatic death scenes. Nevertheless, even if Poe died of natural
causes and was not a victim of the kind of attack described in
this account, other men were. The practice of "cooping" definitely did occur in large cities, like Baltimore, with heavily immigrant and transient populations, and many unsuspecting
individuals were victimized in the manner in which Poe was
allegedly treated. Thus, the episode, which supposedly took
place during the Maryland legislative contest in 1849, is a valid
example of the darker side of past American election days, when
some partisans would do whatever it took—no matter how ab-
horrent—to get their tickets elected.

What are the actual facts in regard to Edgar A. Poe's death? The Baltimore "Sun" of October 8, 1849, has only this announcement:

"We regret to learn that Edgar A. Poe, Esq., the distinguished
American poet, scholar, and critic, died in this city yesterday morning,
after an illness of four or five days. This announcement, coming so sudden and unexpected, will cause poignant regret among all who admire
genius and have sympathies for the frailties too often attending it. Mr.
Poe, we believe, was a native of this State, though reared by a foster-
father in Richmond, Va., where he lately spent some time on a visit. He
was in the thirty-eighth year of his age."

Let us suppose . . . that Poe arrived in Baltimore on Wednesday, October 3, 1849, not entirely free from the effects of bad hours in the capital
of Virginia. He must have reached the city in the forenoon, and, whether
he came by rail or by steamboat, he would have naturally and almost
instinctively gone to the United States Hotel (the present Maltby House),
opposite which, at that time, was the depot of the Baltimore and Ohio
Railroad.

Poe was a Whig in politics. There was an election going on that day,
a very wet and disagreeable one, for members of Congress and members
of the State Legislature. If Poe had been drinking at all, and it is alto-

gether likely that he had, he would talk, and on election day all men talk politics.

Eight blocks east of the hotel where he [presumably] was, was High Street, and in the rear of an engine-house in this vicinity the "Fourth Ward Club," a notorious Whig organization, had their "coop." There was no registry of voters at this time in Baltimore, and almost any one could vote who was willing to face the ordeal of a "challenge" and the oath administered by a judge of elections. Hence, personal voting "material" was valuable, and the roughs of the period, instead of acting as rounders themselves, used to capture and "coop" innocent strangers and foreigners, drug them with bad whiskey and opiates, and send them round to the different voting-places under custody of one or two of their party, "to help the cause." The system of "cooping" probably culminated in this year, 1849, and, if the writer's memory does not play him a trick, the "coop" of the Democrats on Lexington Street, near Eutaw, in the rear of the "New Market" engine-house, had 75 prisoners, while that of the Whigs, on High Street, had 130 or 140—the equivalent of 600 votes.

The prisoners in these "coops," chiefly foreigners, strangers, country-men, fared wretchedly. They were often, at the outstart, and in the most unexpected way, drugged with opiates and such other delirifaciants as would be most likely to keep them from being troublesome and prevent them from resenting their outrageous treatment. They were thrust into cellars and backyards, and kept under lock and key, without light, without beds, without provisions for decency, without food. Only one thing they were supplied with, and that was a sufficient deluge of whiskey to keep their brains all the time sodden, and prevent them from imparting intelligibility to their complaints.

The Whig "coop" in the Fourth Ward, on High Street, was within two squares of the place where Poe was "found." It is altogether possible . . . that Poe was "cooped" and that his outlaw custodians, discovering too late the disastrous effects of their infamous decoctions upon the delicate tissues and convolutions of his finely organized brain, sought to repair some of the damage they had done, and caused inquiry to be made for the friends of the man they had murdered. Too late!

Source: James A. Harrison, *Life and Letters of Edgar Allan Poe* (New York: Crowell, 1903), 329–32.

The Golden Age of Parties, 1856–1896

The period from the mid-1850s to the mid-1890s is often referred to by political historians as "the golden age of parties." In those years, which included the Civil War era and its aftermath, the Republicans replaced the Whigs as the chief opponents of the Democrats, inaugurating a long series of hard-fought and tightly contested national elections. These elections differed from their predecessors, especially in their intensity. The Republican crusade to stop the spread of slavery brought with it a "moral fervor hitherto unknown in American politics," writes historian Allan Nevins. "The campaign of 1840, with its hard cider, log cabins, and rolling balls, had been riotously exuberant, but its enthusiasm had been untempered by ideas or ideals. Now an exalted purpose, a clear cut sense of national aims, lent strength to the ardor of the campaigners"(Nevins, *Ordeal of the Union*, p. 488). The Democrats, meanwhile, worked equally hard to thwart the Republican goals and to defend the status quo. Contests were particularly close in the border states, where sectional interests tugged people in opposite directions. Wherever the two parties were competitive, they made bigger efforts than before to get the voters to the polls. The Civil War (1861–1865) did not end the political strife; conflict continued at the ballot box. Turnouts at election time in the postwar decades were at their highest level in American history; on average about 75 to 80 percent of the adult white males participated in presidential elections. Consequently, Election Day was a truly momentous occasion, and postelection celebrations often reached spectacular proportions. Violence and fraud were also more widespread than before as each side went to extraordinary lengths in order to win.

---

(22) Ardent Republican Goes to the Polls in New York, 1856 and 1860

Few sources before the twentieth century tell very much about the actual fact of voting from the position of the individual voter. One that does, however, is the voluminous and detailed diary of George Templeton Strong, member of a prominent New York merchant family. Strong's description of attempting to cast a ballot demonstrates that in a large city like New York it could be an extremely time-consuming process. Waiting in long lines to reach the ballot box might consume as much as two hours. Strong, like most others of his generation, was not discouraged by this imposition, though sometimes he would leave the area of the polling place and return later when presumably the line would be shorter. Strong and the many others like him did not vote simply out of duty. His diary entries for Election Day both in 1856 and 1860 clearly reveal the enthusiasm of supporters of the new Republican party as they struggled to obtain their first national victory. Although the party lost the presidential contest in 1856, when John C. Frémont was the standard bearer, it won in 1860 with Abraham Lincoln. It is interesting that in the first entry, besides listing partial results, Strong mentions the lack of usual disturbances around the balloting sites in the city. On the other hand, he casually records having heard the news that in one ward two men had been killed in street fighting.

November 4, 1856. Tuesday. Four P.M. Voted after breakfast. Spent an hour or two at the polls of my election district at the corner of Twenty-second Street and Third Avenue. Went downtown to a Trust Company meeting, and then spent two or three hours more in political service. In spite of the foul weather, there is an immense vote; never larger in this city, I think. People form in queues, and so far as I've seen, everything is orderly and good natured; no crowding or confusion. Governor Fish told me he was two hours in line before he could get his vote in. Peter Cooper and Dr. Webster must have been still longer about it this afternoon. They were half an hour off when I left them. There has been some fighting in the First Ward and a couple of men killed; no other disturbances that I hear of.

Indications are not discouraging. The strength of the Frémont vote went in early in the day. This afternoon Fillmore is gaining and Buchanan still more. So it seems, but ordinary inferences from the appearance of voters are not *perfectly* reliable this time. For example, a party of Irishmen came along this morning asking for Republican electoral tickets. They were going to vote the Democratic ticket in the Fifth Ward where they belonged, except for President, and they didn't like to ask for a Republican ticket there. Frémont, I think, will run largely ahead of his ticket, and I don't expect over 10,000 against him in this city. The signs from Pennsylvania are good as far as they go, and the feeling this morning is that Frémont may well get elected. It's a momentous business; thank God, the responsibility of its decision doesn't rest wholly on me. Either way, fearful disaster may come of this election. . . .

11 P.M. Have been downtown exploring and enquiring; learned little that's new and less that's good. Nassau Street and the other streets round the great newspaper establishments (*Tribune, Times, Herald*, and *Sun*) pretty well crowded, in spite of sloppiness under foot and an occasional brisk shower. Bulletins put out from the windows as fast as the returns came in and received with vociferations, the dissatisfied parties keeping silence as a general rule. The city is all one way. Buchanan gets less than 20,000 majority, and the river counties will give him as much more, I suppose. So the western counties will have to come out very strong if Frémont is to get this state. . . . This storm (its now blowing hard and the wind is coming round to the northwest) is inconvenient, for it will interfere with the telegraph and the community will have fits if it doesn't know about Pennsylvania and Indiana tomorrow at breakfast time.

* * * November 6, 1860. Tuesday. A memorable day. We do not know yet for what. Perhaps the disintegration of the country, perhaps for another proof that the North is timid and mercenary, perhaps for demonstration that Southern bluster is worthless. We cannot tell yet what historical lesson the event of November 6, 1860, will teach, but the lesson cannot fail to be weighty.

Clear and cool. Vote very large, probably far beyond that of 1856. Tried to vote this morning and found people in a queue extending a whole block from the polls. Abandoned the effort and went downtown. Life and Trust Company meeting. The magnates of that board showed no sign of fluster and seemed to expect no financial crisis. Uptown again at two, and got in my vote after only an hour's detention. I voted for Lincoln.

After dinner to the Trinity School Board at 762 Broadway. Thence downtown looking for election returns. Great crowd about the newspapers of Fulton and Nassau Streets and Park Row. It was cold, and I was alone and tired and came home sooner than I intended. City returns are all one way, but they will hardly foot up a Fusian majority [the ticket of Lincoln's Democratic and Constitutional Union opponents] of much above 25,000. Brooklyn said to be Fusion by 14,000. An anti-Lincoln majority of 40,000 in New York and Kings, well backed by the river counties, may possibly outweigh the Republican majorities in the western counties, but that is unlikely. The Republicans have gained in the city since 1856, and no doubt gained still more in the interior.

Source: Allan Nevins and Milton H. Thomas, eds., *The Diary of George Templeton Strong* (New York: Macmillan, 1952), 2:307–8; 3:58–59.

(23) Calm Day in the Windy City for Lincoln's Election— Chicago, 1860

The victory of Abraham Lincoln and the Republican party in 1860 was a major turning point in American political history, leading to southern secession, the Civil War, and the start of a seventy-two-year domination of national politics by the GOP. Yet the 1860 presidential contest itself was less competitive than many of those in prior or subsequent years, as the Democrats were so divided nationally they could furnish only limited opposition in certain states. In the South, most of the party refused to accept the regular ticket headed by Senator Stephen A. Douglas. Instead, a regional Democratic slate had emerged, with John C. Breckinridge of Kentucky as the standard bearer, which siphoned off many votes. (Another new competing organization was the Constitutional Union party, made up mainly of former Whigs, headed by former senator John C. Bell of Tennessee.) Even in Illinois, home of both Lincoln and his chief rival, Douglas, the match was not very close. Douglas, who had won the senatorial race against Lincoln two years earlier after their famous series of debates, had lost standing not only among southerners but with many northern and western voters for his middle-of-the-road stance on sectional issues. The following description of voting in the city of Chicago that November day in 1860 shows a much more orderly scene than was usually found on such occasions, according to the reporter. The weather was unseasonably pleasant, the men quietly and patiently standing in line, the police units on hand but seemingly unnecessary, as only a few minor arrests had to be made the entire day. The author, a staunch Republican, appears to take great pride in his party's accomplishment that day.

Yesterday was a marvel. It was contrary to all precedent, a glorious fall day. The weather we are usually supplied with, for the day of testing the Presidential question, very much resembled the late powwow about dissolving the Union, in beginning a little too soon, and blowing itself out before the time came. Such a "spell of weather" as has visited us within the past week, if it had descended upon yesterday, would have made a difference of thousands of votes. Monday night, however, gave matters meteorological a sharp turn, and the morning broke as clear as if rain and wind were never known in this latitude.

It was cool enough to render thick clothing comfortable, and yet not sufficient to render the task of waiting in the lines to vote, unbearable or serious. And so the day passed. Nobody got wet, and very few we saw the worse for other fluids. The lines were full and "long drawn out" upon the hour of opening of the polls, and the voting began without disturbance, without annoyance to voters or judges, without aught to mar the promise and pledge of Republican rule, that every voter shall have his chance to vote quietly and in order.

We visited the several wards early in the forenoon, and found matters progressing most quietly. Challengers were present, representing both and all parties, and there was no interference with the exercise of their right to challenge, and men swore their votes in, or left without voting as they chose. There were no drunken men, no brawlers, only a moderate amount of cheering and vociferations, less street argumentation than we have ever seen before. Every man was there to carry out his preferences and deposit his chosen ticket. Everybody seemed to feel that his neighbor had made his mind up and that it was "no use talking" any more.

And as they went on for hours and hours in the more populous wards, the line at times reaching back three blocks or more, closely ranged and moving slowly on toward the polls, the presence of a numerous peace force being of value, yet scarcely necessary where every man seemed willing to be his own police officer. Many were from two to three hours in reaching the polls, in the slow moving line. We saw them waiting, rods away from the polls, . . . patient and quiet, determined to "drop that little ballot," and these, very many of them, men who often have allowed elections to pass without casting a vote, all these were out yesterday.

Never did Republicans do better service than at the polls yesterday. There was the disadvantage the Squats [Douglas supporters] had placed upon us by forged tickets, as stated in our last issue, having purchased a duplicate engraved block of the Republican ticket from the engraver. But this availed them nothing, since the Wide Awakes [young Republican volunteers] did not belie the name. Every bearer of a Republican ticket as he approached the polls was solicited to see that his ticket was "the clean thing." Hundreds of tickets with a single scratch were thrown aside, defeating alike the purposes of ambitious Squats and Republican soreheads, some of which latter will find a reckoning yet to come.

It was observable yesterday, that though the "byes" did well for "Little Doog," they lacked the staying that their leaders have been wont to give them. Many of these early in the day left work at the polls, and were seen no more, not even in the evening, for what could they hope from the telegraph. It has become sort of lightning they are in wholesome dread of. And when the sun went down, it found a city eager and waiting for the returns of a gallant day's labor, which has turned over a fresh page in our American politics and opened a new account, with an entirely new heading.

Source: "The Election Yesterday," *Chicago Tribune*, November 7, 1860, 1.

---

(24) How Lincoln Experienced His Election as President— Springfield, Illinois, 1860

On Election Day in 1860 in Springfield, Illinois, the state capital and Abraham Lincoln's longtime home, the Republican presidential candidate was in "one of his most amiable moods," according to contemporaries. While displaying a lively interest in the election, "it was noticeable that he scarcely ever alluded to himself or his candidacy." When he cast his ballot, he voted for every Republican but himself. That night, leaders of the party in Illinois, including Lincoln, crowded into the state House of Representatives to keep track of the returns. Other Springfield residents, anticipating word of the impending triumph, stood outside the telegraph office or sat around in taverns and meeting halls waiting for the latest bulletins. Numerous others thronged the streets, anxious for the celebrations to start. As the different dispatches came over the wires and were made public, yells of victory went up. After several hours, reports were received showing that Lincoln's party had carried the West. But as midnight approached, the major eastern results had not come in yet, especially those from the populous state of New York. Lincoln sat eagerly awaiting the all-important returns from the Empire State along with several of his close Illinois associates, including Senator Lyman Trumbull, state treasurer Jesse Dubois, and local newspaper editor Edward Baker. Finally, the good news arrived—Lincoln and the Republicans had won New York and with it the presidential election. As one of those present, Henry

McPike, described the scene, all the pent up emotion broke loose. Lincoln himself without hesitation joined in the festivities.

Dubois jumped to his feet. "Hey," he shouted, and they began singing as loud as he could (sic) a campaign song, "Ain't You Glad You Jined the Republicans?"

Lincoln got up and Trumbull and the rest of us. We were all excited. There were hurried congratulations. Suddenly old Jesse grabbed the dispatch . . . out of Ed. Baker's hands and started for the door. We followed, . . . Lincoln last. The staircase was narrow and steep. We went down it still on the run. Dubois rushed across the street toward the meeting, so out of breath he couldn't speak plain. All he could say was "Spetch. Spetch." . . . Lincoln, coolest of the lot, went home to tell his wife the news.

Source: Reinhard H. Luthin, *The First Lincoln Campaign* (Cambridge, Mass.: Harvard University Press, 1944), 307.

There is some question as to whether Lincoln came directly home after the announcement of his victory since one report claims that he was "almost dragged" by enthusiastic townsfolk to a local establishment to celebrate. In any case, at ten o'clock the next morning, Lincoln was back in the State House to receive friends and other callers who had come to congratulate him. Samuel R. Weed, a St. Louis newspaperman assigned to cover the election at Springfield, tells us what happened that morning in an article written some years later. The article, based on detailed notes he had made at the time, was first published nationally in the *New York Times* on February 14, 1932, and subsequently reprinted in other works.

While he [Lincoln] seemed in good spirits and received these friendly greetings with a sincere pleasure and good nature, there was a sort of sadness in his face which was remarked by more than one of those present. But he kept it under, amid the warm congratulations which poured in upon him, and talked with all who got near enough to him for the purpose with his old-time freedom.

He sat a portion of the time in a big armchair with his feet on the lower edge of a large stove and had a word for everybody. Very early in the day he had said to one group of callers: "Well, boys, your troubles are over now, but mine have just begun." He repeated this remark a half-dozen times in two hours and I have no doubt it came direct from his heart.

After a while the callers became so numerous that he stood up and held a regular levee and took every offered hand. . . . An old gray-haired, grizzled farmer shook hands with him, and as he did so exclaimed: "Uncle Abe, I didn't vote for yer, but I am mighty glad yer elected just the same."

The President-elect quickly replied: "Well, my old friend, when a man has been tried and pronounced not guilty he hasn't any right to find fault with the jury."

Source: Charles M. Segal, ed., Conversations with Lincoln (New York: Putnam, 1961), 37–38.

---

(25) How Lincoln Experienced His Reelection as President— Washington, D.C., 1864

Abraham Lincoln was probably less excited and more reflective on the night of his reelection to a second term in November 1864 than he had been when first elected to the presidency four years earlier. Perhaps the fact that he had already experienced one such triumph and endured the devastating effects of the long Civil War made him respond more somberly. Of course, even on the first occasion his enthusiasm was somewhat restrained by the seriousness of the situation. In 1864, as in the previous election, there was not much tension regarding the outcome. Although as late as the month of August Lincoln had sincerely doubted he would win, recent Union successes on the battlefield made his second victory (over his Democratic opponent, Gen. George McClellan) a foregone conclusion by the time the balloting began. Lincoln did, however, show more than a casual interest in the returns as they came in over the telegraph at the office of the War Department, where the president and his advisers spent most of the evening. Back at the White House, he never spoke to his supporters outside in the streets, but late that night he came to the window and nodded to the band playing outside. The details presented here are taken from the diary of Lincoln's personal secretary during these years, young John Hay, a graduate of Brown University and later secretary of state in the McKinley and Roosevelt administrations.

Nov. 8. The house has been still and almost deserted today. Everybody in Washington, not at home voting, seems ashamed of it and stays away from the President.

I was talking with him to-day. He said, "It is a little singular that I, who am not a vindictive man, should have always been before the people for election in canvasses marked for their bitterness: always but once; when I came to Congress it was a quiet time. But always besides that the contests in which I have been prominent have been marked with great rancor."

At noon [Gen. Benjamin F.] Butler sent a despatch simply saying, "The quietest city ever seen."

Butler was sent to New York by [Edwin M.] Stanton [the secretary of war]. The President had nothing to do with it. Thurlow Weed [a prominent Republican party leader] was nervous about his coming, thought it would harm us and even as late as Sunday wrote saying that Butler's presence was on the whole injurious, in spite of his admirable General Order.

Hoffman sent a very cheering despatch giving a rose-coloured estimate of the forenoon's voting in Baltimore. "I shall be glad if that holds," said the President, "because I had rather feared that in the increased vote over that on the Constitution, the increase would rather be against us."

During the afternoon few despatches were received.

At night, at 7 o'clock we started over to the War Department to spend the evening. Just as we started we received the first gun from Indianapolis, showing a majority of 8,000 there, a gain of 1,500 over [Indiana governor Oliver] Morton's vote. The vote itself seemed an enormous one for a town of that size and can only be accounted for by considering the great influx since the war of voting men from the country into the State centres where a great deal of Army business is done. There was less significance in this vote on account of the October victory which had disheartened the enemy and destroyed their incentive to work.

The night was rainy, steamy and dark. We splashed through the grounds to the side door of the War Department where a soaked and smoking sentinel was standing in his own vapor with his huddled-up frame covered with a rubber cloak. Inside a half-dozen idle orderlies, up-stairs the clerks of the telegraph. As the President entered they handed him a despatch from Forney claiming ten thousand Union majority in Philadelphia. "Forney is a little excitable." Another comes from Felton, Baltimore, giving us "15,000 in the city, 5,000 in the state. All Hail, Free Maryland." That is superb. A message from Rice to Fox, followed instantly by one from [Charles] Sumner to Lincoln, claiming Boston by 5,000, and Rice's & Hooper's elections by majorities of 4,000 apiece. A magnificent advance on the chilly dozens of 1862.

Eckert came in shaking the rain from his cloak, with trousers very disreputably muddy. We sternly demanded an explanation. He had slipped, he said, & tumbled prone, crossing the street. He had done it watching a fellow-being ahead and chuckling at his uncertain footing.

Which reminded the Tycoon [as Lincoln's personal secretaries called him], of course. The President said, "For such an awkward fellow, I am pretty sure-footed. It used to take a pretty dextrous man to throw me. I remember, the evening of the day in 1858, that decided the contest for the Senate between Mr. Douglas and myself, was something like this, dark, rainy & gloomy. I had been reading the returns, and had ascertained that we had lost the Legislature and started to go home. The path had been worn hog-back & was slippery. My foot slipped from under me, knocking the other one out of the way, but I recovered myself & lit square, and I said to myself, 'It's a slip and not a fall.'"

The President sent over the first fruits to Mrs. Lincoln. He said, "She is more anxious than I. . . ."

Despatches kept coming in all the evening showing a splendid triumph in Indiana, showing steady, small gains all over Pennsylvania, enough to give a fair majority this time on the home vote. Guesses from New York and Albany which boiled down to about the estimated majority against us in the city, 35,000, and left the result in the State still doubtful.

A despatch from Butler was picked up & sent by Sanford, saying that the City had gone 35,000 McC. & the State 40,000. This looked impossible. The State had been carefully canvassed & such a result was impossible except in view of some monstrous and undreamed of frauds. After a while another came from Sanford correcting former one & giving us the 40,000 in the State.

Sanford's despatches all the evening continued most jubilant: especially when he announced that most startling majority of 80,000 in Massachusetts.

General Eaton came in and waited for news with us. I had not before known he was with us. His denunciations of Seymour were especially hearty and vigorous.

Towards midnight we had supper, provided by Eckert. The President went awkwardly and hospitably to work shovelling out the fried oysters. He was most agreeable and genial all the evening in fact. Fox was abusing the coffee for being so hot—saying quaintly, it kept hot all the way down to the bottom of the cup as a piece of ice staid cold till you finished eating it.

We got later in the evening a scattering despatch from the West, giving us Michigan, one from Fox promising Missouri certainly, but a loss in the first district from that miserable split of Knox & Johnson, one promising Delaware, and one, too good for ready credence, saying Raymond & Dodge & Darling had been elected in New York City.

Capt Thomas came up with a band about half-past two, and made some music and a small hifalute.

The President answered from the window with rather unusual dignity and effect & we came home. . . .

W.H.L. [Ward Lamon] came to my room to talk over the Chief Justiceship; he goes in for Stanton & thinks, as I am inclined to think, that the President cannot afford to place an enemy in a position so momentous for good or evil.

He took a glass of whiskey and then, refusing my offer of a bed, went out &, rolling himself up in his cloak, lay down at the President's door; passing the night in that attitude of touching and dumb fidelity, with a small arsenal of pistols & bowie knives around him. In the morning he went away leaving my blankets at my door, before I or the President were awake.

Source: Tyler Dennett, ed., *Lincoln and the Civil War in the Diaries and Letters of John Hay* (New York: Dodd, Mead, 1939), 232–36.

(26) Election Fraud in the Post–Civil War North—New York, 1868

In the post–Civil War period, as the two political parties were still fairly evenly balanced nationally and competition in many states remained severe, election fraud became more widespread than ever. This was especially true in the state of New York, which had nearly one-fifth of the electoral votes needed to win a presidential race, and more particularly in immigrant-filled New York City, where the Democratic machine known as Tammany Hall often engaged in improper methods of obtaining votes. Fraudulent registration and other wrongdoing by partisan local officials led the Republican majority in Congress to try to combat this situation. It passed the Federal Elections Law of 1871, outlawing certain nefarious practices, and appointed party stalwart John I. Davenport as chief federal elections supervisor in New York. Davenport made enormous efforts to reduce the amount of voter fraud in the city, appointing his own subordinates to take charge of the registration process and report on any questionable behavior. He also compiled voluminous notebooks, which listed all the city's registrants, to make it easier to detect unqualified voters coming to the polls. One can get some idea of the problems Davenport encountered by looking at the following excerpt from the book he wrote describing the conditions that had existed in many precincts prior to the reforms he instituted.

There had probably been no election for years in which, to a greater or lesser degree, ballot-boxes had not been "stuffed," and the votes fraudulently canvassed and returned. The election of 1868 was not exceptional in this respect, as will appear.

By law there were four inspectors of election who received the votes on election day, and two canvassers of votes, who counted the ballots after the polls were closed. One half of each of these officers were appointed as Republicans, the other half as Democrats. . . .

In the Ninth Election district of the Sixth ward, on the day of election, the two Democratic inspectors refused to allow the oath to be put to any challenged voter, whereupon, finding remonstrance to be vain, the two Republican inspectors left the polling place and went to Police headquarters to complain of the conduct of their associates and have them removed. This broke up the Board of Inspectors, the law providing that no vote should be received without the presence of a quorum, nor unless at least three of the Board were satisfied and agreed to receive the vote. Notwithstanding these provisions of law, the two Democratic inspectors continued to accept the votes of all who presented themselves during the absence of their colleagues. Over 580 votes were cast in the district, of which about four to one were upon naturalization papers.

In the Third Election district of the Eleventh ward, on election day, a young man, a son of one of the deputy sheriffs, stationed himself behind the counter where the inspectors were receiving votes, and was furnished by one of the Democratic inspectors with his copy of the registry. As a voter would come up, this young man would call out, "all right," and before the Republican inspector could find the name of the would-be voter upon his register, the Democratic chairman of the Board would receive the ballots and deposit them in the boxes. During a portion of the day this young man received votes and deposited them in the boxes, acting as an inspector without even the color of the law. Protesting was of no avail, and after the poll was closed it was found that votes had been received from persons not registered, while some names had been voted upon twice.

In the Fifth Election district of the Fourth ward, many illegal votes were received by the two Democratic inspectors against the protest of their Republican colleagues, and without a concurrence of the majority of the Board, as required by law.

In the Seventh Election district of the twenty-first ward, one of the Republican inspectors who had previously marked upon his book a large number of names of persons whom he desired to challenge, not believing them entitled to vote, was arrested upon a false charge on the morning of election day when on his way to the polls, and kept confined some five hours, when he was released on bail. Upon arriving at the poll of his district, he found that the votes of the persons he had so marked for challenge had all been offered to and received by the other members of the Board of inspectors.

In the Third Election district of the Fourth ward eighty-five names of persons who did not vote were added to the poll-list during the day of election. Late in the evening, but before the canvass was begun, the Republican canvasser became intoxicated, and eighty-five full sets of Democratic ballots were obtained, thrown upon the table with the contents of the boxes as they were emptied, and were canvassed and returned.

In the Fifth Election district of the Thirteenth ward the returns of the canvass of votes cast for Representatives in Congress, gave George Francis Train, who was running as an independent candidate, one (1) vote.

After the election, Clark Bell, Esq., Mr. Train's attorney, procured a large number of affidavits from registered persons in that district, "who swore that they voted for Train." Peter Hale, a resident of No. 242 Division street, in that district, subsequently testified that he voted there for Mr. Train, and personally put into the hands of some forty voters ballots for Train, and "saw such votes deposited in the box."

In many districts of the city, on the day of election, it was almost impossible for the challengers to discharge their duties. Special deputy sheriffs, repeaters and roughs thronged the polls and threatened the lives of those who attempted to challenge illegal voters. In this work of preventing challenging, prominent Democratic politicians as well as Democratic inspectors of election frequently aided and encouraged the outside disturbing elements. A few instances will make the facts clear to the minds of all.

In the Sixteenth Election district of the Sixteenth ward, the Republican challenger was ordered out of the room early in the day, by the Democratic Chairman of the Board of Inspectors, and was compelled to leave.

In the Third Election district of the Eleventh ward, the Republican challenger protested to the Board against the reception of votes by the chairman, before the name of the voter was found on the registry by the inspector in charge of the "check" copy. For this, the chairman—a Democrat—ordered the police officer present to arrest the challenger, but the latter showed his authority to act, and the officer declined to remove him. He was then repeatedly threatened by the chairman of the Board, and outsiders, and told that if he "should attempt to challenge," his life would be forfeited. Intimidated, but determined not to be driven off, he made no direct challenges, contenting himself with noting the facts, and protesting against the action of the Board, but no attention was paid to his objections, other than to inform him that he must keep his mouth shut. In speaking of the affairs of the day, the challenger has testified "My friends told me that I had better not challenge anybody; and it was said in my hearing, that if I challenged anybody, the——life should pay for it: my friends advised me to stay there and take observations. I have

not the least doubt that if I had challenged, personal violence would
have been inflicted upon me. I left fifteen or twenty minutes before the
polls closed; . . . I had been picked out as a victim, and so I thought I
had better go away."

Source: John I. Davenport, *The Election Frauds of New York City and Their Prevention*
(New York, 1872).

---

(27) Blacks Intimidated by Ku Klux Klan—New Iberia, Louisiana, 1869

> After the Civil War the slaves were freed, and, with the passage
> by Congress of several "reconstruction" measures culminating in
> the fourteenth and fifteenth amendments to the U.S. Constitu-
> tion, black males in the South became citizens and eligible to
> vote. Many of the freedmen were in fact eager to exercise their
> newly won voting rights. In some states for a time such men
> could cast ballots without much hindrance, partly due to the
> protection provided by federal troops or by local Republican
> organizations known as Union Leagues. In other states, how-
> ever, especially those in the Deep South, violence and intimi-
> dation were often used by groups of whites, collectively known
> as the Ku Klux Klan, to keep blacks from showing up at the polls
> on Election Day. Members of the Klan could not accept the idea
> of blacks voting, particularly in districts where they felt the non-
> white majority threatened to take power. The following docu-
> ment, which provides testimony from a Louisiana Republican
> appearing before Congress in 1869, explains the kind of terrorist
> actions undertaken by the Klan in his state against potential
> black voters.

There were numerous secret political organizations of the Democratic
party throughout the parish, [New Iberia] known . . . as the "Ku Klux
Klans," whose objects were to intimidate the Republicans and prevent
them from voting at all, unless they would vote the Democratic ticket.
These organizations were armed with fire-arms and patrolled the parish
night and day, committing murders and outrages among the Republicans, and produced such terror and alarm among the freedmen and others belonging to the Republican party that it was unsafe for them to hold
meetings. . . . It was utterly impossible to distribute Republican tickets
among the voters of the parish without danger of being mobbed and

killed. . . . Witness knows of a great many freedmen who were Republicans, and who desired to vote the Republican ticket, who were, by violence, fraud, and intimidation, compelled to vote the Democratic ticket. . . . Before and on the day of election the principal roads in the parish leading to the different places of voting were patrolled by armed men of these Klans for the purpose of intercepting Republicans going to vote; and, in many instances, plantations where freedmen were employed were guarded by armed men to prevent the freedmen from going to the polls.

Source: Walter L. Fleming, ed., *Documentary History of Reconstruction* (Cleveland: Arthur Clark, 1906), 370.

---

(28) Blacks Cheated by Democratic Opponents— Vicksburg, Mississippi, 1875

Violence and intimidation were not the only methods being employed to keep blacks from voting. As the noted historian of African Americans, John Hope Franklin, has pointed out, other devices, though hardly legal, had a more "respectable" appearance. "Polling places were frequently set up far from black communities, and the more diligent blacks failed to reach them upon finding roads blocked and ferries frequently out of repair at election time. Polling places were sometimes changed without notifying black voters; or, if they were notified, election officials thought nothing of making a last-minute decision not to change the place after all. Election laws were so imperfect that in many communities uniform ballots were not required, and officials winked at Democrats who made up several ballots to cast with the one given them. The practice of stuffing ballot boxes was widespread. Criminal manipulation of the counting gave point to the assertion of an enthusiastic Democrat that 'the white and black Republicans may outvote us, but we can outcount them'" (John Hope Franklin, *From Slavery to Freedom*, 8th ed., p. 287). An example of the latter situation is described in testimony given by a black Mississippian to a Senate committee in 1875. D.J. Foreman, a Negro Republican leader, had had three hundred Republican voters and only forty-seven Democrats in his district at the time of the previous election. Yet as he explains below, the Democrats won.

... We held meetings but we did not hold them publicly. We used to go into the swamps to hold them, and we had a house off the road where we could meet, with no lamps or anything.

Q. What did you do at those meetings?

A. We would meet for the purpose of discussing what we were going to do at the election.

Q. What did you propose to do at the election?

A. Some said not to go to the polls, some said they would go, some said they were afraid to go, and some said they were not, and they would go [even] if they got killed....

Q. Are your people armed generally[?]....

A. No, sir; they are poorly armed....

Q. When did you first know what the result was [in the 1875 election]?

A. I met Bazelis, clerk of the election, the next morning coming from Vicksburgh, and I asked him what was the result of the election. He told me: "We beat you badly yesterday." I says, "No, you didn't; you polled forty-seven votes." He says, "It was you polled forty-seven votes, and we polled three hundred. You all voted democratic votes...."

Q. Do you know anything more about what took place at the election?

A. [The whites] ... met the colored people, and would not allow them to come with arms; and the white people kept on theirs, and that scared the colored people....

Q. And the democrats carried their arms?

A. Yes, sir; and Mr. Henderson told me that I would have to shut my mouth; and I told him that I thought they were going to let us have a fair election; and they said it was a fair election, only the fuss I was making. I told him I was making a fuss for something; that I thought as they did not allow colored people to bring their arms, that they ought not to have theirs.

Source: Mississippi in 1875, Senate Report 527, Part 2, 44th Cong., 1st sess. (Washington, D.C., 1876), 1380–83, in William Loren Katz, *Eyewitness: The Negro in American History* (New York: Pitman, 1967), 283–84.

(29) Women First Vote in Western Territorial Election— Laramie, Wyoming, 1870

At about the same time that southern black males were first seeking to exercise their right to vote, in parts of the West another politically disadvantaged group—women—sought to begin casting ballots as well. The territory of Wyoming in 1869 was the first to grant women the use of the elective franchise. The Democratic legislature had approved the measure partly to embarrass the Republican-appointed governor, partly to attract more women settlers (the ratio of men to women at the time stood at six to one), and partly because some members felt it was right and proper. Of course, many men in Wyoming were not comfortable with this decision and ridiculed the idea of "petticoat government." Yet after women started to participate in the balloting, there developed a growing tolerance, especially as female voters brought a certain amount of order and dignity to the electoral process. As the following account, taken from Elizabeth Cady Stanton's and Susan B. Anthony's history of the suffrage movement, asserts, the previous territorial election had been accompanied by drunkenness, rowdyism, and even bloodshed. Some men had reportedly stayed away from the polls rather than expose themselves to such abuse. But once women were taking part, beginning with the contest in 1870, unruly behavior was no longer a problem, except in the saloons. The account also includes a letter, written to the editor of the *Laramie Sentinel* by the local pastor of the Baptist church, the Rev. D.J. Pierce, who witnessed the event and affirms the positive contribution made by women in their initial appearance at the polls.

The first election under the woman suffrage law was held in September 1870, for the election of a delegate in congress, and county officers. There was an exciting canvass, and both parties applied to the whisky shops, as before, supposing they would wield the political power of the territory, and that not enough women would vote to influence the result. The morning of the election came, but did not bring the usual scenes around the polls. A few women came out early to vote, and the crowd kept entirely out of sight. There was plenty of drinking and noise at the saloons, but the men would not remain, after voting, around the polls. It seemed more like Sunday than election day. Even the negro men and women voted without objection or disturbance. Quite a number of women voted during the day, at least in all the larger towns, but apprehension of a repetition of the scenes of the former election, and doubt as to the proper course for them to pursue, kept very many from voting. The result was a great disappointment all around. The election had passed off with unexpected quiet, and order had everywhere prevailed. The whisky shops had been beaten, and their favorite candidate for congress, although he had spent several thousand dollars to secure an election, was left out in the cold. I cannot deny myself the pleasure of quoting at length the following letter of the Rev. D.J. Pierce, at that time a resident of Laramie City, and a very wealthy man, to show the powerful influence that was exerted on the mind of a New England clergyman by that first exhibition of women at the polls, and as evidence of the singular and beneficial change in the character of the election, and the conduct of the men:

Editor, Laramie Sentinel: I am pleased to notice your action in printing testimonials of different classes to the influence of woman suffrage in Wyoming. With the apathy of conservatism and prejudice of party spirit arrayed against the idea in America, it is the duty of the residents of Wyoming to note the simple facts of their noted experiment, and lay them before the world for its consideration. I came from the vicinity of Boston, arriving in Laramie two weeks before the first regular election of 1870. I had never sympathized with the extreme theories of the woman's rights platform, to the advocates of which I had often listened in Boston. But I had never been able to learn just why a woman is naturally excluded from the privilege of franchise, and I sometimes argued in favor in lyceum debates. Still the question of her degradation stared me in the face, and I came to Wyoming unsettled in the matter, determined to be an impartial judge. I was early at the polls, but too late to witness the polling of the first female vote—by "Grandma" Swain, a much-esteemed Quaker lady of 75 summers, who determined by her words and influence to rally her sex to defend the state of morality and justice.

I saw the rough mountaineers maintaining the most respectful decorum whenever the women approached the polls, and heard the timely warning of one of the leading managers as he silenced an incipient quarrel with uplifted finger, saying "Hist! Be quiet! A woman is coming!"

And I was compelled to allow that in this new country, supposed at the time to be infested by hordes of cut-throats, gamblers and abandoned characters, I had witnessed a more quiet election than it had been my fortune to see in the quiet towns of Vermont. I saw ladies attended by their husbands, brothers, or sweethearts, ride to the place of voting, and alight in the midst of a silent crowd, and pass through an open space to the polls, depositing their votes with no more exposure to insult or injury than they would expect on visiting a grocery store or meat-market. Indeed, they were much safer here, every man of their party was pledged to shield them, while every member of the other party feared the influence of any signs of disrespect.

Source: Elizabeth Cady Stanton et al., *History of Woman Suffrage* (New York: Fowler & Wells, 1881–1922), 2:738–39.

(30) Women Take Part in Municipal Election—Topeka, Kansas, 1889

Although equal voting rights women had obtained in the territory of Wyoming in 1869 were carried over into statehood in 1890, by the end of the nineteenth century the number of full-suffrage states had risen only to four—Colorado, Utah, and Idaho being added in the mid- to late 1890s. However, in the intervening years several states had granted women partial suffrage, especially in the realm of school board elections, as it was felt that women, being the prime rearers of children, ought to participate in the decisions affecting the education of their offspring. In addition, the state of Kansas, beginning in 1887, agreed to give all women the right to take part in municipal elections. The following newspaper account describes women's participation in the mayoral contest in the town of Topeka in April 1889, the third year of female voting, calling it "an experiment in progress." As the document shows, many women in the community, including a substantial number of African Americans, demonstrated a great eagerness to vote. Indeed, the reporter claimed, women voters often displayed more enthusiasm than the men, and in casting their ballots seemed "more impressed with the responsibility of their act" than their male counterparts. Also mentioned, at the end of the article, is the fact that people in a few towns even chose an all-female slate of local officials, something that would attract a good deal of national attention in the years to come.

Topeka, Kansas, April 7.—Thousands of women participated in the municipal elections held throughout Kansas last week. In Topeka alone over 2,300 voted, and in Leavenworth, Wichita, Atchison, Fort Scott, and smaller cities the numbers far exceeded those of 1887. No issue other than that of decent municipal government was presented, and the accepted explanation of this large vote is that the women now fully appreciate the fruits of the victory they won two years ago.

The scenes at the polls certainly sustained this view of the situation. In Topeka the women displayed more enthusiasm than the men. They not only went to the polls and worked, but many of the most influential of them sent their carriages to remote parts of the city and brought in numbers of their less-happily circumstanced sisters, who needed but the one incentive of rapid transit to make them good nineteenth-century

Kansas citizens. Hundreds of colored women visited the voting places during the day, and many of these electioneered with all the art of practiced politicians. Every hack or carryall in the city was called into service, and it was noticeable that the "black vote" required more transportation than its paler adjunct of civilization. Much to the disgust of the Republicans, most of the white women voted for the Democratic candidates for Mayor in Topeka, Leavenworth, and Atchison. In the former city the Republican nominee was confessedly a "ringster," while in Leavenworth the notorious Col. Dan Anthony, brother of Susan B., headed the Republican ticket. Susan B. Anthony came out from Rochester to help the Colonel, but the women proved too much for them, and he was snowed under by 700 majority. It is possible that Miss Anthony is not so much in favor of woman suffrage in Kansas as she was a week ago.

At each voting place in Topeka, and presumably the other cities, a partition separated the men and women as they deposited their ballots. The women seemed more impressed with the responsibility of their act, and scrutinized their tickets carefully before passing them through the windows. Out in this benighted country the names of all the candidates are printed on long sheets of paper. With charming frankness many of the ladies who voted for the first time produced pencils and "scratched" their tickets and then handed them to the clerks unfolded and with the changes visible to the canvassers. In an alley near one of the polls three white women were seen in earnest conversation with a colored dame, who evidently could not read, but desired to vote the straight Republican ticket. She was finally provided with a ticket that added another nail to the coffin of the Republican candidate for Mayor, and she marched up to the window and handed it in with the air of a Queen.

During the day many cases of husband and wife voting oppositely came to notice, and these have already been cited in attempted refutation of the claim that women are largely influenced by their husbands. It is asserted further that many men were induced to change their votes on Tuesday, through the arguments of their better halves. The result, particularly in this banner Republican city, would certainly indicate something of this nature.

Kansas, the great experimental ground of the Nation, seems to have settled the question of municipal suffrage for women, to the satisfaction of a large majority of its own people at least. In Cottonwood Falls and Rossville, two small cities, the entire Government has just been placed in the hands of women. Oskaloosa has been governed by women for the past two years, and the people seem to be pleased, for they have re-elected them.

Source: "Women with the Ballot," *New York Times*, April 8, 1889, 1.

(31) Henry George in Defeat Speaks to His Supporters— New York, 1886

One feature of Election Day that would increase in frequency and importance was a brief address by the candidate to his supporters after the results of the balloting were made known. For the winner, it was often a statement filled with joy as he savored the moment of victory. All the burdens born and sacrifices undertaken during the campaign were now counterbalanced by the exhilaration of triumph. Besides thanking those who had worked and voted for him, the winner's statement usually focused on goals to be pursued by the individual and his party. For the loser, the speech was often the antithesis. It mainly dwelled on the pain of defeat and the effort that had been made in vain. Yet for some losing candidates, especially those connected with some larger cause, there might be an attempt to look at the positive side, to emphasize any partial success rather than what had not been accomplished. The speaker might express the need for the movement to go forward and tell his listeners not to give up hope despite the lack of victory this time.

A good example of the latter phenomenon in the late nineteenth century was a speech made by the social reformer Henry George to his backers after running a vigorous race in the New York City mayoralty contest in 1886. George, who believed that the workingman was financially overburdened and that society could be maintained through a "single tax" on land, had taken his case that year to the people of the nation's largest metropolis. Lacking a regular party organization and competing against both entrenched machines and their attractive candidates—well-known businessman Abram Hewitt on the Democratic side and the young patrician Theodore Roosevelt on the Republican side—George came in a strong second. He captured more votes than Roosevelt, garnering 31 percent of the overall total. Though he did not win the office he had sought, George talked in his postelection speech about what his forces had achieved in going up against the overwhelming power of the existing parties. Rather than viewing the result as a loss, he saw it as the start of something of monumental importance, even though that turned out not to be so.

Friends and Brothers: I am prouder to-night in your greeting, in your support, in your friendship, in the devotion to a great cause that I have seen among you rendered to me as an exponent of your principles, than I would be if by ordinary methods I held in my hand the official returns making me President of the United States.

I congratulate you to-night upon the victory we have won. Under a fair vote of the people of New York I would be to-night elected Mayor. If, as now seems probable, the official returns do not give me that office, it is because of the money, of the bribery, of the intimidation, of a press perverted and unscrupulous, of the unreasoning fears of the ignorant rich, and the hopeless degradation of the miserable poor. But men, I did not accept your candidacy for the office, nor did you nominate me for the office; what we sought was to bring principle into American politics. I congratulate you upon the greatest of victories that we have won. They may bribe, they may count us out, by their vile arts they may defeat what would be an honest verdict of the people; but we have gained what we fought for. Thank God, we have made a beginning. We have demonstrated the political power of labor. Never again—never again, will the politicians look upon a labor movement with contempt.

I have waited to get the full returns and have not got them yet. But my vote will hardly fall under seventy thousand. You know, you men know—you men who have worked night after night without a penny, you men who have stood by the polls all day without a cent—you know under what disadvantages this struggle has been made. If this is the beginning, what will be the end?

I am a proud and happy man to-night. I thank you from the bottom of my heart. I thank you more truly and kindly than if you had given me the highest office, for the devotion you have shown, for the manner in which you have forgotten all factional disputes, for the manner in which all the diverse elements have rallied, and all petty jealousies that have hitherto divided the ranks of labor have been lost sight of.

The future, the future is ours. This is the Bunker Hill. We have been driven back as the Continental troops were from Bunker Hill. If they won no technical victory, they did win a victory that echoed round the world and still rings. They won a victory that made this Republic a reality, and, thank God, men of New York, we in this fight have won a victory that makes the true Republic of the future certain—certain in our time. Most of you men are younger than I, and to you more years will be given. You will look back to this campaign with pride. We have not been trying to elect a Mayor; we have been making history. We have lit a fire that will never go out. We have begun a movement that, defeated, and defeated, and defeated, must still go on. All the great currents of our time, all the aspirations of the heart of man, all the new forces of our civilization are with us and for us. They never fail who die in a good cause. So, on and on and on together. We have done in this campaign more for popular education, more to purify politics, more toward the emancipation of labor from industrial slavery, than could have been accomplished in twenty years of ordinary agitation.

Some time let us meet again and talk over these matters.

We have done a greater thing than my election to the Mayoralty. A constitutional convention has been called. That gives us a great opportunity. Let us improve it. That is the next fight. Let us win that beyond any peradventure.

And now I want to express my appreciation and my thanks to the gentlemen of the Executive Committee and its chief and chairman, Mr. McMackin, for the intelligence, for the self-sacrifice, for the energy, and the industry, and the devotion which they have shown in your cause, and to the many men whom I have met in the streets to-day, and the still greater number of men I did not meet. I thank them all. Let me express my hearty thanks—my appreciation of the way in which they worked against all obstacles.

I tell you again that such devotion, such earnestness, must and will carry this cause forward, no matter what little skirmish we may happen to nominally lose. This has been but a skirmish that prepares our forces for the battles which are to follow.

Source: Louis F. Post and Fred Leubuscher, *Henry George's 1886 Campaign* (New York, 1887), 169–70.

(32) Partisan Struggle in Small New Jersey Town— Cranford, New Jersey, 1888

Few sources give as good an account of the atmosphere around the polling place in a small town in the late nineteenth century as the following firsthand description of the general election of 1888 in Cranford, New Jersey. Cranford, just across the river from New York City, was a divided community that took its politics very seriously. During the campaign, party meetings and torchlight parades were scheduled almost every night, and on Election Day itself the voters responded en masse. As the author notes, despite cold and foggy weather, between forty and fifty men had already gathered at the town hall well before the polls opened at 6:00 A.M., and the turnout would continue to be heavy in subsequent hours. There were 325 eligible voters in Cranford, and by the end of the day 320 would cast ballots (146 Republicans, 146 Democrats, twenty-six Prohibitionists, and two others). These men represented not just different political persuasions, but all races, ages, and levels of wealth. The writer takes great pains to stress the democratic nature of the process at the election site, especially the intermingling of the well-dressed man of means with the average farmer in work clothes. In his eyes, the system worked very well.

CRANFORD, N.J., Nov. 10.—It is, I believe, pretty well known in New York that on Tuesday we had an election in this State. Some of our friends from the back lots will not yet believe that the election is really over, but it is a settled fact. Nobody in this township ever saw the patriots gathered in from the hills and valleys as they were on Tuesday. They came in blocks of five and blocks of ten, singly, on foot, on horseback, and in all sorts of vehicles, white and black, young and old, sick, well, maimed, blind, and indifferent. Those who had no conveyances of their own were sent for, and those who would not come were sent for, and those who would not come were sent for again and yet again. Sick men were almost dragged out of their beds, and unwilling men were buttonholed and bothered till they had to vote to save their own lives. But it is not to give any news about the election that I write this letter. I remember seeing a political article in THE TIMES a week or two ago, and it will not do to print too much on the same subject. I want rather to give a few incidents of an election day in New Jersey in one of the smaller towns, and coming from the standpoint of an amateur politician perhaps they may not be without interest.

Meeting had followed meeting with alarming rapidity throughout the campaign; torches and bands and banners had done their whole duty, and on Monday night we who were managing the affairs of the nation, that is to say, the members of the Executive Committee for this township, had held our final meeting and pronounced everything ready for the fray. Under the new law the polls were to open at 6 o'clock in the morning, and some of us must be on hand to see things done properly. There was a vacant inspectorship to be filled, and those who were present when the polls were opened would have the privilege of voting for a candidate to fill the vacancy. At 5:30 in the morning lights began to glimmer in the Town Hall, the sole polling place for the township—lights that just served to make visible outside a thick fog that obscured a tree at 20 yards and completely obliterated a house at 25. It was a most disagreeable morning; cold, raw, damp, and every way unpleasant. Nothing but the responsibility that lay upon this township of making a President for four years more could have induced anybody to leave a comfortable bed and go out into the chill morning air. But we had besides to elect a Congressman and a gentleman to represent us in the New Jersey Assembly, and the fate of districts and counties, perhaps even of a Nation, rested in our hands, and we turned out heroically. At

5:40 a person in every way resembling the writer, with a stout cane in one hand and a bright lantern in the other, sallied forth into the darkness and fog and went over to the polling place, wondering why the new law could not have done a trifle better by us in New Jersey and opened the polls at midnight, so that a man might vote before going to bed. In the Town Hall, the polling place, the faithful had already gathered to the number of 40 or 50. Lights were burning, men were shivering, and the judge of election was putting in place that remarkable piece of mechanism known as the New Jersey ballot box, with glass sides and an iron top and a handle on one side to grind in the votes.

"Now, gentlemen," said the Town Clerk when 6 o'clock arrived, "the hour has come for opening the polls. It is necessary to select one more inspector of election; who will you have?"

Tom Tomson was promptly nominated on the one side and Jim Jonson on the other.

"Now, all of you," said the Town Clerk, "who are in favor of Tom Tomson please take the east side of the hall, and all who are in favor of Jim Jonson take the west side."

The division made and the heads counted, we turned out—horrible discovery—to be 23 on each side, when the door opened, and in walked one of our own clan and joined our ranks, carrying victory to our banners. Tom Tomson was elected, and thus the first battle of the day was won by a hair. We were a curious crowd gathered together in the Town Hall on that foggy Tuesday morning. Nowhere but in the immediate neighborhood of New York, I think, could such an assemblage be found. Here was a solid old Jersey farmer from way up the river, with his trousers stuffed in his boot tops and hay seed dripping from his hair, and beside him an officer from the United States Sub-Treasury. There the village blacksmith, and next to him a wealthy New York merchant whose name is familiar to everybody. Here an importer, there a young farmer boy, and away over on one side, holding on gallantly to his lantern, THE TIMES's correspondent, ready to drop in a vote where it might do the most good.

The Democratic "watcher" took his place with his little book and began checking off the voters as their ballots were deposited; the Republican watcher was there, also with his little book; and so was the Prohibition man, book in hand, all hard at work. In went the first vote, around went the handle, click went the machinery inside the box, and the business of the day was begun. A hard day's business it was for everybody concerned. In the first half hour more than 50 votes were polled, for three quarters of our Cranford voters are in business in New York; and go down in the early trains.

After the first batch of votes were in, and the workers really got settled down to business, it seemed as if everybody challenged everybody else.

It was a contagious fever, and it spread with marvelous rapidity. John Q. Smith, who was born and has always lived on the banks of the Rahway, challenged the vote of Robert R. Robinson, whose grandfather was one of the early Jersey settlers, and who like enough was never out of this township in his life. The White family challenged the Black family, and the Greens challenged the Grays. Nothing ever moved faster than this challenging fever, and before long I caught it myself and began to look over the book for a Prohibitionist of foreign birth, that I might challenge him just for the fun of making him go home after his papers. This was done in a purely philanthropic spirit, to give every Prohib a chance to show that he was legally entitled to vote. It is always pleasant to learn a good thing about anybody, and I gladly record that among the Prohibition voters in Cranford I could not find a single foreigner.

It was not until after breakfast time that the horses began to vote. Of course they did not walk bodily into the hall and personally cast their ballots, though there are very few horses in Cranford that could be challenged on account of their age, most of them having lived here fully long enough to vote; but on this occasion they did their voting by proxy, bringing their lords and masters to town. Several of the Cranford horses deserve great credit for their conduct on election day, for they worked as hard as any of the politicians, and did more than their share to bring out a full vote. Two or three of them decorated with flags, scoured all parts of the township and brought in the lame, the halt, and the blind. Three hundred and twenty-five was the highest estimate of the possible number of votes, and about 320 were actually cast, a result that was owing largely to the efforts of the horses and their owners. Nothing but the moisture in the atmosphere kept it from being the dryest kind of a dry day, for all the hotels and saloons were closed, not only theoretically, but in fact. Still, most of the faithful were armed with flasks, excepting, of course, the Prohibitionists, who, in New Jersey, are notoriously temperate and abstemious. It was hardly more than dark when the last vote was counted, and then was made known the remarkable result of 146 Democratic votes, 146 Republican, and 26 Prohibition. It was the closest vote ever polled in Cranford, and showed slight gains for the Democrats and Prohibitionists. All parties had done the hardest kind of work, and no stone was left unturned. One incident of the day shows how important it is for every man to cast his vote who can. One of the old-time Republicans, living a short distance out of town, refused for some reason to vote for anybody. Carriage after carriage was sent after him, but his invariable answer was: "No, I have made up my mind not to vote, and my vote cannot make any difference at any rate." His vote would just have given the Republicans in this town the booming majority of one. New York gathered in a large share of the faithful as soon as the local vote was counted, for everybody was in a hurry for general news, and some of the Republicans telegraphed home: "[Benjamin] Harrison is elected; light up the town!" But as none of these private dispatches were delivered till Wednesday morning the town remained in its customary darkness. Like many another place, perhaps including even New York, Cranford is well satisfied to wait four years for a repetition of the dose.

Source: "Over the Hills to the Polls," *New York Times*, November 11, 1888, 16.

---

(33) A Black Female Precinct Worker Tells Her Story— New York, 1895

How did local precinct workers go about getting voters to the polls in late-nineteenth-century urban America? While it is hard to find any firsthand accounts involving a male figure in such a position, a very revealing one exists for an African-American female—Mary L. Hall, a former slave originally from Savannah, Georgia, who subsequently worked for many years for the Republican party in New York City. Hall first became active in politics in Georgia in 1869, when black men, most of whom could neither read nor write, were just beginning to exercise their suffrage rights. "The people were voting in the Court House there in Savannah and the polls were open all day long, and when I went out I saw the advantage the white persons were taking of my people. The white people were giving the colored voters Democratic tickets, and the Negro men did not know any better. I saw that I could be of use." In a newspaper interview conducted in the mid 1890s, Hall goes on to describe her later political experiences in a black neighborhood on the west side of New York City. As president of the Colored Women's Republican Auxiliary, Hall was responsible for bringing a certain number of voters to the ballot box each Election Day, and tells how despite many obstacles she succeeded in that endeavor. Besides telling about Hall's political activities, the document also provides an interesting glimpse of certain other aspects of black life in New York during this period.

I really can tell a Republican whenever I see one in the face. I am a pretty good character reader, anyway. There is something open and frank about a Republican that draws me to him. All that we have ever received that has been elevating has been from the Republican Party. I give twenty-six voters to the party every election day. I give more than that, but I am always sure of twenty-six.

I make a room-to-room canvass. I even go into the gambling places and dives where I think colored men are likely to be, and make them come out and register. Then, on election day, I make them vote. This is the dirty work I have done for the Captain [Caleb Simms, the district leader]. He would not do that himself.

Every election day I serve soup, coffee, sandwiches, and cigars to voters. You cannot get colored men to vote without spending money one way or another. . . .

Sometimes I give the men something to drink. Sometimes they say they want something to eat. Sometimes a man says he has a white shirt in the laundry that must come out. There must be money for all these things. I have 105 women in my association, but they are all poor women with young children, and they must have some money, though it be only a little, if they go out and work.

Did you see that little woman on the platform at the meeting the other evening? She is one of the best workers I have. She is always at the post of duty. She lives in Thirty-second Street, and she takes more men to the polls than any one else.

On election day I am out before the polls open and I stay there all day and watch the people voting. I never forget a face. The way they try to work it is to get the Democratic negroes and Tammany heelers to vote early in the morning. Then after that they go in line again with something folded in their hands that looks like a ticket, and they take up the time, and then it gets so late the Republican voters don't have a chance.

I have a white man and a colored man to watch, and I have them go inside the polls to see who has voted. If they say a man has voted, I put a "V" down beside his name and cross it out. Then I go to where in line he is standing and say: "What are you doing here?" and push him out. If he won't go I call a policeman.

There, did you see that man going by? I was going to show you a Democratic nigger. That was the one that knocked me down.

It was on one registration day, and I had been out to get some things for tea—some tomatoes and eggs. I was standing with some colored women watching the Democratic niggers across the street. One of the women took some of my eggs and began to throw them. I had not done anything, but one of the men came across the street and asked me what I was doing and hit me. Then I got some more eggs and began to throw them at him. They were not rotten eggs, though, for they cost me 28 cents a dozen.

Then this man came across the street and knocked me down with a blackjack. I thought I was going to die. One time I was hit when I took a voter away from a Democratic [ward] heeler [a local party worker] and tore up his tickets. But they only hit me a little.

I was hooted at and cried down by both black and white people when I first began to do election work. The white men told the policeman to arrest me, for I was either crazy or drunk.

But when the policeman came to me he found there was not a smell of liquor about. I won't say I wouldn't drink a glass of beer sometimes, but on election day I never let a drop of anything pass my lips.

Source: "She Is a Politician," *New York Times*, October 18, 1895, 8.

---

(34) The Atmosphere of Election Day in a Major Metropolis—New York, 1896

The presidential contest of 1896 would be one of the most intensely fought in American history. The Republicans, hoping to capitalize on the failures of the Democratic administration of Grover Cleveland, designated former Ohio governor William McKinley as their candidate. The Democrats, moving away from the party's traditionally conservative nominees, chose thirty-six-year-old congressman William Jennings Bryan of Nebraska, who had ignited the party convention with his fiery "cross of gold" speech. The well-organized, well-financed Republicans thought they would achieve an easy victory, given the still-difficult economic conditions facing the country. But Bryan, crisscrossing the nation by rail, giving more speeches than any previous White House hopeful, attacking the business community, and calling for the coinage of "free silver," left the outcome of the race in doubt until the very end. The following essay, "The Day," written by a visiting Englishman, captures the tension and excitement of Election Day in New York City on this occasion. The author carefully depicts what was occurring on the city streets as the balloting went on and then, in even greater detail, tells what was happening as the ballots were counted and the results made known.

The belated demonstrators were hardly silent when the day of destiny dawned. And almost before it had actually dawned the day's work had begun. The polls open at six o'clock in New York, and even by that hour millionaire and beggar had lined up in front of the polling-booths as if they were the pit-door of a theatre. The strain of the last few days had become no longer bearable. Nobody could lie abed when the moment for action had at last come. Unbreakfasted, unwashed, unclothed, all hastened to get the momentous vote off their chests. The clustering figures in the half-daylight, muffled in overcoats, recalled an Oxford undergraduates' eight o'clock roll-call.

It must be explained that Americans do not vote, like us, in a public building. During the last few days broad, dark-green wooden sheds have squatted on the streets all over the city. In these tabernacles they take the sacrament of citizenship. In the poorer quarters, where the streets are narrower, shops are consecrated to the solemn rite. Usually cigar-stores are chosen—sometimes, with genial irony for the defeated candidate, an undertaker's.

By the time the city ordinarily wakes up nearly half the votes had been cast. Already New York, its duty done, had settled itself down to enjoy a holiday under the clear sunlight of an Indian summer's day. The polling-places were soon deserted, but for a little knot of party watchers, tallymen all decked out with ribbons like prize shorthorns, and the police. Rarely a candidate or some high party official bustled up on a tour of inspection; then the oracle of the voice of the people sank back into dumbness again. The party headquarters were no longer crowded as in past days. Only a few devotees were there, keeping lists and receiving reports from the polling-places. Tammany Hall itself was half empty, and almost silent. Wall Street and the other business quarters were ablaze with the national colours, but there were no business men. The Broadway shops and restaurants were all decked out in bunting, but all were closed. Fifth Avenue was as depopulated as in the middle of August. The mean streets of the East Side were filled with unshaven men, slatternly women, and barefooted children. But this assemblage was merely because here the street takes the place of the country and the seaside. Only at rare street corners stood three or four men, with puckered faces, wondering why Mike O'Flaherty had not voted yet. Meanwhile crowds of people were streaming to the ferries and the railway stations, seeking the country. The streets gradually filled with citizens' wives and children, all in their Sunday clothes. It was a Sabbath without any Sabbatarianism. You would say the city was quietly enjoying victory instead of being in the midst of battle.

But this is a day of vast activity for the street Arabs of New York. It is their day of days in the four long years. From early dawn they began to collect every available sort of material for bonfires. Their Guy Fawkes' day is a movable feast, dependent on the day of election. All day long they steal barrels, and planks, and straw, and boxes, under the very noses of the tolerant proprietors. Impatient enthusiasts had little fires crackling, in full sunlight and in the middle of the street, as early as nine o'clock. For the rest, the only signs of public excitement were the dense black masses of people fringing the pavement opposite all the newspaper offices—awaiting tidings not yet due for six hours. Altogether it was a day of waiting, but of waiting that was endurable compared with yesterday's. To-day each man had done all that in him lay, and he could await the result with clean-conscienced resignation.

But the polling was hardly over when the supreme day became merged in a supreme night. It was a day for work, which had been done in perfect order, and with a calmness and a dignity that fitted the momentous occasion. Mr. [Theodore] Roosevelt, New York's Chief Commissioner of Police, told me that this was the most peacefully conducted election in American history. Hardly an arrest was made all day. The very Italian roadmakers and the Yiddish hucksters put on character for one day, and carried themselves as citizens worthy of their citizenship.

But the night was given to a gluttony of sensation, after the suspense between triumph and despair in the last hour. Before the polls closed, at five o'clock, New York had settled down to an emotional debauch. The city was drained dry of voters early in the day, and the closest polling organisation hardly squeezed out a single elector in that last hour. Now to see if the great struggle of six months should issue in a burst of prosperity or in collapse and ruin!

Hours before any news was possible great crowds had massed in the City Hall Park and in Printing House Square. Here are most of the great newspaper offices, packed together even closer than in London. One big building is shared by both Silver and Gold newspapers [i.e., supporters of silver or gold-backed currency]. Caricatures, separated only by a window, showed any given statesman as the saviour of his country or as an embezzler of public funds, according to the taste of the exhibitor and the observer. The stereopticon bulletin shows being so close together, they could be depended on for an entertaining rivalry of picturesque sensation, which New York resolved to enjoy to the full. The towering face of the 'World' building was masked by an enormous screen, and half-a-dozen other newspaper buildings were almost as generously furnished with raw material for the cartoons and bulletins that should move to laughter or to tears. One could hardly move there by five o'clock; by six, when the first meagre results began to come in, the crush was almost terrifying in its unmeasurable and ungovernable force.

Meanwhile, inside the newspaper offices the most important work in four years was progressing feverishly. To realise the work before the newspaper you must remember that thirteen millions of votes were coming in from points three thousand miles apart, some of them three hours in time behind the others. On the basis of whatever flimsy indications arrived before press-time the paper must calculate a result for the whole country, whose accuracy might make or mar. The biggest room in each office was laid out with trestle-tables, whereat sat men adding, subtract-

ing, and multiplying. Each man had in his head, or at least on paper at
his side, the vote of 1892 in every county and precinct, in order to estimate from the early returns of the smallest village the probable trend
and force of the stream sweeping over the whole country. The opinion
of thousands of counties had thus to be dealt with, and the complexity
and magnitude of the task strained every rivet in the newspaper organisation. The scene inside the office was a combination of mad confusion
and perfect harmony. A little army of boys were flying with telegraphic
results to the calculators, and flying back with each result reduced to its
proper place in the general scheme. The calculators mopped their brows
without speaking, and calculated fiercely.

The anxious crowd outside surged denser and more terrible in its ungovernable weight. Thousands stood craning their necks to the walls of
the huge buildings before them, faintly outlined against the deep sky.
Search-lights spun round the horizon, lighting up signal-kites floating
aloft. On the screens appeared scenes shown by the cinematographe,
which were received with alternate delight and derision. When the first
returns were shown the crowd lost mastery of itself. The City Hall Park
is cut up by public buildings, with parallelograms and triangles of grass.
The crowd broke against the wire fences, swept them down, and surged
over the sacred enclosures. It could not help it. The laws of space and
force were the only things that had not taken a night off for the election.

From the first moment of the arrival of returns, the direction of the
stream was clearly apparent. New York City, where never before had a
majority been given for a Republican President, was going steadily and
surely for Mr. M'Kinley. One hundred districts, two hundred districts,
three hundred districts, were heard from, and Mr. M'Kinley forged
steadily ahead, till his majority in the city was certain to be at least
20,000. Then the serried masses began to open their lungs, and fierce
yells and whoops and cheers crashed from side to side of the great
square.

Passing north-eastward through the city was like passing from a mill-
race to a mill-pool. The poverty-stricken streets, where three hours before
one could hardly move for the crowds of dirty aliens lounging away the
holiday on the pavement, were now silent and dark, save where the
chartered sons of the gutter danced and whooped around the bonfires.
Early in the day these had been made from purloined boxes and barrels;
now they were being fed with straw mattresses and cheap furniture. But
the adults, the Italians, Poles, and miscellaneous Yiddishers, were still
under the spell of their brief dignity of citizenship.

At the main police office was an election bureau for receiving the first
official counts of the city voting. The bare flagstones of the stairs rang
with the hasty heels of journalists scurrying up and down with despatches. In the court-room was assembled a job lot of curious listeners,

and from time to time the officials enthroned on the bench hastily snatched papers from hurrying messengers and read aloud a bulletin putting a fresh nail in the coffin of Bryanism. The listening loafers chaffed the police and indulged in good-natured horseplay, while the constables laid aside their official majesty and worked away industriously with paper, pencil, and figures like ordinary commoners. In Commissioner Roosevelt's room was a tape telegraph-machine, ticking away feverishly.

Now began the announcements of voting in the country outside of New York. Chicago came along, swinging heavily to M'Kinley. Then came Kentucky, and like portents, in crushing sequence, from East and West and South. "That settles it," snapped out a hard sharp voice, at the announcement of the certain defeat of Governor [John P.] Altgeld in Illinois, and smiles wreathed the hard bitter face of an old inspector standing beside the instrument. Word quickly ran along the sentinels in the corridors and on the stairs of the downfall of the enemy of the law [who had pardoned three supposed anarchists charged with bomb-throwing in the Haymarket Square riot in May 1886]. The telegraph clicked more breathlessly, the official roared out the results more lustily, the journalists scurried about more wildly as the returns from everywhere came tumbling over each other, all pointing the same way.

Thence I went up deserted Broadway to Madison Square. Here a dense crowd was packed across the thoroughfare before the bulletin-boards of the up-town newspaper offices. Here doubt was dispelled in a frenzy of triumph. Many of the announcements were premature and incorrect, but enough was quickly known to send the watchers mad, and the air was torn with cheers. But loud above the cheers and the crackle of laughter that swept the crowds when the stereoptician joked, above the grinding of the cablecars elbowing their way and banging their gongs, arose the deafening blast of tin horns, which were sold by hundreds in the crowd. At each new triumph of Republicanism the ear-splitting bray of these tin trumpets boomed out. This was the form which the voice of the people chose to manifest its exultation. White men and black men, sober men and hilarious men, young men, staid middle-age and grey-beards, matrons and maidens, all were gravely tooting these babies' tin trumpets. Everybody was too exultant to care whether he behaved like an infant or not. There was no escape from the infernal din.

At the Republican headquarters I found the worn, pale, sleepless heroes of the fight summoning their last energies to revel without affectation of self-control in the brilliancy of their victory. Here, again, of course, were the newspaper-men, gathering the threads of information despatched to headquarters, and weaving them together into the complete tale of triumph. But hardly anybody was now concerned to add and compare returns. White-bearded, frock-coated men were rushing

about shaking hands with everybody in sight. The rooms echoed with
the ripple of light-hearted girls' laughter. A little army of waiters was
perspiringly trying to keep pace with the unquenchable demand for
champagne. Distracted with delight, the solid pillars of Sound Money
could only laugh and babble, and hurry from the tape to the window
and from the window back to the tape. Their joy would not allow them
to keep still one second.

At Democratic headquarters things were very different. Here was only
lassitude after effort. There was no victory or champagne to fillip it into
a flicker of animation. Everything and every one was most gloomily
silent, with the exception of a few unconquerable optimists, who were
still vainly trying to demonstrate that maturer returns might retrieve all.
Tammany Hall gave up the struggle early, and by eleven o'clock was
black and voiceless. Jeering enemies encamped on its steps undisturbed
and unanswered.

Passing on to the University Club, I found every member present exulting and dancing like schoolboys, as a waiter read item after item of
the colossal pile of victories. These fine gentlemen of New York cried for
cheers for M'Kinley, hurled stentorian congratulations at entering
friends, clasped each other round the waist by threes and fours, and
waltzed round the room under the approving smiles of the head-waiters.

My next task was to fight my way up to Herald Square. Here were
two cinematographes at work, but by now the people hardly deigned to
glance at them. This was the climax. No longer was the crowd made up
of men and women, but of rejoicing machines. The wide square was one
riot of delirium. The crowd spread itself over the tram rails, and almost
sought to push back the crawling cable-cars which attempted to jostle
them from an immediate view of the next undreamed-of success posted
on the bulletins. Now rockets and Roman candles were blazing on every
side. Gunpowder flared, bands crashed, bugles rang; overhead the late
trains puffed and clattered, and above all rang volleys of cheers and the
interminable discordant blare of tin trumpets, all blended in a furious
jangle of jubilation. The whole place was mad, demoniac, inspired with
a divine frenzy.

But by now it was well past midnight. Reports came rarely; the lights
began to go out; gangs of young men with linked arms charged and split
up the thinning crowd. The elevated trains and the cable-cars making
for the northern suburbs looked as though human bees had swarmed
over them. Every inch of floor and outside platform had a foot clinging
precariously to it. People were even hanging desperately from the brakes
and couplings. So New York began to empty, the vast assemblage falling
asleep with the reaction from an excitement that was almost too intense
for life. And through the crowd came pushing a man with matted hair
crying the morning papers.

The night of nights was justified of its supreme destiny. The expectation had been the tensest for a generation, but the realisation had risen to it and had overwhelmed it. The last screams of jubilation grew fainter and more distant; gradually the glamour of the dream wore off, and the city paled to ordinary dawn and ordinary day. New York was her daily self again, with the most stirring night of her recent fate behind her.

Source: G.W. Steevens, The Land of the Dollar (Edinburgh and London, 1897), 284–95.

---

(35) How William McKinley Spent the Day of His Election—Canton, Ohio, 1896

By the late nineteenth century, a tradition had developed in the press of having reporters follow and record the moment-to-moment activities of the two major parties' presidential candidates over the entire day. The stories particularly focused on each nominee's trip to the polling place, how they spent their time back home, and their reaction, later on in the evening, to the results as they came in. The experience of White House aspirants and of their friends and families was somewhat different than what such individuals have to face today. While there is the commonality of having to endure long hours of anxious waiting, a much more casual atmosphere can be observed in times past. People often dropped by, unannounced, with no secret service agents present to screen out potential undesirables. To be sure, the candidates usually maintained a public area in their homes for general visitors, keeping a private area for family and close advisers. As the returns began to be received, a crowd usually formed outside the residence, awaiting word from someone inside as to the nature of the outcome. Eventually, when the results were fairly clear, the presumed winner, as we see here with Ohio governor William McKinley, would come out to show their appreciation and thank the people gathered. But only in the twentieth century did the president-elect begin to deliver a public statement on election night, commenting on his victory.

CANTON (O.), November 3.—Major McKinley cast his vote at 9 o'clock this morning. Bands and marching clubs were on the streets by 6 o'clock summoning voters to cast their ballots early. It was an ideal fall day. After breakfast McKinley read with interest the Associated Press bulletins from all sections showing that the weather was generally clear and that a heavy vote was being polled early. He commented on this with satisfaction, adding that it was amazing that such a heavy percentage of the vote could be in by 9 o'clock as the reports indicated. Then he sat down to his desk to run through a heap of telegrams.

At 8 A.M. a telephone from the McKinley troop asked the Governor if he would go to the polls with the troop as an escort. He acknowledged the courtesy, but said he wished to go as a private citizen, and suggested that the troop march to the house and let him review them on the way to the polls. The invitation was accepted. When the troop reached the house they faced about and, with umbrellas waving, gave "Three cheers for McKinley." The Major bowed his acknowledgment with a sweep of his beaver, and as the cheers continued, waved his handkerchief. "Three cheers for the next President," were added, and the marchers moved to the polls with a parting shout, "Eighty per cent of the vote is in, Governor!" "We will be around tomorrow, Major!"

The Republican nominee started for the polls at 8:30 o'clock, accompanied by his brother, Abner McKinley, and his nephew Samuel Saxton. The men raised their hats as he passed and ladies on residence steps waved their hands.

As Major McKinley entered the small store in which the booths were located there was a stir of agitation among the officials and a mild rustle of applause. The nominee took his place in the line and the systematic march of the Australian balloting proceeded in truly democratic fashion. Ahead of Major McKinley was a swarthy-faced workingman, whose hands showed he had just laid down his tools. With some confusion he greeted the Major and offered to yield his place, but the offer was declined with a whisper in the man's ear, which made him beam.

"William McKinley, 723 North Market street," called the inspector, just as the clock marked 9. The Major stepped forward and received his ballot, a huge sheet with eight horizontal tickets, the first one being the Republican, headed with his own name. He moved through the inclosure to the curtained booths in the rear and stepped into the first one. He was in no hurry. Adjusting his eye-glasses, he scrutinized the ticket carefully. For just one minute and eighteen seconds he went over the names. Then, marking the head of the Republican ticket, indicating a straight Republican vote, he came from the booth and handed the ballot to the official in charge of the box. As he emerged from the place there was another cheer from the outside, another kindly acknowledgment, and then, having exercised his American privilege as a voter, Major McKinley and his brother walked down Tuscarawa street to greet the white-haired mother, 88 years old, who is a keen observer of the scenes in which her son is playing so large a part.

Major McKinley spent his afternoon with Chairman [Marcus Alonzo]

Hanna and his party, who, with the local committee, were photographed on McKinley's porch, with the Major as the central figure. At 4 o'clock Mr. Hanna and his associates left for Cleveland. Mrs. McKinley accompanied him to the train. At 6 o'clock the returns began to come in and preparations were made for reading them aloud in the McKinley library, the doors being open to all who chose to come in. The Major sat at his desk smoking a cigar and listening attentively to each bulletin, but showing no outward concern as to the result. One dispatch from Joseph Manley at New York headquarters said: "Maine's majority for McKinley will reach 50,000." And this was soon followed by another Manley dispatch saying: "New York State will give you 200,000 majority." The Major himself smilingly read a telegram from Max Pracht of Oregon saying: "Oregon is yours and the fullness thereof."

At 7 o'clock Major McKinley retired for his supper, while the reading of returns proceeded. Up to that time he had made no comment on the returns further than to say that the bulk of them came from the East thus far. When favorable returns from Nebraska were read he sat impassive and apparently oblivious to the exclamations of approval from the friends crowded about him. In the parlor across the hall Mrs. McKinley and her near relatives and friends received the returns. By 8 o'clock the character of the private dispatches and general returns reaching McKinley's house were such that a feeling of absolute confidence took possession of those centered in the Major's library. The officials at Chicago headquarters sent frequent private messages to Major McKinley, each one swelling the total of States claimed as certain for the Republican candidate.

The detailed returns, which were read as they came, appeared to bear out the claims from headquarters, and the spirit of the victory achieved was on every lip. Governor McKinley had joined his wife and mother in the parlor across the hall, which was closed to the general public. At 9 o'clock the Major's nephew, Mr. Saxton, emerged from the parlor with a private dispatch just received. It was from Garrett A. Hobart, Vice-Presidential candidate, who, at this early hour, felt that victory was won and telegraphed his congratulations. There was a round of applause from the group within the library as Mr. Hobart's words were read. Soon thereafter Major McKinley came from the parlor and joined the crowd in the outer room. His face now wore an unmistakable look of satisfaction, and he smiled and chatted with those about him about the favorable character of the reports. He was not yet ready, however, to express his own judgment on the result, although it was evident he shared the general feeling of confidence that he had carried the day. . . . [Favorable reports continued over the next few hours and eventually McKinley went out on the front porch to greet the many well-wishers who had gathered.]

At 12:30 o'clock Mr. McKinley received a tremendous ovation from his townspeople. He took a position on top of the porch of his residence and waved his salutations to the enthusiastic concourse. The midnight was light as day by the hundreds of flamebeaux and blazing fires of red and green. Major McKinley made no address. For an hour the remarkable spectacle proceeded. The whistles of all the factories joined in one long continuous screech, which echoed throughout the town. Mingled with this was the booming of cannon, the firing of guns and pistols, the shouts from thousands of throats. The crowd was massed solidly for three squares down Market street.

Source: "President-Elect M'Kinley at Home," *San Francisco Chronicle*, November 4, 1896.

---

(36) How William Jennings Bryan Reacted to His Defeat— Lincoln, Nebraska, 1896

While William McKinley was observed by reporters enjoying the sweets of victory and speaking to well-wishers, what was the reaction of his adversary, William Jennings Bryan, to the voters' decision at the polls? Instead of depending on newspaper accounts, we can look at Bryan's own words on the subject. Shortly after the election, Bryan wrote a book about his endeavors on the campaign trail and what happened at the ballot box. In two brief chapters at the end of the volume, he recounts his feelings as he went back to his native state Nebraska to vote and then finally to his home in Lincoln to receive the latest bulletins, firmly believing that he would win the presidency. The news he heard that night was not what he had hoped for. Most of the large eastern states, he learned, had gone to his opponent. As he says, "Confidence resolved itself into doubt, and doubt, in turn, gave place to resignation." Subsequently, a day and a half later, seeing that his cause was hopeless and defeat now inevitable, Bryan sent a note of concession to his rival (the first on record). In the last pages of the book, he analyzed the outcome, trying to prove that he lost only by a small margin. (He had won nearly as many states as his adversary; unfortunately, most of them, especially in the West, contained small populations and provided few electoral votes.) Indeed, by calling his book *The First Battle*, he implied that his crusade would continue; he would ultimately lose twice more in his relentless effort to capture the presidency.

The campaign was over, and its conclusion brought to me a sense of relief. No matter what the result might be, I felt I had done all within my power to bring success to the principles for which I stood, and that however small my contribution to the cause might have been, I could expect the same commendation which, the Bible tells us, was accorded to the woman who had done what she could.

The following morning we returned to Lincoln on an early train. The Bryan Home Guards met us at the depot and escorted me to the city clerk's office, where I made the affidavit required of those who fail to register, and then they accompanied me to the polling place, where I deposited my ballot. Just as I was about to vote, one of the strongest Republicans of the precinct, then acting as a challenger for his party, suggested that as a mark of respect to their townsman they take off their hats. The suggestion was adopted by all excepting one. I relate this incident because, although the compliment was somewhat embarrassing at the time, I appreciated it, as it showed the personal good will which, as a rule, was manifested towards me in my home city by those who did not agree with me on political questions.

The Home Guards took me to the door of my house, where I thanked them for the consideration which they had shown, and the sacrifices which they made during the campaign. I may add here that I am proud of the Bryan Home Guards. During my travels I met no better disciplined club. They marched with the precision of veterans and were always ready for duty.

When necessity no longer spurred me to exertion, I began to feel the effects of long continued labor and sought rest in bed. As soon as the polls were closed the representatives of the press, drawn by friendliness and enterprise, assembled in the library below to analyze the returns, while Mrs. Bryan brought the more important bulletins to my room—her face betraying their purport before I received them from her hand. As the evening progressed the indications pointed more and more strongly to defeat, and by eleven o'clock I realized that, while the returns from the country might change the result, the success of my opponent was more than probable. Confidence resolved itself into doubt, and doubt, in turn, gave place to resignation. While the compassionless current sped hither and thither, carrying its message of gladness to foe and its message of sadness to friend, there vanished from my mind the vision of a President in the White House, perplexed by the cares of state, and, in the contemplation of the picture of a citizen by his fireside, free from official responsibility, I fell asleep.

Later reports justified, in a measure, the expectation that the news from the country would be more favorable, but the changes were not sufficient to affect the result. During Wednesday and Thursday I was in communication with Chairman Jones, ready to concede Mr. McKinley's election as soon the National Committee received definite returns from Chairman Jones announcing that sufficient was known to make my defeat certain, and I at once sent the following telegram to Mr. McKinley:

Lincoln, Neb., November 5.
Hon. Wm. McKinley, Canton, Ohio: Senator Jones has just informed me that the returns indicate your election, and I hasten to extend my congratulations. We have submitted the issue to the American people and their will is law.
W.J. Bryan

Mr. McKinley immediately wired:

Canton, Ohio, November 6.
Hon. W.J. Bryan, Lincoln, Neb.: I acknowledge the receipt of your courteous message of congratulations with thanks, and beg you will receive my best wishes for your health and happiness.
William McKinley.

This exchange of messages was much commented upon at the time, though why it should be considered extraordinary I do not know. We were not fighting each other, but stood as the representatives of different political ideas, between which the people were to choose. Our contest aroused no personal feeling upon the part of either, and I have no doubt that had I been elected he would as promptly have sent his congratulations. A courteous observance of the proprieties of such an occasion tends to eliminate the individual and enables opponents to contend sharply over the matters of principle, without disturbance of social relations. I look back with much satisfaction to the fact that the four political contests through which I have passed, two successfully and two unsuccessfully, have been free from personalities.

Source: William Jennings Bryan, *The First Battle* (Chicago: W.B. Conkey, 1897), 603–6.

Moving into the Modern Age, 1900–1948

In the early twentieth century, Election Day, while still a time of excitement in many locales, did not have the same hold on the public that it did during previous decades. One Georgian in 1900 declared that elections in his state were now tame compared to the years after the Civil War, when riots had often ensued. But it was not only a reduction in violence that characterized the election landscape of the new era; the traditional party rivalry between Republicans and Democrats now had much less intensity. In part this resulted from the scaling back of party competition as the Republicans came to dominate certain regions, such as the Northeast and Midwest, while the Democrats controlled the entire South; campaigning, and ultimately voting, fell off in areas where the opposing side had little chance of winning. Mass participation in the political sphere was less encouraged than it had been before, and stricter registration laws made it more difficult for some individuals to vote. At the polls, casting a vote became more orderly, especially with the secret ballot and the installment of voting machines in large communities. In addition, election festivities had increasing competition from vaudeville, motion pictures, and spectator sports, though election night still saw many people out in public and engaging in some form of celebration. The invention of radio, however, would eventually put a damper on that too, keeping more people at home.

(37) How the Ballots Are Counted and Reported—New York, 1913

One of the most important aspects of Election Day, along with the casting of ballots, was (and is) the counting of ballots. Yet few documents prior to the election of 2000 tell anything about how this was done or how difficult a task it could be. Particularly in the distant past, long before the age of the computer, even the mechanical calculator—when paper ballots were the only ones used and had to be counted by hand—tabulating the vote constituted an immense chore. This was especially the case in large cities like New York, with two-thirds of a million voters in 1,780 election districts early in the twentieth century. Adding up the tally in New York City involved a virtual army of individuals—interestingly, most of them employed by the police department. Indeed, an election bureau set up at police headquarters was then in charge of the city's vote-counting operation. As the precinct totals became available, police officers assigned to the task worked in conjunction with local news-gathering organizations to get the results to the press and to the public, all within a few short hours. Though the polls closed at 5:00 P.M., the outcome was usually known by ten or eleven o'clock. It was, as the author of the accompanying article states, "a complicated system, but nevertheless a simple one." It was also much less corrupt than the system in the previous century, when party politicians had been in charge. The situation in New York was unusual, however. In most communities, partisan officials continued to control the ballot count for a long time to come. Even in New York, irregularities still occurred despite the efforts made to prevent them.

Another man squeezed through the door, and the shuffling, swaying line once more moved forward. It was slow, tedious work, this waiting to vote.

"Seem to be splitting tickets quite a lot," volunteered a watcher, poking his head out of the polling-place for a breath of air.

"Pshaw!" said a man in the line. "We kick about this, just because it takes five or ten minutes out of a holiday. But did you ever stop to think of the men who have to count those votes, not only for this district but for the whole city? We growl because the voting's slow, but when we're through we're through. And we spend the day playing golf or pinochle or something, then tonight, after dinner, we drift downtown and get the returns. The polls close at five, and at midnight we know who's elected. Did you ever happen to think about the work that has to be done in those few hours?"

None of us ever had, except in a detached and casual way. Again the man smiled.

"Does any one here happen to know, for instance, what happens to his ballot after he slips it into the ballot-box?"

"It is counted, of course," answered somebody.

"How is it counted? Who counts it? Who adds your vote to all the other votes in the city to make the total? Anybody know?"

Nobody did.

"I don't either," confessed the man; "but it just occurs to me now that I'd like to. There must be a pretty keen system somewhere, not only to count the votes, but to count 'em right and count 'em quick."

There is.

In New York City alone this year the total registration was, in round figures 670,000. This registration was divided among 1,780 election districts: 734 in Manhattan, 216 in the Bronx, 624 in Brooklyn, 161 in Queens, and 45 in Richmond. The vote, of course, was somewhat under the registration figure, but not much.

Here we have, say, 650,000 individual votes, many of them what are known as split tickets, to be counted, tabulated, and totaled all within the few hurried hours from the closing of the polls to the press time of the morning papers. Now for the average man it is not particularly difficult to conceive of counting the votes in any single election district; it's a job, of course, but still it's a job within reason. But when you remember that practically no two candidates on the whole ballot get anything like the same number of votes, then it begins to seem a pretty tough proposition.

And on top of that there's the driving necessity of speed, for the papers cannot wait. The polls close at five o'clock. Not much more than four hours later, to the waiting thousands in the city's streets, the jamming, jostling, hooting, shouting thousands of election night, a hundred different bulletins flash the first substantial predictions of the final outcome. Between ten and eleven o'clock the thing is a practical certainty. Shortly after midnight the last possibility of doubt disappears. It's all over. In two more hours the full returns are printed and on the street. The last of the noisy crowds straggle sleepily home. Within the space of these few brief hours there have been counted, assembled, and tabulated the votes on 650,000 ballots.

This is how it is done:

At five o'clock, with the closing of the polls, the board of inspectors of each election district proceeds to the canvassing of the ballots. The ballot-box is opened and the ballots themselves are taken out, without being unfolded, and counted. The number of ballots is now compared with the number of voters registered in that district. If there happen to be more ballots than there are registered voters, all the ballots, still folded, are replaced in the box from which they were taken. Within the box they are shuffled—"thoroughly mingled," as the law has it. One of the inspectors now stands with his back to the box and draws out, at random, as many ballots as may be in excess of the registration. These ballots, without being unfolded, are forthwith destroyed. In most cases, of course, there are not more ballots than there are registered voters, but it happens often enough to be a part of the regular procedure.

Next comes the actual counting of the votes. The chairman of the board of inspectors unfolds the ballots, separating them into piles of straight and split tickets. The straight tickets, those on which the vote is exclusively for the candidates of one party, are counted first, the tally for each name being kept by the poll clerk to whom that name has been assigned. This is a fairly simple matter, for there will be one pile of Democratic ballots, a pile of Republican, a pile of Progressive, a pile of Socialist, and so on. But the counting of the split votes is harder. The chairman of the board takes each ballot separately, announcing orally the vote for each individual candidate voted for. This, as can well be imagined, sometimes takes hours, even in a small district. After all the votes have been counted, they are added together, individual by individual.

The total count for the election district is now immediately despatched by the police officer on duty at the polling-place to the police station of the precinct in which the district is situated. The ballots themselves are replaced in the ballot-box and sealed, to be held for six months in case of protest, dispute, or other trouble. But as far as the immediate computation of the vote is concerned, the ballots are done with.

We are now at the precinct police station, where the returns from all the election districts of that precinct are brought in. Here is a veritable babel of confusion. Police officers, reporters, favored lookers-on, nobody knows who else, all are crowding together: everybody is in the way of everybody else. Every moment or so a patrolman comes jamming in through the throng, reaching into his pocket for a slip of paper, and handing it hastily to the lieutenant at the desk. It is the verdict of another election district—so many votes for each candidate for Mayor, so many for President of the Board of Aldermen, so many for District Attorney, so many for Comptroller, and all the way through. The lieutenant, who is connected by direct wire with what is known as the election bureau at police headquarters, scans the figures, jiggles the receiver of his telephone up and down, and then suddenly starts barking numerals into the mouthpiece. All evening long some officer keeps at this task, sending figure after figure after figure, as fast as the district returns arrive. And if it is a populous precinct, they arrive so rapidly that the reports begin to stack up in the piles.

So much for what takes place at police stations. Before going on, however, to the work of the headquarters election bureau it is perhaps best to sketch a brief analysis of the system in its entirety. It is a system of three units: the polling-place, the police station, and police headquarters. In the polling-place the votes of the election district are counted, tabulated, and totaled. In the precinct police station the returns from the election districts of the precinct are collected for transmission to the headquarters bureau. This, in reality, is nothing more or less than a sort of relay. But in the election bureau at police headquarters the returns from the election districts, sent in through the precinct stations, are not only recorded, added together, and tabulated, but are also turned over to the newspapers, then and there, in final form for publication.

Now this may not seem particularly complicated until you happen to remember the number of names on the average ballot; until you remember that those names except in the cases of the more important offices, are limited to certain Aldermanic and Assembly and congressional and Senatorial districts. In other words, each different section of the city has a practically distinct ballot. And every important name on every ballot is taken care of.

The election bureau at Manhattan police headquarters does all the work for the two boroughs of Manhattan and the Bronx. These two boroughs, between them, possess 950 separate election districts. In the past years their vote has run something over 350,000. Every individual vote for every individual candidate in this whole thickly populated territory is handled, within the space of a few short hours by an organization contained in one single room.

The secret of the whole thing is a high degree of systematization, coupled with an even higher degree of co-operation between the police department and the two great news bureaus which cover the metropolis. The police department is responsible to the people by the law of the State of New York. The newspapers are responsible to the people even more directly. So the two public agencies put their shoulders together and do the work.

When the lieutenant at the desk of the Twelfth Precinct station house telephones in to headquarters that Peter J. Sullivan, the Democratic candidate for alderman in such and such a district, has this or that many votes he is answered on the other end of the wire at headquarters by a policeman, who makes a memorandum record of the district, the candidate, and the vote.

The policeman who takes this memorandum is but one of a score or more who sit, each man with a double telephone receiver clamped over his head, in a great gridiron of tables, row upon row, in one corner of the room. Each one of these men is assigned to take the returns from a certain precinct or a certain number of districts.

Out near the center of the room, at another gridiron of long, narrow tables, sit the accountants who do the actual tabulating, adding together, and computing of the figures. There are two or three dozen of these men, each one of them with a huge blank-book before him, divided according to offices for the more important votes and according to districts for the less important. Around and around this series of tables, as if in an old-fashioned walking race, circles a host of messenger boys, all going in the same direction. At one point, near the corner of the room, this circle touches the gridiron of tables where the policemen with telephone receivers clamped to their heads are getting the precinct returns. And as each messenger boy passes the chief of this body he takes a memorandum slip, bearing the report of a vote, and carries it around the moving circle to the chief accountant, in charge of the gridiron in the center of the room. When you realize that these messengers are walking only a few feet apart, and walking as fast as messengers can be induced to walk, then you can begin to understand how rapidly the vote is coming in.

The chief accountant takes the slip informing him that Peter J. Sullivan, the Democratic candidate for alderman in such and such a district, has this or that many votes, and straightway gives it to the man under him who is taking care of Peter J. Sullivan's district. The man enters the vote, opposite the proper election district, in his book. One by one the different election district votes come in, all in this same way, until at last Peter J. Sullivan's vote, together with the vote of his rivals, is complete. The accountant foots up the total, passes the page of his book over to the chief of his table for verification, and the figures are ready.

Two newspaper men are standing there, one from each of the two great news bureaus. To make things simpler we'll follow one of them. He takes the report of Peter J. Sullivan's district, copies down the figures on a specially prepared blank, and hurries over to the far side of the room.

Here along the wall, arranged in a series of shallow little stalls, is a row of telephones, each one of them attended by a newspaper man. Each one of these reporters is responsible for sending in to his office just one set of votes. One man takes the Mayor, the next the President of the Board of Aldermen, the next the District Attorney, the next the Comptroller; one man will have the vote for such and such a court, another the vote for the municipal judges, another the vote for the Board of Aldermen itself. Each one of these men has a working partner whose duty is to stay at the table where his set of votes is being computed and bring the figures over, by Assembly districts, as soon as they are totaled.

So the reporter who gets the result of the vote in Peter J. Sullivan's district takes his figures immediately to his team-mate, who in turn copies them down (so that when he has time he can check them over) and telephones them in to his office.

In the newspaper office again there is a reporter whose special duty it is to get this vote over the wire, write it down on a slip, and hand it directly to an office boy. The office boy hands it to one of the four or five men who make up the election tables. And now at last, as soon as the figures are checked, the returns on Peter J. Sullivan's district are ready to be set up in type and printed.

The checking is done through the news organization's own election bureau, which works in parallel lines with the police headquarters bureau. In each precinct police station there are reporters who take the election district figures as they come in and telephone or telegraph them immediately to the election bureau, with the general exception that the sheets bearing the returns are made out in full, just as they are to be printed, in the city room, or main editorial office, by messenger. The editors who make out the election tables thus have two separate sets of figures. This precludes almost all possibility of error, for when there is any discrepancy it can be easily traced.

You cast your vote for Mayor. At five o'clock, when the polls close, your ballot is taken out of the ballot-box, and your vote for Mayor is tabulated with all the other votes for Mayor cast in your polling-place. When the votes are totaled, a policeman is despatched with them to the precinct police station. There the lieutenant telephones all the votes for Mayor from your election district to a policeman on the other end of the wire at police headquarters.

The policeman gives the report to a messenger. The messenger hurries it to the gridiron at the center of the room, where one of the tables bears a large printed sign, "Mayor." The accountant at the head of this table passes it down to the man under him who has in charge the Assembly district in which your election district is included. This man enters the figures in his book, a book labeled "Mayor," with a page for each Assembly district. There may be, say, a dozen election districts in your assembly district. One by one the returns from each come in, until at last the vote for Mayor in your Assembly district is complete. The accountant foots the columns and passes the book up to his chief at the end of the table. The chief verifies the figures and gives the Assembly district total to the reporter at his elbow.

The reporter hurries over to his teammate; the team-mate, sitting at a stall marked "Mayor," telephones the figures to the man in his office who is also sitting at a telephone marked "Mayor." The reporter in the newspaper office gives his figures to a boy, who rushes them over to one of the men who make up the election tables. The figures are checked with the paper's own figures. And at the last moment before press time the latest total on the vote for Mayor, with possibly all but two or three

Assembly districts included, is sent to the composing room. The late editions of the paper will have the figures in full.

It is a complicated system, but nevertheless a simple one. After passing through the clearing-house of the precinct police station, each set of votes for each individual office goes through a channel which is separate and distinct in every way from the channel used by any other set of votes. It takes work, it takes intelligence, it takes an army of wide-awake men; but the results are sure and the results are quick. Without this system you might have had to wait the better part of a week this year before finding out at all the results of the election. We accept the trolley car, the telephone, and the aeroplane as wonders of modern science. Sometimes we overlook what man can do in other, less spectacular ways.

Source: Gerald Mygatt, "Counting the City's Vote," *The Outlook*, November 8, 1913, 535–38.

---

(38) Voting amidst the Influenza Epidemic—San Francisco and Fresno, California, 1918

One of the most dangerous situations voters in this country ever had to face occurred on Election Day in 1918, which coincided with the spread of a major influenza epidemic. The epidemic had already caused the death of thousands of Americans and the prolonged illness of thousands more. Many in the electorate therefore felt wary about casting their ballots, since it involved being in public for a considerable time, which in turn meant possible exposure to the disease. Indeed, in the areas affected the level of participation would be much lower than normal for midterm congressional elections and statewide gubernatorial races. Some party leaders in the state of California, referring to the smaller turnout, called it a "primary vote"—that is, comparable to that in a primary election. In cities such as San Francisco, the polling places were unusually quiet and otherwise abnormal. To conduct the proceedings all election officials were required to wear masks during their entire periods on duty, and voters were told to have their noses and mouths covered when they entered the voting booths. Such regulations were probably not always complied with. Also, a number of odd occurrences are reported here, such as the case of a woman in Fresno, California, who refused to sign her name in the polling book because she would have to use a "public pen." In addition, information regarding the election results was less widely available than usual, since newspapers gave up their normal practice of posting the latest returns on bulletin boards outside their offices, so as to keep crowds from forming on downtown streets. The following two newspaper accounts fill in some of the other details of this unique story.

San Francisco voted en masque yesterday, but not en masse.

Early estimates set the total vote in this city at less than that cast in the primaries on August 27, when 96,000 citizens exercised their privilege. The late evening voting, however, raised the total so that at 9 o'clock last night Registrar J.H. Zemansky announced that the total vote of San Francisco might run to 102,000.

This is only 58 per cent of the registration of 175,000 when the books closed for the general election.

The "flu" was the cause, said Zemansky. Many persons are ill with the malady or convalescing and many more, he said, were reluctant to leave their homes while the epidemic is on, even to vote.

The condition was shown in the many last-minute changes that had to be made among the election officers. The Registrar made 150 changes in inspectors alone in the last three days, and probably half of the 4400 election officers were substituted by the inspectors at the last moment yesterday morning.

At that there were complaints to the Board of Health that election officers were serving, who either had the influenza or were convalescing.

Because of the influenza and the absence of great numbers of men in the Army [during World War I] or on Government work, which makes them ineligible, at least half the election officers were women. In some booths as many as five out of the six were women.

All election officers were required to wear masks constantly and the Election Commission issued orders that all persons entering the booths to vote must be properly attired in accordance with the influenza ordinance.

Throughout the city the election passed off as quietly as a meeting of a home missionary society. The election officers were not very busy and the voters noticeably took their time to the ballots. Reports to the Registrar's office indicated that in the Western Addition, the Richmond and the Sunset voters were generally stamping fully the list of amendments, but that in the southern portion of the city they were troubling themselves about only the personalities on the ballot.

The storm Monday night damaged a good many election booths through out the city. Though none of them were destroyed, canvas covers were torn off and the buildings somewhat bashed about. A truck loaded with spare canvas covers worked all night so that by 6 o'clock yesterday morning all the booths were roofed again.

After the storm of the night before, election day was bright and clear throughout the State. The last appeals of this campaign, speechless because of the influenza, were made in newspaper advertising yesterday morning. Influenza had another result upon the election in that almost all newspapers gave up their customary practice of bullettining the returns. In some places health officers forbade the publishing of bulletins in order to obviate crowds, and in others newspapers voluntarily abandoned their plans for flashing the results.

Source: "Stephens Sweeps California," *San Francisco Chronicle*, November 6, 1918, 1, 6; [lb]

(Fresno, California) Returns from the general election yesterday were so meager at 1 o'clock this morning that it was almost impossible at that time to give any indication of results, except in two or three instances.

Partial returns from 193 precincts in the Seventh Congressional district gave Barbour 4,326, Hawson 4,151.

Many voters yesterday got "cold feet." This was easy enough, according to an election official on Tulare street. Booths were placed outside the polling places in the full sweep of the wind as a health precaution.

"Some of the voters complained of cold feet after standing in the open booths and running down through the list of amendments," was the comment. "We are not referring to those who had to stay at home."

Sanitary precautions were general. Masks were worn by the judges and clerks, and children were warned to stay out of stores on Blackstone avenue where polling was in progress. Congregating about the polls was frowned upon. In one precinct, a voter refused to sign her name in ink, objecting to using a "public pen."

At the high school a well known faculty man, evidently carrying a problem in his mind, walked up to the polling place. He discovered that he had lost his mask. Not waiting to attempt to vote, he rushed home to get his nose and mouth covered in the prescribed legal manner.

Judges of a down-town precinct reported that about twenty voters had "moved out" since registration. Some of them had been called in the draft. The vote in the precinct was very light.

There were few challenges and apparently fewer mistakes on the ballots than usual yesterday. It was suggested in some quarters that the vote was very largely a "primary vote," meaning that those who voted yesterday were very largely the same voters who took enough interest to vote in the primaries. At 5 o'clock in the afternoon, it was estimated 50 per cent of the voters in the city had cast their ballots.

At at least one of the polling places the lone man on the board went out to lunch at noon, and the remaining officers and judges smilingly declared they had "woman suffrage" boards.

Voting was slow at Precinct 19 in the early hours, and the women on the board did a considerable amount of knitting and other needle work. In fact, it was declared that the morning might as well have been a knitting bee.

At night, there was a transformation. Women and a sprinkle of men began counting votes. Any interruption caused polite protests.

"We are called slow at the primary counting," said a woman judge. "And we are going to make this count as business-like as any men could make it. It is also the time of an epidemic, and we do not propose to stay out any later than we can help tonight."

Source: "Congressional Race in Seventh Close," *Fresno Republican*, November 6, 1918, 1.

---

(39) Women Vote for First Time on National Basis—New York, 1920

The presidential contest in November 1920 marked a major milestone in Election Day history: it was the first in which women all across the nation participated in the balloting. A certain number of women, as noted earlier, had been allowed to cast ballots before this year, particularly in some of the new western states. However, thanks to the passage of the Nineteenth Amendment to the Constitution that August, bringing the struggle for equal suffrage to a positive conclusion, women could now vote everywhere. Significant changes accordingly occurred as to how and where voting was to be conducted. Most notably, the voting site in many locales was moved out of traditionally male-only establishments, such as saloons and barbershops, and into places more accommodating to women, like schools and churches. In addition, the very presence of women seemed to make the overall voting process more orderly and refined. Far fewer incidents of fistfights or drunkenness were reported during this election than in previous ones. As the following summary of the day's events from the *Woman Citizen* discloses, not only was greater decorum displayed, but the women, in exercising their voting rights, disproved many of the theories long postulated by the antisuffrage movement. Among other things, it was shown that far from being casual and undiscriminating as they made their selections, female voters generally went about the task in a serious and thoughtful way. More frequently than men, they chose candidates on the basis of merit rather than simply by party labels. They also brought the overall presidential turn-out figure to an all-time high. Although it was later found that women had not voted in the same proportion as men in this election—only about 43 percent took part nationwide compared with over 70 percent of men—female voters would gradually become a force to be reckoned with on Election Day.

These are [the] headlines: "Women outnumbered men at the New Hampshire polls"; "Pennsylvania was prepared to handle the largest vote ever polled at a presidential election"; "Big rush of women at the polls in Massachusetts"; "Voting places crowded in Maryland."

In New York state and city, the percentage of registered voters actually voting was said to be the largest ever reached in the city's history.

"Henry S. Renaud, State Superintendent of Elections, who had a corps of deputies and inspectors traveling from polling place to polling place to supervise the work of the election boards, said, 'that the vote this year will be nearer 100 percent of the registration than it ever has been before.'"

This is the story told by the New York *Times* of November 3d.

"The largest vote on record was polled yesterday in this city. In a veritable flood, which in some places swamped the election officials, the voters went to the polls early in all five boroughs. In the Bronx the early rush was so great that some officials asked the Board of Elections for additional voting booths.

"When the polls closed at 6 o'clock last night it was estimated that more than 90 percent of the 1,373,565 registered voters had cast their ballots."

"Vote of Women in City Enormous," the *Morning Telegraph* headlined its election story the morning after.

"Women are too unintelligent to vote," was [one] phrase with which the anti-suffragists hypnotized themselves.

Quoting the *Telegraph* again, this is the way they actually voted:

"'These women,' said one of the watchers at a polling place in Eighth avenue near Fiftieth street, 'are the most intelligent voters I ever saw. They are interested and have a lot of common sense. They have it all over the men, I think. I didn't have one woman, young or old, ask me a foolish question the entire day. Much to my surprise I find that they know more about the local political situation than do the men.'

"He was asked if he could account for this.

"'Well, the only way I can explain their familiarity with local affairs is that they have more leisure to read the newspapers,' was the answer. 'I heard one girl of about 21 say she was going to vote against the candidate I represent, and I asked her why. She brought forth several things about his record that she did not like, and I made a vain effort to swerve her. But I am sure she voted as she originally intended. This showed that she was of the kind who made up their minds for themselves. Politicians will have a difficult time if they expect to swing the women's vote en masse. It can't be done.

"'I can forgive a woman like that. She voted according to her principles. But I cannot forgive the man who says: "I'm going to vote against Senator John Doe because he is of such-and-such a party."'"

"Women will create confusion at the polls," was a long cherished anti notion. But it wasn't true according to the Superintendent of Elections, as quoted by the New York *Times.*

"'Everything,' said he, 'has been working smoothly, and there has been an almost complete absence of disorder.'

"A similar announcement was made by John R. Voorhis, President of the Board of Elections, after a personal tour of inspection.

"There was hardly any disorder, and no disturbance of a serious nature such as have been common in the past. Few arrests were made.

"Women showed intense interest in the election. In many districts more women than men went to the polling places in the morning. The average number of voters was from forty to fifty an hour.

"With three ballots to vote, the election officials regard this as remarkable and as evidence that the election machinery was working with unprecedented smoothness. Secretary William C. Baxter of the Board of Elections said that where in other years there had been 100 complaints of missing ballots or ballot boxes in the first hour of voting, not a single complaint had been received this year, nor any request for aid, except for more voting booths."

"It takes too much time to vote," was another old anti-suffrage bogeyman. The *Morning Telegraph* spoke of the leisurely manner in which women voted. And even at that, how much time was given? *An average of three minutes.*

"Watchers at the polls who *timed* them estimated that each woman consumed about three minutes in making her selection of candidates. Some of them remained at least seven or eight minutes in the canvas booths.

"From this it was at first thought that the women were delayed by their unfamiliarity with the ballot and ignorance about the proper way to make it out. But as time went by, this theory was discarded. Surprisingly few spoiled ballots were returned with the request for others. Also the remarks the women voters dropped in a casual fashion showed they knew quite well what they were doing. Consequently the watchers finally decided that they were spending their time in looking at the names of the candidates, weighing their records, and then voting by merit instead of by party.

"What will mother do with the baby when she votes?" is now an almost forgotten anxiety.

For the "cops" have taken care of that.

"At 3 o'clock in the afternoon the policeman at one polling place reported that he had held more than forty babies and that he had every expectation of doubling this record.

"'It's quite the usual thing for these women to check their babies with me,' he laughed. 'They probably know their children will be safe under the care of the New York Police Department. But I don't mind. I like to hold babies. You see I've three of my own at home.'"

Some editorial comments show how general was the good record of this, the American woman's first independence day:

"It was interesting to see the new voters of the other sex on the job around eight o'clock—quiet, self-contained and not asking even the expected questions," said the *Evening Telegram*. "They had taken the trouble to find out, knew what to do and how to do it.

"Above all, the ladies have brought to the act of handling the votes the decorum that was so devoutly to be desired."

"Yesterday's experience with women voting in their first presidential election was markedly satisfactory," said the *Evening World*. "Their presence at the polls more than justified itself.

"Yesterday's elections were orderly to a degree almost unprecedented. The influence of women restrained rowdyism.

"It is to be hoped that this particular effect of woman suffrage will continue. If politics comes to be more of a family affair, it is sure to absorb more of the moral tone of the home.

"All over the United States yesterday men escorted mothers, sisters, daughters and sweethearts to the polls. The refining influence of woman was manifest. Men were on their good behavior. Quiet superseded rowdy language. 'Rough stuff' was taboo."

Source: "Woman Comes of Age: Her Record at the Polls," *Woman Citizen*, November 13, 1920.

---

(40) Black Women Barred from the Vote—Atlanta, Georgia, 1920

Although the Nineteenth Amendment supposedly granted suffrage rights in 1920 to all adult women, that ideal was not always achieved. In much of the Deep South, African-American women often found themselves barred from the polls. This was true despite the fact that many black women had taken pains to register in the months before the election. Even among those who were not turned away, there was no guarantee that their vote would count; such ballots were sometimes invalidated by the authorities. In Atlanta, Georgia, as the following selection shows, seventy-nine African American women cast ballots in the Sixth Ward, seemingly in a legal fashion. But afterward their votes were thrown out by a local judge, who declared that these women had not been properly registered. Previously, the state's attorney-general had ruled that any woman could vote in the contest even if they had not conformed to the usual six-months-in-advance registration procedure. Evidently this was not the case—at least insofar as these black female Atlantans were concerned. The story here was not unique, and it foreshadowed a long, hard struggle on the part of all blacks over several decades to be able to participate fully on Election Day.

The success of seventy-nine negro women in casting their ballots in the sixth ward of Atlanta proved of no avail when, following the order of [Judge] Thomas H. Jeffries, election managers threw out each of their tickets before tabulating the returns Tuesday night.

Tuesday morning a large number of negro women presented themselves at the sixth ward polling place and demanded the right to cast their ballots, and, with the permission of Dr. J.C. Peck, Republican manager at the place, seventy-nine succeeded in polling their tickets before a peremptory order of Judge Jeffries halted the proceedings.

When the first negro woman had cast her ballot, over the objection of W.H. Brown, Democrat, the other manager at the polling place, four more rapidly followed her action, and Mr. Brown immediately quit his post, declaring that he was disgusted, and reported the Republican manager's procedure to Judge Jeffries, who immediately dispatched Deputy Ordinary Claude Mason with orders to stop all women, white or black from voting in the ward, and if Dr. Peck failed to carry out his oath as manager to remove him.

The Republican manager first objected to Judge Jeffries' orders, but finally agreed to observe the terms of his oath, it is stated. Negro men, who accompanied the women as they demanded the right to vote, argued the latter were entitled to cast their ballots on the ground of Attorney General R.A. Denny's ruling that any woman could vote in Tuesday's election, regardless of whether she was registered. [Judge] Jeffries issued his order on the state law, which provides all voters must be registered six months prior to election day.

Claims were made by some Republican leaders that the election of
Congressman W.D. Upshaw would be contested on the ground women
were refused permission to vote. Official cognizance of the situation in
the sixth ward was taken by department of justice agents, who have
received orders to carefully report all alleged election irregularities.

Source: "Votes of Negro Women Are Void," Atlanta Constitution, November 3,
1920, 7.

(41) Resistance to Blacks Voting—Orange and Duval Counties, Florida, 1920

> Even more serious than the official response to black women
> voting in Atlanta was the violent reaction of whites in other parts
> of the Deep South to African Americans of both sexes attempting
> to cast ballots around that time. For many years black men had
> been reluctant to test the various legal barriers to enfranchise-
> ment that had been erected in the late nineteenth and early
> twentieth centuries. But the wartime experiences of the Negro
> soldier together with the passage of the woman suffrage amend-
> ment now prompted many blacks—male and female—to try to
> register and vote for the first time. These actions led to a resur-
> gence of violence by the notorious Ku Klux Klan, particularly in
> areas where African Americans were in the majority and might,
> if successful, overturn the existing white power structure. The
> following article by Walter White, then an investigator and later
> head of the National Association for the Advancement of Col-
> ored People (NAACP), carried in The New Republic a few weeks
> after the attacks, describes the ugly racial confrontations that
> occurred in certain communities in northern Florida on these
> occasions.

"I want to register."

"All right, Jim, you can, but I want to tell you something. Some God
damn black . . . is going to get killed yet about this voting business."

The questioner is a colored man in Orange county, Florida. The answer
is from a registrar, white, of course. The Negro, cognizant of the sinister
truthfulness of the reply he had received, would probably decide that it
was not particularly healthy for him to press his request. Thus, and in
many other ways equally as flagrant, did the election of 1920 proceed in
Florida and other southern states.

The Ku Klux Klan, of infamous post–Civil War memory, has been actively revived in the South. Its avowed purpose is to "keep the nigger in his place," and to maintain, at all costs, "white supremacy." In spite of vigorous denials on the part of its leaders, the branches of this organization have entered upon a campaign of terror that can mean nothing but serious clashes involving the loss of many lives and the destruction of much property. The recent elections brought into full play all of the fear that "white supremacy" would crumble if Negroes were allowed to vote, augmented by the belief that the recent war experiences of the Negro soldier had made him less tractable than before. In many southern cities and towns, parades of the Klans were extensively advertised in advance and held on the night of October 30th, the Saturday before election. The effect of these outturnings of robed figures, clad in white hoods and gowns adorned with flaming red crosses, was probably astounding to those who believed in the efficacy of such methods. The principal danger to America of anarchistic organizations like the Klan lies in their distorted perspective of conditions. The Negro emerged from slavery ignorant, uneducated, superstitious. It was a simple task to terrify him by the sight of a band of men, clothed in white coming down a lonely road on a moonlight night. Today, the Negro is neither so poor nor so ignorant nor so easily terrified, a fact known to everybody but the revivers of the Ku Klux Klan. Instead of running to cover, frightened, his mood now is to protect himself and his family by fighting to the death. It is as though one attempted to frighten a man of forty by threatening him with some of the tales used to quiet him when he was an infant. The method just doesn't work.

This can best be shown by the attitude of the Negroes of Jacksonville. An old colored woman, standing on Bay Street as she watched the parade of the Klansmen on the Saturday night before election, called out derisively to the marchers:

"Buckra (Poor white people), you ain't done nothing. Those German guns didn't scare us and we know white robes won't do it now."

Among the educated Negroes there is a seriousness and a determination not to start trouble, but equally are they resolved not to run from trouble if it comes. But, whatever were the intentions of the sponsors of the parade, it acted as an incentive to bring to the polls on Election Day many colored men and women voters who had before been indifferent.

The population of Jacksonville at present is estimated at 90,000—Negroes numbering between 45,000 and 50,000. The enfranchisement of women caused this majority held by Negro voters to be of grave significance to the Democratic party of Florida. Coupled with this was the fear which is general throughout the South that the colored woman voter is more difficult "to handle" than colored men have been. The Jacksonville Metropolis of September 16th carried a scare head, "DEMOCRACY IN DU-

VAL COUNTY ENDANGERED BY VERY LARGE REGISTRATION OF NEGRO
WOMEN," and the article beneath it carried an appeal to race prejudice
based upon the fact that more Negro women than white had shown
enough interest to register. The first line, which read: "Are the white
men and white women of Duval County going to permit 'negro wash-
erwomen and cooks' to wield the balance of political power?" is indic-
ative of the nature of the appeal thus made. . . . Similar appeals were
made throughout the preelection period. A few days before election, the
local press told of the issuing of 4,000 blank warrants "for the arrest of
Negro men and women who had improperly registered when they presented themselves for voting." Yet, all of this failed to stop the colored
people who went quietly and intelligently about their task of registering.

On Election Day each polling booth was provided by the election officials with four entrances—one each for white women, white men, colored women and colored men. Two each were to be taken
simultaneously from the head of each line, according to the published
instructions. This was not done. No white voter was delayed or hindered
in voting while every possible handicap was put in the way of colored
voters. More than 4,000 colored men and women stood in line from 8:
00 A.M. to 5:40 P.M., the closing hour, determined to vote if possible.
Colored women served sandwiches and coffee to the lines at all of the
booths. Later the names, addresses and registration certificate numbers
were taken of the more than 4,000 refused voters. Affidavits were being
secured from each of these at the time of my visit to Florida during
election week. . . .

More serious and distressing, however, was the situation found in Orange County where the election clash at Ocoee occurred. News dispatches of November 4th told of the killing of six colored men, one by
lynching, and of two white men, when Mose Norman, a colored man
attempted to vote although he had not registered or paid his poll tax.
The facts, secured on the spot, reveal an entirely different story. Three
weeks prior to the election the local Ku Klux Klan sent word to the
colored people of Orange County, that no Negroes would be allowed to
vote and that if any Negro tried to do so, trouble could be expected.
Norman refused to be intimidated. The registration books at Orlando
show that he had qualified and registered. He was unpopular with the
whites because he was too prosperous—he owned an orange grove for
which he refused offers of $10,000 several times. The prevailing senti-
ment was that Norman was too prosperous "for a nigger." When Norman went to the polls he was overpowered, severely beaten, his gun
taken away from him (he had gone prepared for he knew there were no
limits to which the Ku Klux Klan would not go) and ordered to go home.
He went instead to the home of July Perry, another colored man, who
likewise was unpopular in that he owned his own home and was fore-

man of a large orange grove owned by a Northern white man. The community felt that the job belonged to a white man. A mob formed, went out and surrounded the colored settlement, applied kerosene, burned twenty houses, two churches, a school-house and a lodge hall. Perry and the other beleaguered Negroes fought desperately. Two members of the mob were killed and two wounded. Perry, with his arm shot away, was taken to Orlando and placed in jail. Shortly afterwards, a detachment of the mob went to the county jail at Orlando, to which the sheriff voluntarily turned over the keys. The mob took Perry just outside the city and, more dead than alive, lynched him.

In the meantime, the colored men, women and children trapped in the burning houses fought desperately against insurmountable odds. Negroes attempting to flee were either shot down or forced back into the flames. The number killed will never be known. I asked a white citizen of Ocoee who boasted of his participation in the slaughter how many Negroes died. He declared that fifty-six were known to have been killed—that he had killed seventeen "niggers" himself. . . .

And thus the story runs. This and many other issues of the *New Republic* could be filled with tale after tale of unbelievable horror—how a wealthy colored physician of Quincy was surrounded at the polls by a mob, members of which spat on his face and dared him upon pain of death to wipe it because he had advised colored citizens to qualify, register and vote; how in Live Oak two colored business men, undertakers, merchants and landowners, were, for the same offense, beaten into unconsciousness and ordered to leave homes, property and families; how one of them has left and the other lies near the point of death from a paralytic stroke brought on by the beating; how among those burned alive at Ocoee were a mother and her two weeks old baby. The examples given are enough.

The question involved is not simply that of barring a few Negroes from voting. It involves a condition which will allow any white man, whether highly intelligent or densely ignorant, owning much property or abjectly poor, to vote, while all Negroes are disfranchised, it matters not how intelligent or worthy of the franchise they may be. This situation is not one which is wholly sectional but one which is so fundamental that no citizen of America, North or South, can disregard it.

Source: Walter White, "Election by Terror in Florida," *The New Republic*, January 12, 1921, 195–97.

(42) The Experience of a Progressive Poll Watcher— Philadelphia, 1922

Corruption and fraud at the polling place would decline over the course of the twentieth century, as the enforcement of new laws and greater vigilance on the part of numerous volunteers at the scene made it difficult for local party bosses to conduct business in their traditional ways. An example of this new vigilance can be seen in the following account given by a female poll watcher in Philadelphia who, during the Republican primary election for the Pennsylvania governorship in 1922, supported the progressive candidate Gifford Pinchot against the nominee of the conservative faction, championed by longtime city bosses. The author, a member of the new League of Women Voters and an advocate of clean government, was part of a well-organized effort to monitor closely what went on at each polling station and to summon, if necessary, legal or police assistance. She and other poll watchers were trained in what to look for in regard to suspicious behavior, how to keep an eye on the registration book, and what to say to try to prevent illegal voting. The document gives us a glimpse of what party officials at the time normally tried to get away with. On this occasion at least, they were stopped in their tracks.

The women did more than vote for Mr. Pinchot. They watched at the polls and had an eye on the counting of the ballots. In almost every election division of Philadelphia one or two carefully instructed women sat at the polling-place, and several more, under the name of Vigilants, patrolled the pavement, ready to summon legal or police assistance should the watchers be in need of either. . . .

In my own ward brawls and fights have not been uncommon, and before the Personal Registration Act went into effect the independent watchers had sometimes to be carried from the polls to the hospital. Happily, no such fate befell my alternate nor myself, and our faithful Vigilants had no more serious duty than to give us an occasional reminder of their supporting presence.

Our polling-place, instead of being in a saloon, as in the old days, was in a sufficiently respectable office. The election officers, who were all Negroes—for in my ward the Negroes have a numerical majority—were courteous and carried their courtesy to the unexpected and agreeable extreme of refraining from smoking. The judge sustained all my challenges, even one against the hitherto all-powerful division boss, who was the only white organization watcher and the only one who showed hostility toward us women. Early in the day he brought in an old colored man as feeble in mind as in body and said to the judge, "This man cannot read or write. Make out an affidavit for him."

I found the man's signature in the registration book, and challenged. The boss said, contemptuously, "No one can read that scrawl." "I can," I replied. But the boss repeated his order to the judge. I again protested, and the boss, losing his temper, shouted, "Give that man an affidavit, I tell you."

I went to the dazed victim of our election laws and said, "Don't you know that if you put a mark on that paper you will surely go to jail?" Seeing that I knew the law and that the Vigilants were ready at a signal from me to call legal assistance, the boss hastily left the room and sent in a colored sub-boss, who told the old man that it was not necessary to make an affidavit. "Take this and copy it," he ordered, and, thrusting into his hand a sample ballot, he pushed him into a booth.

Sample ballots marked for the organization candidates were handed out openly and freely to all who asked for them and to many who did not ask. I knew that under the law such open distribution of sample ballots is not permitted within fifty feet of the polling-place, but I knew also that the courts had construed the law liberally and the judge would probably not sustain me if I should make a protest. I contented myself, therefore, with saying to a watcher whose pockets bulged with ballots, "Don't you think what you are doing is perilously like assistance?" He made no answer, but I noticed that he handed out no more ballots in the room. . . .

When the polls opened, the judge assigned me a seat near the desk, where I was able to keep an eye on the registration book. My proximity to the book troubled the organization watchers, and during a temporary absence of the judge one of them said to me: "You are in the way there. Sit over here against the wall."

"But the judge gave me this seat," I remonstrated.

"What if he did?" said the man, squaring his shoulders. "I am the division boss, and what I say goes."

"Very probably," I answered, sweetly; "but I am required to take my orders from the judge, and, with your permission, I will sit here until he returns."

But when he returned nothing further was said about my moving.

Late in the day an organization watcher said suddenly, "No one has voted from Mulberry Street." "No," said another, "and I'll tell you why. A lady on Mulberry Street was put in jail last month; the division leader didn't get her out, and nobody's votin' on that street."

Four hundred and sixty-nine names were on the registration list, but only 309 ballots were cast. It is not so long ago that these figures would have been reversed, and it is barely possible that the revolt on Mulberry Street and the falling off of the number of voters is an indication of the waning power of the boss.

The election officers and organization watchers in my division were old friends and co-workers at the polls. Two of them were father and son, two were husband and wife. They were intimate with most of the voters, asked after the children, and inquired why John or James or Amelia had not yet turned out to vote. It was quite a family party, and I felt like an unbidden guest.

Except for my challenges and an occasional difference with the division boss, the election in my division was peaceful and uneventful, and so it was in the majority of election precincts. For this peace and order the Prohibition Law was largely responsible. The law is broken in Philadelphia, as in other cities, but the mass of the people support it, and no better evidence is needed than the order that prevailed at the polls. In a division often disgraced with drunken brawls I saw no sign of liquor and the most disreputable-looking voters exhaled no alcoholic odor, and from a majority of the divisions the women watchers made the same report. We were told the next morning that the quiet election was not due to the women watchers nor to the Prohibition Law, but to a special order from the chief of all the bosses that there were to be no disturbances at the polls. That may have been, but the fact remains that public sentiment would have tolerated no disturbances, and he knew it.

The bosses are learning, but there is still much that they fail even to apprehend. As the polls closed, the same sub-boss who had tried to get me away from the registration list said, "What are you going to get out of this?"

"A good Governor, I hope," I replied.

"Don't try to come that over me," he retorted. "Nobody works for nothing. What's in it for you? If you don't get paid for watching, you're out of a job."

It is this lack of imagination that may be the final undoing of the boss.

Source: Imogen B. Oakley, "Experiences of a Pinchot Watcher at the Polls," *The Outlook*, August 16, 1922, 638–39.

(43) Radio Becomes an Important Provider of Returns— New York, 1928

As mentioned in the introduction, the advent of radio would have an enormous influence on election-night behavior, beginning with the presidential contest of 1928. At party headquarters and other sites where people had always gathered to get the latest news, there was no longer such "a jam of anxious, perspiring humanity," as a considerable part of the public now tuned in to get the results on the airwaves. The accompanying article concentrates especially on the preparations made by the NBC network for its election-night broadcast that year. It includes a reference to the prior distribution of "score cards" so that listeners could keep track of the results as they were announced. The article also mentions that "musical interludes" would be provided by the network's regular Tuesday night entertainers in case "lulls occur in the bulletin service." The famous announcer Graham McNamee was put in charge of entertainment, while *New York Times* political writer David Lawrence was to furnish election returns and commentary, aided by a staff of fifty. NBC was to begin its coverage at 6:00 P.M., whereas the competing CBS network would start at 8:00 P.M.; both planned to continue giving out pertinent information well into the next morning. Other stations arranged to have briefer reports during the evening. Just how big an audience tuned in to the broadcasts is unknown. However, the number of election-night listeners undoubtedly increased over the following decades, as more and more people owned radios and began staying at home.

Radio stations throughout the nation will broadcast election returns tonight. Beginning at 6 o'clock, many of them will depart from the regular entertainment schedules to send out the returns. The National Broadcasting Company's networks will start the election service at 6 P.M. Artists usually heard on the air Tuesday nights will be in the studios to entertain in case any lulls occur in the bulletin service.

David Lawrence, political writer and editor, will be in charge of the staff of fifty experts for the National Broadcasting Company, Associated Press, United Press and International News Service. The group in the studio will include political analysts and tabulators. The bulletins supplied by the three news services will be used in preparing the running story, which will continue until 266 electoral votes are given to the successful candidate. Music will fill in for brief interludes. Graham McNamee, announcer, will be in charge of the entertainment. Mr. Lawrence will broadcast the political story.

"Instead of announcing numerical returns from scattered States and precincts," said a representative of the National Broadcasting Company, "we will send out interpretive reports. For example, when a certain number of precincts in Newark have reported and the majority for one of the major candidates is given, the listeners will be told what this signifies as compared with election returns of four years ago and what its probable effect will be on the present Presidential race. Score cards have been made available by the NBC through cooperation with several newspapers. Mr. Lawrence will work with a score card in his hand. The national situation will be summarized from time to time and in addition reports on the outcome of Congressional contests and State contests will go on the air."

More than seventy-five radio stations will be associated with the NBC for the election broadcast. [The newspaper also reported that the network would rebroadcast the program on short wave for foreign listeners.]

Source: "Election Returns on Radio Tonight," *New York Times*, November 6, 1928, 32.

---

(44) Small New England Town First to Vote—New Ashford, Massachusetts, 1936

During the early to middle decades of the twentieth century, one of the interesting sidelights of the overall Election Day story (and one always widely reported in the press) was the competition among certain small towns in the Eastern Time Zone for the honor of being the first election district in the nation to cast and tabulate its ballots. The winner on several occasions was the western Massachusetts town of New Ashford, population ninety-four during the 1930s, approximately one-third of whom regularly voted (or about half of those eligible). Usually the polls opened at 5:45 A.M., with the voting and tabulation concluded before 6:30 A.M. The article below discusses the town's efforts to be first in the nation in regard to voting and how competing communities sometimes offered "fat breakfasts" of bacon, eggs, and coffee to prospective voters in their attempts to beat out New Ashford. In later years, Nutbush (North Carolina), Millsfield (New Hampshire), and then Dixville Notch (New Hampshire) would take the prize, the few electors in these towns casting and counting their votes shortly after midnight right at the beginning of Election Day.

"It is so still in New Ashford that one can hear a feather drop from a bluejay's tail," wrote Josh Billings, the humorist, a century or so ago.

And still it still is, except on Election day in Presidential years. Then what a tumult and shouting crash out in New Ashford! Content to drowse in the Berkshire Hills of Massachusetts for three years and 364 days out of every four years, New Ashford on the day remaining leaps to life, twitches in every member and yells for national recognition.

On Presidential Election days, it is the proud glory of New Ashford to be the first town in the United States to cast its votes, tally them and report them to the universe.

Other Berkshire towns have twitched at New Ashford's laurels. On one occasion, only a poor telephone connection kept them from the grasp of Mount Washington. Last week, the ladies of nearby Tolland, buying up bacon, eggs and coffee, were promising fat breakfasts to every voter who cast his ballot before 6.10 A.M. But New Ashford had been first since 1916, and if the Andersons and Beaches, the Rathbuns and Pickenses, the Packards and Raineys who people it can make it so, it will continue to be first till the cows come home.

Predominantly Methodist, stoutly Republican, as Yankee as pie for breakfast, New Ashford—population ninety-four, assessed valuation $125,000, annual budget $6,000—clings to the hillsides twelve miles north of Pittsfield.

An ultramodern motor road twists through its heart, and air-flow autos swoop over it, but New Ashford remains horse-and-buggy in atmosphere. It has never had a railroad, trolley-car or telegraph office. It had never had a public telephone until this year, when one was installed in Benjamin Boyce's gas station. But neither has it any town debt or relief problem.

On Election day every four years, New Ashford citizens hop out of bed at cock-crow, milk the cows in jig-time, gulp down breakfasts, give the dishes a lick and a promise, and go steaming down to the one-room, century-old white school-house. There they cluster excitedly around the square, wood-burning, sheet-iron stove until 5.45, when the polls open.

Mrs. Mattie Beach, Town Clerk, sits at the teacher's desk and hands them their ballots. Quickly, for these people know their own minds, they mark them, drop them in the ballot box. Quickly they are tallied and, usually from a telephone in a near-by town, flashed from 'Quoddy [referring either to Passamaquoddy, Maine, or to West [sic] Quoddy Head, the easternmost extension of Maine] to San Diego.

Eight years ago, New Ashford used a short-waved radio, but one of the radio operators fell from a tree and sprained his arm, deepening distrust of new-fangled gadgets. Nevertheless, last week, broadcasting chains were instructing their agents to be on hand in the little white schoolhouse when New Ashford casts its votes.

Sitting in the living-room of his flat-roofed house on the Stanford University campus on the morning of Election day, 1928, Mr. Hoover got a telegram that delighted him. "Good omen," it said. "New Ashford: 28

Hoover, 3 Smith." Beaming, he pinned the message on the mantel of the fireplace. Four years later, Mr. Hoover carried New Ashford again. The vote: 24 Hoover, 8 Roosevelt.

In 1928, the New Ashford result was officially announced at 6.26 A.M. In 1932 it was not announced until 6.28. One man, a Democrat, was entirely responsible for the delay. Gregory Makaroff, the son of a gun, scorned all offers of a lift, walked two miles to the polls carrying a Roosevelt banner with a horseshoe painted on it for luck.

Source: "Early Voters: New Ashford Proud of Its Speed in Balloting and Counting Returns," *Literary Digest*, November 7, 1936, 9–10.

---

(45) How the Associated Press Tabulates the National Vote—New York, 1940

One of the amazing aspects of Election Day over the course of the twentieth century was the increasing rapidity with which election results were reported. In earlier times, even with the invention of the telegraph, the tabulation was often slow and the outcome sometimes not fully known for several days. But not long into the new century, many of the results were known by midnight (Eastern Time) or within a few hours afterward, reducing the waiting and the doubt, and allowing the celebrations to go forward. What made this possible, as the article below points out, was the creation of a vast collecting and reporting system by the news organization known as the Associated Press. As the author notes, the AP election machinery was initially established for the New York State contest in 1904 and then spread to other states before going national for the first time in 1916. By 1940, the year of the Franklin Roosevelt–Wendell Willkie presidential contest, when this article was written, some sixty-five thousand persons were involved in the quick tabulating and reporting of the votes coming in, including one correspondent in each of the more than three thousand counties nationwide. The count made by the AP was not the official count, but it was usually at least 99.6 percent accurate. Thus, newspapers and broadcasters throughout the country showed little hesitation in using the figures provided and presenting them to an eager public.

On Tuesday, November 5th, the poll clerk at Davis, West Virginia, will gather a handful of eating tobacco and take a few warm-up chews. Then he'll settle down to counting ballots to see how Messrs. Roosevelt and Willkie have done in the little mountain town, isolated in the cut-over timberlands of the high Alleghenies.

A few minutes after he completes his task the vote of Davis, West Virginia, will be lumped with other votes cast by shrimp fishermen in Louisiana, cowboys in Montana, and lumbermen in Maine. And totals will be known in the newspaper offices of San Francisco, Lima in Peru, and London. They will be heard in millions of homes via the radio. Quite a job, you will admit. And it is. This is the job done election night by the Associated Press. It will look easy when morning papers headline the names of the winners. But there will be a lot of work behind those headlines.

In the space of a dozen hours this co-operative news service will have tallied probably 50 million votes; using an army of 65,000 men to do the job. If the election is a landslide the facts will be known by midnight. Even if it is tight, conclusive figures will probably be known by breakfast time.

If it wasn't for the AP it would take weeks and possibly months to find out who had won. . . . The official machinery can grind slowly, the AP can't. It must be fast—and sure. Besides telling us who is the next President, and the make-up of the new Congress, it handles 48 separate state stories that night. Politicians down in Independence, Kansas, want to know who has been elected in Cheyenne County up in the north-western part of the state; and people in Amarillo, Texas, want to know how the voting is going 800 miles away in Brownsville.

The news service has to collect votes from islands off the Carolina coast, from Alaska, the backwoods counties of Arkansas (where it once had to charter a locomotive to bring in the returns), and from Cook County, Illinois, where there are two million votes to be counted. No news story gets the meticulous coverage given a national election. It must be complete to the last vote. And accurate.

The major domo of this vast show is Claude A. Jagger, baldish, rosy-cheeked AP financial editor. During the 1929 stock crash Jagger, then twenty-seven years old, wrote 8,000 words of running story in one sitting. After a siege like that a national election is a relatively simple matter.

Plans can be laid months in advance and if the planning job is good enough everything goes smoothly.

Jagger began setting up machinery to cover the November 5th election while most of us were on vacation last summer. By now every detail is complete. All Jagger has to do on election night is sit back at his desk in the main newsroom at the AP bureau in Rockefeller Center, New York. And watch it roll. It's quite a spectacle.

Election day will start calmly enough. Probably a few minutes past midnight November 4th the dozen people of Millsfield, New Hampshire, will have voted, closed the polls and claimed the honor of being the first United States election district to report. Somerset, Vermont, will come along in the early morning and so will New Ashford, Massachusetts. Later in the day the shooting will be in Kentucky where politics, like mountain dew, is taken straight. Slight points of controversy are grounds for homicide. Ten to twenty of these lethal affairs—par for the day—must be taken into account.

Roosevelt and Willkie will vote and be photographed and interviewed at the polls. Their pictures will be sent on the 20,000-mile Wirephoto network. Congressmen will shed cultured pearls of wisdom as they disappear into voting booths, and governors will pose with their wives—decorated, for this occasion, with orchids. All this is a tepid prelude to the real business. The wires warm to their task at 5 P.M. Eastern Standard time, when polls begin to close. Then Jagger's army swings into action.

The lone correspondent tucked away in a remote Wisconsin county seat may think he is missing all the fun, but he is the real basis for AP election machinery, the hero of this piece. There is a man like him for each of the 3,070 U.S. counties and on them the whole show depends. In many cases they work for newspapers which are members of the AP; in others they are employed directly. In any case their job is the same: to collect the vote from every precinct in the county.

To get a better idea of how it works, let's take the correspondent in Aroostook County, Maine. Weeks before the election he had lined up a man in every precinct in his county who would report directly to him—usually one of the election clerks. Speed was stressed; the vote had to be in the moment the count was complete. If it could be telephoned into the office that was fine. If there were no telephones it could be brought in by car, motorcycle, or horse.

Advance instructions told the correspondent what he was to do. When five precincts were complete he was to report to state headquarters. He was to follow this half an hour later with whatever else had come in; and thereafter make telephone reports at hourly intervals until his county was complete. In some states a $25 prize goes to the first man to clean up a county—no insignificant pickings in the life of a rural journalist.

The county man has a comptometer operator to help him tabulate returns; and prepared charts covering all offices. When he has five precincts the great AP election machine starts to grind. He calls Portland over special election telephones installed that day. Only the county correspondents know the numbers of these telephones. This precaution is taken against the wires being jammed by incidental telephone traffic.

Slips of paper with the vote noted on them go to tabulators in Portland to be added to those that have come in from other parts of the state.

Returns in which there is purely local interest go out over state wires. Those nationally interesting are relayed to Boston, biggest New England bureau and key point on that divisional wire circuit.

Boston is a madhouse. It looks like a movie director's conception of a newspaper office. Jack Chester, bureau chief, barks orders. A bank of a dozen or more girls with calculating machines run totals on votes pouring in from other New England points. Top-notch reporters write running stories to feed hungry wires.

This bureau is hooked into the main trunk wire system of the AP—a 285,000-mile cobweb touching virtually every town of any size in the U.S. The main trunks consist of as many as five parallel wires. A message tapped out on any one of them is reproduced on telegraphic printers from Boston to Seattle, from Havana to Mexico City.

Boston has been chosen as an example because it is usually the lead-off point in the election service. According to schedules it starts the round robin of returns about 5 P.M. In the space of two minutes printers clicking at top speed will give the latest returns collected. Then New York will swing onto the wire with the vote it has gathered, then Philadelphia, Baltimore, Atlanta. The wire goes west, picking up Pittsburgh, Cleveland, Detroit, Chicago, Des Moines, and Omaha. Kansas City is the great U.S. news divide.

The bulk of Eastern stories are pulled off wires here. The West wouldn't be interested. Similarly, Western stories, dull stuff to the East, are discarded. But on election night the news goes straight to Denver, Salt Lake City and the Coast.

In an hour's time or less the circuit will be completed; then Boston will start sending again. So it will go all night, the tempo increasing moment by moment to reach a white heat during the period between 10 P.M. and 2 A.M. when the Far West is breaking.

Bureaus keep in scheduled line unless really hot news breaks: a pivotal state, for example, going unmistakably to one candidate or the other. Then they can cut in out of turn—signaling "95," old Morse operators' symbol for important news, or "bulletin," or even "flash."

By midnight large state bureaus are a bedlam. They are required to keep cumulative totals for hundreds of offices: state legislatures, county governments, important judgeships. To help with the job some of them use fantastically complex punched-card tabulating machines. Cards are punched for each county and for each office as returns arrive. Then they can be run through a tabulating machine in a matter of seconds to give the relative standing of various candidates.

Meanwhile, the writing staff must keep running stories on the network of state wires—and regional wires—stories which never reach the main trunks. All this work is done to the accompaniment of an insufferable din: jangling of telephone bells, the metallic clink of Morse instruments and the clatter of teletype machines.

Washington is the nerve center for the works, the main tabulating point of the system. Here, returns from states are pulled off wires as they come in and national tabulations are made covering the presidency, congressmen, governors. The steady stream of minor returns goes to tabulators, and presidential returns go directly to a man presiding over a 6x10-foot blackboard. State totals for Willkie and Roosevelt are chalked up here; being corrected from minute to minute as new returns arrive. The blackboard is a graphic representation of democracy at work. It keeps tabs on a nation choosing a leader. A glance at this board tells how the tide is running.

A battery of crack political correspondents face this board under the watchful eye of Brian Bell, a vigorous man of fifty, bureau manager at Washington. Three men write presidential "leads"—the running story of the presidential election. The outpouring of words from their typewriters keep one wire nearly full. Another writer follows gubernatorial elections, and others follow the races for House and Senate seats. Within ten minutes of the time a pivotal state reports some significant shift in the vote, a story of the change is in the offices of 1,400 member newspapers; and on the air through an arrangement with broadcasting companies. Even the men most directly concerned—Messrs. Roosevelt and Willkie— will get the word by the same medium. AP will string wires to any place the candidates designate.

The election story will be almost as big in other parts of the world as it is in the United States. Via the Press-Wireless station on Long Island the New York office will feed the news directly to approximately 100 Spanish-American client papers. Cables will carry it to the AP of Great Britain and Australia; and Canadian Press wires will take it over the Dominion.

Along "No-Man's Land"—wartime designation for the corridor in the AP's New York building occupied by foreign new agencies—more wires will be working. Domei (Japan); Havas (France); DNB (Germany); Reuters (Britain); Tass (Russia); and others will shoot AP returns to every corner of the earth.

Prior to the establishment of AP election coverage, returns were collected haphazardly by individual newspapers and commercial telegraph companies. Opportunities for fraud were plentiful. A key district, county or state, could withhold returns until it saw what a favorite candidate needed to put him over. With returns now all but instantaneous there isn't time for such skullduggery. Any delay causes immediate suspicion. A few years ago Memphis was late and newspapers over the state bitterly assailed Boss Crump's political machine. The boss was innocent.

What actually happened was that the bureau tabulator had fallen down on the job and a recanvas of polls was necessary.

The AP machine was first set up to cover the New York state elections in 1906, was extended to others in 1908 and 1912. It got its first trial on a national scale in 1916 during the Hughes-Wilson contest. Its baptism of fire couldn't have been tougher. The first returns indicated a Hughes landslide but the margin narrowed until the result hung on California. All day Wednesday and Thursday votes trickled in from remote mountainous precincts with the vote seesawing back and forth between the two candidates. At 11:20 Thursday night the AP flashed Wilson's victory—by a margin of 3,000 votes!

Since then the machinery for coverage has been greased and enlarged. Conditions are nowhere so difficult as they once were. Voting machines have speeded the count. Telephones and good roads have brought once-isolated counties within easy reach. Martin County, Kentucky, still has but one telephone, and Pendleton County, West Virginia, has recently gotten service. But these are isolated and not too significant examples of conditions that are fast disappearing.

How accurate is the AP count as compared with the official count? Two recent checks in New Jersey showed to be 99.6 and 99.8 per cent accurate, respectively.

No matter what happens elsewhere on the night of November 5th the election will be the world's biggest news. It will take a million wired words to tell the complete story. Only top-ranking items will be able to compete for wire space with a story of such dimensions: a king would have to be assassinated to make bigger news than the pivotal Ohio vote.

It will be a frenzied, sleepless night for the 65,000 men who do the job. They will end up red-eyed, deafened by the din, and soaked with coffee (the New York bureau drank 40 gallons last election). But by breakfast time the job will be more than 90 per cent finished. By then they can tell us whether we have been wearing the right buttons.

Source: J.D. Ratcliff, "They Work While You Vote," *Collier's*, November 9, 1940, 21, 68.

---

(46) American Soldiers Vote on Duty during World War II—Europe, 1944

Because it took place amid the Second World War, Election Day in 1944 was somewhat unusual in that numerous voters serving in the armed forces needed to cast their ballots far from home, often overseas. During the Civil War, a small percentage of votes had come from soldiers in the field, but in World War II the figure was in the millions, over 400,000 from native New Yorkers alone. Some of the ballots from faraway places had been marked a month or two before November, but others were deposited on Election Day itself, occasionally in difficult circumstances. As will be noted in the first document below, officers sometimes had to crawl to frontline trenches to accept votes from the enlisted men.

The military vote was heavier than expected and, as the second document concludes, the broad participation by members of the armed forces clearly showed their strong support for democracy at home. The final tally of the soldier vote was not completed until well after the presidential race had been decided, but most estimates indicated a bigger majority for continuing President Franklin Roosevelt in office than among the civilian population. The material in the first selection is taken from *The Stars and Stripes*, the daily newspaper of the U.S. armed forces in the European Theater of Operations, while the later part comes from reports in the *New York Times*.

"Election day dawned in a cold and cheerless drizzle on the Western Front," Larry LeSeur, CBS reporter, told America in a broadcast yesterday from Holland. "The war in the West seems to have almost paused while you in America will decide the election. The doughboys themselves will be listening to election results on captured German radio sets."

"But most of the men who have been fighting all day will be asleep in their pup tents and in their water-logged foxholes."

"Gen. Eisenhower will get the election news at the front. 'Ike' seemed almost casual about the election when he left Supreme Headquarters today and visited men in the line." . . .

Shortly after midnight last night, David Anderson, American radio reporter, broadcast this picture of voting at the front in Holland.

"Just 20 minutes ago the polls closed here for the soldier vote. The task of assuring each man his democratic privilege was not easy. Officers crawled on their stomachs through rain-soaked peat and bog to accept the votes of doughboys in forward slit trenches. They reached into the jowls of tanks to take them from the hands of crew members. Tanks came from near and far with sealed ballots which will ultimately be opened in America."

Source: "Election Notes," *The Stars and Stripes*, November 8, 1944, 1.[lb]

The size of the soldier vote, which includes . . . ballots cast by members of all branches of the armed forces, was larger than had been estimated originally. It gave evidence that the men and women who are fighting . . . for victory have maintained their interest in the democratic processes at home. Several combatants have died since registering their choice.

These votes are being counted as valid, a far cry and a patriotic one from the days when "counting dead men's votes" was a scandalous piece of political trickery.

The short form Federal war ballot was used for overseas members of the armed forces by fifteen States that issued their own State ballots for service members stationed in the continental United States. The other States declined to avail themselves of the Federal forms and issued their own ballots to members of the military abroad and in this country.

Army and Navy voting officers helped bring about the large vote by making State war ballot applications available to enlisted men and officers from States, among them New York, which required a signed application before sending a war ballot to a service man or woman. On many a ship and in camps on both sides of the world the voting officers handed out cards to members of their units who might otherwise not have troubled to write for a state form.

The tabulation of the service votes was watched closely . . . by observers for an answer to the question whether there was any such thing . . . as a "military vote" or if service men and women made their voting choices about the same as persons in the same age range back home.

The absentee military votes, most of which had been marked weeks and in some cases months ago, were the last to be counted, with a few notable exceptions as in New Jersey. In most States, the tally was taken first of the civilian votes cast yesterday, and only then did the election clerks count up the paper ballots that members of the armed forces had marked in foxholes, on battle decks, and in cantonments and hospitals here and overseas.

Source: Charles Grutzner, "Roosevelt Strong in War Vote Tally," *New York Times,* November 8, 1944, 1.

(47) Franklin Roosevelt's Last Election Day—Hyde Park, New York, 1944

The 1944 presidential election was the last one featuring Franklin Delano Roosevelt, perhaps the most notable and certainly the most successful American politician of the twentieth century.

Cousin of Theodore Roosevelt, Franklin had at first pursued a political career in the same manner as his famous kinsman, starting in the New York State legislature, becoming assistant secretary of the Navy, and then being named his party's vice-presidential candidate. The younger Roosevelt's political quest was subsequently sidetracked—most people thought it completely ended—as he was stricken with polio in 1921. Yet despite being confined to a wheelchair FDR managed to make his way back into politics, getting elected twice as governor of New York and ultimately four times as president of the United States. Roosevelt's 1944 campaign proved to be a difficult one, as he was by that time physically weary from his many years in office; in fact, he was terminally ill. His Republican opponent that year, New York governor Thomas Dewey, made it a fairly close race by criticizing the tired and quarrelsome "old men" running the government. Still, Roosevelt showed some energy in the last days of the contest, and with the help of organized labor, the urban machines, and absentee ballots from voters in the armed forces, managed to win by a comfortable margin. How Roosevelt spent his last Election Day is described below by *New York Times* reporter John H. Crider, with some additional material provided from a book on FDR's last year by journalist Jim Bishop.

Hyde Park, New York, November 7—President Roosevelt told several thousand Hyde Park villagers from his front porch at 11:40 tonight that it was too early to make any statement on election returns, but expressed confidence he would continue his custom of commuting here from Washington for another four years. . . .

Earlier in the day the President went to the Town Hall and exercised the function of good citizenship which he had repeatedly admonished other Americans to do throughout the campaign.

Mr. Roosevelt drove over to the village to vote just after noon, riding in the front seat of an open phaeton and wearing an old brown fedora and the black naval cape with velvet collar and braided frogs which is one of his favorite outdoor garments.

It was a clear bright fall day—what some called "Republican weather," and the President was voting as always in a staunchly Republican part of the State. He usually carries his own election district, Hyde Park No. 3, but loses Dutchess County.

The car stopped first in front of the Hyde Park Elementary School, where Miss Noreen I. Davey, the principal, greeted Mr. Roosevelt with a handshake. Classes were let out and about a hundred children assembled near the Presidential car. The kindergarten tots were permitted to stand nearest, so they could see.

Mr. Roosevelt told the children that they, too, would be voting soon. He arrived at the school about 12:10 and stayed for ten minutes.

The President drove on to the old frame Town Hall, built about 1900, where several hundred citizens—more, some observers thought, than had been present on previous election days—had assembled to see their famous neighbor perform his rite of citizenship.

Source: John H. Crider, "Torchlight Parade Honors Roosevelt," *New York Times*, November 8, 1944, 3.[lb]

Like most politicians, he voted fairly early so that the press could use the photographs and quotations for afternoon editions. However, Hyde Park had new voting machines, and when the President got behind the curtains, he had a problem reaching up from his wheelchair to close the curtains, and even greater problems reading the local referenda. The First Lady, standing outside the curtains was shocked to hear the best-known voice of the century shout, "Damn!"

At lunchtime, . . . he was back home reminding the housekeeper that, at 9:00 P.M., he expected the dining room table to be cleared; he wanted tally sheets and pencils to be laid out and a radio set and news ticker moved into the small room. Throughout the afternoon a surge of excitement was visible in the election questions which flew back and forth across the library. [The President was surrounded by advisors including Admiral William D. Leahy, Henry Morganthau, Robert Sherwood, Steve Early, Sam Rosenman, Grace Tully and Bill Hassett, who took turns asking about those states still considered doubtful.] Mr. Roosevelt was calm and, at times, jolly. He said he hoped he was right in giving his occupation before the election board as "tree grower." He also excused his loud "Damn!" complaining that newsreel photographers had strung their wires over his voting booth, "fouling the curtains and making everything inoperable." . . .

Early dinner had been over for an hour when Mr. Roosevelt wheeled his chair into the dining room and moved it partly under the table on the kitchen side. . . . The Associated Press and United Press news tickers could not be wired into the dining room, so Bill Hassett made frequent trips to the small smoking room and back, with sheets in his hand, to be laid before the President. Grace Tully sat beside FDR with a telephone to her ear. She had a direct line to Democratic national headquarters at the Biltmore Hotel in New York, and whatever information accrued she passed quietly to the President. He ran the election guessing game himself. Now and then, Henry Morganthau would saunter in from the li-

brary to ask, "How are things going?. . . ." Some of the early returns from
the New England states established no trend. It was not until after 10:
00 P.M. that the Democratic majorities in the big cities of the East and
Midwest began to tip the election toward Roosevelt. The tipping became
more noticeable toward 11:00 P.M. The election was not "in the bag," but
it began to look good for Roosevelt.

Source: Jim Bishop, *FDR's Last Year* (New York: William Morrow, 1974), 177–79.

---

(48) Black Veterans Seek to Vote in Postwar South— Mississippi, 1946–1947

Though people of all colors fought during World War II to protect American freedom, most southern blacks upon returning
home found that they were still denied their fundamental rights,
particularly the right to vote and otherwise participate in the
electoral process. Admittedly, some progress was being made
by the federal government to rectify the situation. In 1944 the
Supreme Court in *Smith v. Allwright* ruled that the exclusion of
Negroes from a state primary was a clear violation of the Fifteenth Amendment. Subsequent to that decision, African Americans in modest numbers began being admitted to the voting
booth in certain parts of the Upper South. Even in South Carolina and Georgia, thousands of blacks were casting ballots a few
years later, especially in such larger cities as Charleston and
Atlanta. But in places like rural Mississippi the older exclusion-
ary pattern was more deeply entrenched and difficult to change.
A telling example can be seen in the experience of Charles and
Medgar Evers, who would later become civil rights leaders. In
1946, the Evers brothers, who had recently come back from
military service, along with four friends, approached the Newton
County courthouse, with the idea of exercising the right to vote.
They obtained ballots but were unable to deposit them in the
ballot box, being blocked by a group of armed whites and forced
to leave the premises. Despite being denied and receiving several death threats, the Evers brothers were determined to achieve
their goal. The following year, both Charles and Medgar did
manage to vote, and, as Charles stated in his memoirs, in the
way the officials guarded the ballot box, "they let us know there
was something mighty good in voting."

The election came. Senator Bilbo was raving: "The best way to stop nig-gers from voting is to visit them the night before the election." Medgar and I heard this, and we said silently, "Come on and visit us! We'll kill you all! No one visited us."

On election day, Medgar and I recruited some old friends to join us: my good friend A. J. Needham; A. J.'s brother C.B. Needham; and two others Bernon Wansley and a man named Hudson. We went to the polls early to beat the crowd. When we reached the courthouse, we found 250 rednecks, dressed in overalls, holding shotguns, rifles, and pistols. Some were sitting in pickup trucks, others standing around the courthouse square. God! I'd never seen so many Klukkers, bigots, and hatemongers, never seen so many guns in one place, not even in the army. And mean, silent white men holding those guns.

We tried to ignore them, but a bunch of them were blocking the court-house doors. We stood on the courthouse steps, eyeballing each other. I had a long-handle .38 with me and a switchblade knife in my pocket. I'd learned as a young boy that white folks feared knives more than guns. Now I tucked the .38 away in my pocket, held the switchblade in my hand, and headed for the door.

The old circuit clerk, Mr. Brand, scurried over [saying]: "You Evers boys come from a good family. Why go looking for trouble like this?" We looked at him real solid but said nothing. Mr. Brand kept on: "Charles, you and Medgar, you all go back, you're going to cause trou-ble." I said, "Let me tell you something, Mr. Brand. We are going to vote—or else we're all going to go to hell today. It's up to you. Now, give us our ballots." Mr. Brand turned tail and scooted back into the courthouse.

[Eventually, the Evers brothers reached the clerk's office.]

Source: Charles Evers and Andrew Szanton, *Have No Fear: The Charles Evers Story* (New York: John Wiley and Sons, 1997), 61–62.[lb]

We were inside the courthouse. We had received our ballots to vote, but there wasn't any way we could get to the ballot box, because the Klans-men had put the ballot box *inside* a back office and they were physically blocking the door to that office. I said, "Look, Medgar, I'm going through," and he replied, "No, Charley, don't try. It ain't worth it."

They stood there, and we stood there eyeballing each other. I really wanted to die that day. And again we found out they're cowards. They were shaking like leaves on a tree. There were dozens of them, big-bellied, rednecked and with guns, and scared to death.

I asked, "May I place my ballot in the ballot box?"

One said, "You niggers can't come in here."

And I replied, "Why not?"

And he said, "Cause we said so."

Andy May walked up beside me and asked, "Evers, ain't nothin' happened to you yet?"

And I answered by saying, "Isn't anything going to happen to me."

Medgar said, "Come on, Charley, we'll get them next time."

Medgar and I left. But I said to May, "Listen, we'll be back. And you better not follow us down the street."

The sheriff did not try to arrest us. We vowed we were not coming back home alive if they tried anything on us. They would have to kill us. I told Brand and the rest of them, "That's all right. One of these days you're going to want to come in the door and we ain't going to let you in."

[Charles and Medgar never forgot that day. After risking their lives in a war for democracy and free elections, they had come home and were nearly killed for trying to vote. More than any other single event, that day made the Evers brothers civil rights activists. The following year, in the 1947 county elections, despite being threatened again, they did manage to vote, knowing that voting was the key to power.]

Source: Charles Evers, *Evers* (New York: World, 1971), 94–6.

---

(49) Harry Truman Reacts to His Upset Victory—Excelsior Springs, Missouri, 1948

At Franklin Roosevelt's death in April 1945, the vice president, Missouri Democrat Harry Truman, took over the presidency. The public, however, was not very happy with his performance over the next three and a half years. Among the many difficulties plaguing the Truman administration were labor strife, conflict with Russia, and charges of communist influence in the American government. As the general election of 1948 approached the Republicans seemed sure of winning the presidency for the first time in twenty years. Truman, reluctantly nominated by the Democratic convention, was given little chance of success, for in addition to facing strong GOP opposition he had to deal with the splits in his own party. Some southern Democrats had bolted and formed a "Dixiecrat" ticket to protest the civil rights plank in the platform, and some left-wing elements had gone over to support the Progressive candidate, Henry Wallace. The Republican nominee, again Governor Thomas Dewey of New York, quickly became the overwhelming favorite. Indeed, most of the polls showed Dewey so far out in front that soon he felt no need to stump very vigorously for votes. Most political experts ignored the gains Truman appeared to be making in the last stages of the race and predicted a major triumph for Dewey. But as it turned out the so-called experts were wrong, and Truman scored an upset victory—surely the biggest one in presidential history. In his memoirs, excerpted below, he recalled his impressions of that election night, particularly noting how the famous radio commentator H.V. Kaltenborn kept trying to discount voting figures that showed that Truman was going to win.

At four-thirty in the afternoon on Election Day, Jim Rowley and Henry Nicholson, who were first and second in command of the White House Secret Service detail, drove with me from my home down to the Elms Hotel at Excelsior Springs, Missouri, a resort about thirty miles northeast of Kansas City. We had slipped away from the reporters, who spent the rest of the night trying to find me. They kept telephoning my family at Independence, hoping to get some information. At Excelsior Springs, after taking a Turkish bath, I went upstairs to my room at six-thirty, had a ham sandwich and a glass of milk, turned on the radio to listen to some of the eastern returns, and then went to bed. I was reported some thousands ahead.

I awoke at midnight and again listened to the radio broadcast of Mr. H.V. Kaltenborn. I was about 1,200,000 ahead on the count but, according to this broadcaster, was still undoubtedly beaten.

About four o'clock in the morning Rowley came into my room and advised me to tune in again on Kaltenborn's broadcast. I did so, and learned that at that time I was over 2,000,000 ahead, but the commentator continued to say he couldn't see how I could be elected.

I told Rowley and Nicholson that we had better go back to Kansas City, because it looked very much as if we were in for another four years, and we arrived in Kansas City at about six o'clock Wednesday morning, November 3. At ten-thirty I received a telegram from Governor Dewey congratulating me on my election.

Source: *Memoirs of Harry S. Truman* (Garden City, N.Y.: Doubleday, 1956), 2:220–21.

---

(50) GOP Headquarters: Scene of Gloom—New York, 1948

In contrast to President Truman's upbeat remarks is a description of the "scene of gloom" at Republican national headquarters at

the Hotel Roosevelt in New York City. Hundreds of party workers had gathered there to celebrate Governor Dewey's expected
victory but wound up experiencing another defeat. After losing
to Roosevelt and the Democrats four times in national elections,
the Republicans had been confident that this would be their year
to triumph. All the evidence had pointed that way, and so they
were stunned by Dewey's loss. As one of those in attendance
exclaimed, "And I waited for this night 16 years."

Republicans who stayed up all night at national headquarters to celebrate looked at dawn today like haggard brides left waiting at the
church. It was so quiet around the hotel Roosevelt that you could hear
a poll-taker's chin drop.

But if there was a poll-taker in the place he wisely kept his mouth
shut. There were no Republican chins any longer able even to fall open.
They had all done that hours before.

It was a scene of political carnage over which spread the lengthening
shadow cast by the little man from Missouri. Harry S. Truman, stub-
bornly riding out threats of a Republican landslide, had lived up to the
motto of his state—"You got to show me."

Win, lose or draw, he had—almost single-mouthed—smashed Republican hopes of gaining control of both Congress and the presidency.

The tidal flood of Democratic votes completely ruined the Grand Old
Party's brand new victory party.

Some 300 happy party workers crowded into the Gold Ballroom of
the hotel, confident they would see a Democratic debacle.

A score or more television and newsreel cameras were trained on the
flag-draped balcony, where Gov. Thomas E. Dewey was expected to deliver his victory speech before midnight. Rumors said his aides had composed the speech two days before.

The crowd stirred uneasily as early returns showed Truman ahead.
But they cheered when campaign manager Herbert Brownell, grinning
widely, stepped out on the gallery and minimized the figures—again
predicting victory. It was the last grin of the evening.

Some Republicans left then, sure Dewey had won. But they were probably the only ones who got a good night's rest.

For after midnight deepening alarm swept the gaily-bannered room.
The faces of the crowd were a slow motion study of confidence changing
from surprise to doubt, from doubt to disbelief—and then on to stunned
fear and panic.

By 2 A.M. only 100 people were left in the ballroom, and workmen
quit hanging up the depressing figures on the big scoreboard. . . . [Only
22 people remained at 6 A.M. when defeat became certain.]

Source: Hal Boyle, "GOP Headquarters Scene of Gloom," Associated Press, November 3, 1948.

Emergence of the Mass Media Age, 1952–1964

Beginning in the 1950s, there would be marked changes in how America experienced Election Day. For one thing, elections became more serious business with the heightening of the Cold War, leading to a temporary upsurge in voting through the mid 1960s. People worried about a possible nuclear confrontation and about "whose finger was on the button." Another change was the movement toward greater racial and gender equality at the polls. Women would reach parity with men in regard to the turnout rate, and African Americans would gradually obtain voting rights in the South. Native Americans began to exercise the vote more readily and become a factor in elections in the Southwest. New states would be added—Hawaii and Alaska—and become parts of the electoral picture. The most notable difference, however, was the impact of television and other new technology. From the fifties onward, television would revolutionize the way people learned about an election's progress and obtained the final results. Yet if TV provided faster and more accurate returns, it also accelerated the decline of public celebration as more and more people spent election night at home. In addition, TV-commissioned preelection polling would take away some of the drama from Election Day and discourage some people from voting. Nevertheless, not until subsequent years did the nation begin to see a sharp decline in turnout. People in the 1950s and early '60s still had a strong faith in government and the existing political process. Furthermore, the parties remained highly competitive, most notably in the presidential contest of 1960, in which Democratic candidate John Kennedy defeated the Republicans' Richard Nixon by a very narrow margin.

(51) Native Americans Begin to Vote—Arizona and New Mexico, 1952

Like African Americans, Native Americans had been denied
equal rights for centuries, in particular the right to vote. Even
though they had been present long before white Europeans
came to the New World, the native peoples were assigned an
inferior status under the law. When the Constitution was ratified
in the 1780s, it stipulated that the tribes should be dealt with
through special treaty arrangements and not as citizens of the
United States. Not until 1924, with the passage of the Indian
Citizenship Act, were Native Americans granted full citizenship.
Even then, as had been the case for many blacks, various sub-
terfuges continued to be used—poll taxes, literacy tests—to prevent Indians from voting in several states. In places with large
numbers of Native Americans, such as Arizona and New Mexico, it was ruled that persons living on reservations were wards
of the federal government under "guardianship" and thus incom-
petent to vote. Only in 1948 were these barriers finally removed.
The accompanying article shows how Native Americans by
1952 were becoming politically active and registering to vote,
and how the Republican presidential candidate Dwight Eisenhower even attended an intertribal festival that summer to pro-
mote his candidacy. In subsequent years, although white
officials in some states tried to lessen the impact of Indian ballots
by holding at-large elections in certain counties, Native Americans would organize vigorously to defeat these efforts and were
electing their tribesmen to state legislatures in the Southwest by
the 1960s.

This is the first Presidential election in which the Indian vote will count—
and it may mean somebody's scalp.

Of the 450,000 Indians in the United States, all but about 115,000 have
had the vote for many years, but the disfranchised ones were concentrated in the only two states where their vote might really be effective.
Arizona, with a total population of 749,587, has 70,000 Indians; New
Mexico has 45,000 in a total of 681,187.

The Arizona State Constitution denies the vote to "persons under
guardianship," and this, until 1948, was taken to mean Indians. Then
two Apache war veterans carried their plea to the State Supreme Court,
which decided the phrase didn't apply to Indians. The same year in New

Mexico a Pueblo ex-Marine sergeant challenged the state's voting ban on "Indians not taxed" and showed a federal district court that Indians pay sales, income and many other taxes. They got the franchise.

It was too late that year (July 15 in Arizona and Aug. 4 in New Mexico) to do much. This is not true today. If eight electoral votes in those two states decide an election the Indians aim to deliver them, and in any case there is going to be something said about who their Governors are and who are going to Congress.

A new, mostly veteran-led, sense of political power is everywhere in the Indian country, but nowhere is it so strong as in Arizona, where all tribes have combined in a state-wide Intertribal Council. When the council's chairman, a young Papago Indian, Thomas A. Segundo, told Secretary of the Interior Oscar Chapman that Arizona Indians wanted to select their own attorneys and wanted the government to check only professional standing and the reasonableness of their fees, Chapman rescinded a new procedure setting up many other points on which the Government might reject Indian contracts. Many people testified on the same matter, but there was no doubt Segundo represented the most Indians.

Segundo shrewdly began his campaign to get out the Papago vote by talking to the women. Before long there were more squaws registered than braves, and then it was no trouble at all to get the men to swoop down on the registration booths, like Hollywood warriors attacking a wagon train. The 7,000 Papagos will definitely be heard from this year.

Arizona Indians in 1950 swung the state for Republican Gov. Howard Pyle. He had promised to end discrimination against them. Presently they accused him of not delivering. When Clarence Wesley, an Apache leader, politely asked him why, he called Wesley an agitator. Wesley may be a red man, but he's no red, and he didn't like it. Barry Goldwater of Phoenix, the Republican Senatorial candidate, seems popular in the Indian councils, who have heard to complain about incumbent Democratic Senator Ernest W. McFarland.

General Eisenhower, mindful of those electoral votes in New Mexico and Arizona, dropped in at the Gallup (N.M.) Intertribal Indian Ceremonial, heavily attended by Indians from both states, on Aug. 10. "My own (boyhood) heroes were . . . Red Cloud, Chief Dog, Crazy Horse and Geronimo," he said. During World War II "never did I hear a complaint about the battle conduct of the North American Indian." He closed with a plea that Indians "exercise the right of universal suffrage." It was good medicine.

In New Mexico 15,000 of the 45,000 Indians probably will vote. Democratic Senator Dennis Chavez, who has done much for the Indians, is running against former Secretary of War Patrick J. Hurley who, one In-

dian said, has "never done anything but kiss a few papooses, who complained that his mustache scratched."

Source: Alden Stevens, "Voice of the Native," *New York Times*, November 2, 1952,
section 6, 65. Copyright © 1952 by the New York Times Co, Reprinted by permission.

---

(52) Declining Crowds in Times Square—New York, 1952

By the 1950s, one of the long-standing practices associated with
Election Day—urban dwellers coming together in the streets to
wait for the results—would begin to fade. The growing impact
of radio and then TV, coupled with the movement of families to
the suburbs, sounded the death knell of the tradition of huge
crowds viewing the returns on lighted bulletin boards outside
newspaper offices. The most famous gathering spot in the country since the early years of the twentieth century had been Times
Square in New York City, where upward of 250,000 people had
once stood on election night. But as the article below indicates,
no more than one-tenth that number appeared on the evening
of November 4, 1952, when former World War II hero Gen.
Dwight D. Eisenhower, running on the Republican ticket, bested
Democratic governor Adlai E. Stevenson of Illinois in the presidential race. Even four years earlier, when television ownership
had still been very limited, the size of the crowd in Times Square
had fallen from prewar levels; thus the 1952 postelection turnout
simply confirmed an already developing trend. To be sure,
twenty-five thousand was still a considerable figure, but that was
a peak estimate. During much of the evening the numbers were
smaller, and with each passing election further and further reductions in attendance at such gatherings would occur.

Times Square last night had the smallest Election Night turnout in its
long existence. It was the least demonstrative crowd, too—without voice,
without the traditional horns and bells, and utterly without enthusiasm.

Between 9 and 10 o'clock no more than 10,000 persons were in the
square, and these were packed thickest on the sidewalks from Forty-third
to Forty-fifth Streets, watching the new election bulletin board on the
north wall of Times Tower. At the peak, the police estimated, less than
25,000 were in the square.

Even when the theaters emptied, the crowds did not overflow the curbs to cover the pavement as in pre-television days. Though no solid line of police horses stood at the curb to restrain them, bulletin watchers held to the curbs with only gently urging from patrolmen.

Motor traffic moved freely all night without a break in all directions. In former years the pavements would be solidly packed with humanity, and motor traffic would have to be diverted. Up to eight years ago police never estimated presidential election night crowds at less than 250,000.

The election night crowd that assembled four years ago last night, when President Truman was running against Governor Dewey, had fallen far enough away from old figures to indicate that the tradition was dying. Last night's version confirmed the diagnosis.

Assistant Chief Inspector John King, who organized the police detail for the square this year, used the smallest number of men ever assigned for election night. He dispensed entirely with mounted men who in former years had lined the curbs. . . .

Nowhere in the square was there even a hint of the dense masses of a decade ago. The police pointed out that only television and radio could have caused such a drain. The night was starless, but a yellow moon hung over the city. The temperature stood at a pleasant 50 degrees.

Times Square shopkeepers had anticipated a sizable turnout. Boarding was up to protect plate glass fronts from Forty-third Street to Forty-seventh, but the storekeepers need not have put themselves to the trouble. Their windows were never threatened.

The pigeons around Father Duffy's statue were little disturbed in their nocturnal food-hunting and the ambulances, radio cars and Civil Defense equipment brought into the square remained stationary, with no call for their services. . . .

What little cheering there was in front of THE NEW YORK TIMES' new election bulletin seemed about even—brief shouting when a lead for General Eisenhower came up on the board, equally brief applause when Governor Stevenson's name was put up. It was damp stuff compared with the deafening roars of old Times Square crowds.

A last burst of shouting echoed in the square at 12:40 A.M. today when the line of lights on the east side of the new election board suddenly streaked to the top, to show that General Eisenhower had more than 266 electoral votes, and had won in a sweep. . . .

Then the searchlight high in the Tower, which had been brooming the starless sky to the north all night, to show Eisenhower in the lead, held steady to show that he had won. The crowd cheered again, and slowly came apart to drift toward the subways.

A tradition was dead, with only a few thousand pallbearers to see it peacefully interred.

(53) Beginning of Widespread Television Coverage—New York, 1952

Election night in 1952 was notable not only for the precipitous decline of community celebrations but for the first extensive television coverage of national voting returns. (The two phenomena were, of course, closely interconnected.) To be sure, television had existed before 1952, but only a relatively small number of Americans had owned TV sets prior to that time. In addition, the newly formed television networks and their local affiliates had not really given much attention to political contests in previous years. Although many people, especially in the western states, did not yet have television service in 1952 and still relied on radio for the latest results, it became clear that the new visual media had distinct advantages over the nonvisual. Most notably, as the author of the accompanying article emphasizes, it was hard to grasp all the numerical data being read over the airwaves without the visual component on the screen. Television coverage in 1952 was certainly not as thorough or the presentation as technologically sophisticated as they became in later decades. Readers will probably be amused by the fact that one network listed voting figures on a traditional blackboard. Also, the networks' first use of advanced computers—"super-duper electronic brains"—turned out to be "more of a nuisance than a help" during the evening's proceedings. Interestingly, the main focus of the article is on which network provided the best coverage and fastest results, subjects that would continue to be of interest to the public in the future.

Television's coverage of the election returns on Tuesday evening and Wednesday morning resulted in a landslide victory for the Columbia Broadcasting System. Both in the complex task of tabulation and the incidental commentary, the network left its rivals far behind.

Columbia's greatest advantage was the ease with which a viewer could follow the constantly changing figures. There were forty-eight individual panels, on which were recorded the tallies from the different states. Each panel was shown in close-up and the figures practically filled the screen.

Similarly, large panels were used for the total popular and electoral votes. The visual effect was excellent.

In contrast, the National Broadcasting Company employed a system of cash register machines in which the numbers were comparatively small. In addition, there were disconcerting movements of the registers between each state tally. The American Broadcasting used an old-fashioned blackboard, which was difficult for John Daly, the network's anchor man on the election, to read. For the viewer it was too much of a strain to make order of A.B.C.'s jumble of digits.

For a good part of the evening C.B.S. also outpaced its rivals in the speed with which they tabulated the returns. Some unsung heroes certainly did superb advance planning at Columbia.

Tuesday also saw the first use on Election Night of the supposedly super-duper electronic brains, which can think in terms of a couple of quintillion mathematical problems at one time. Both gadgets were more of a nuisance than a help.

The C.B.S. pride was called "Univac," which at the critical moment refused to work with anything like the efficiency of the human being. This mishap caused the C.B.S. stars, Walter Cronkite, Ed Murrow and Eric Sevareid, to give "Univac" a rough ride for the rest of the evening in a most amusing sidelight to the C.B.S. coverage. . . .

[Gould goes on to assert that the CBS team of Cronkite, Murrow, and Sevareid came through with their accustomed high-level performance, which was superior to that of the NBC crew, headed by John Cameron Swayze and Bill Henry, who seemed much less at ease. Radio, the author concluded, did a generally good job, but suffered in comparison with TV. Trying to absorb figures read over the air was far more difficult than having them presented in written form on the video screen.]

Source: Jack Gould, "C.B.S. Television Coverage of Election Returns Resulted in Landslide Victory for Network," *New York Times*, November 7, 1952, 31. Copyright © 1952 by the New York Times Co. Reprinted by permission.

---

(54) Voting Is a Lonely Business—New York, 1960

During former eras, as we have seen, Election Day was usually a time of communal activity, not simply the casting of ballots but a getting together of friends and neighbors. There was often a holiday atmosphere, filled with noise and good cheer. But in the modern period, especially during the Cold War, when the outcome of the vote determined whose hands would be "on the

button" that controlled nuclear weapons, Election Day for some
people became a much more somber, solitary time, involving
deep reflection about the choices to be made and anxiety over
the results. Admittedly, for many Americans a national election
still meant a day of fun and excitement, including all kinds of
celebration with others. However, an increasing number of individuals, like New Yorker staff writer Philip Hamburger, who
describes below his experience on November 8, 1960, found it
to be a very lonely day. As he states, it was not just lonely but
quiet, "one of the quietest of all days." Outside the voting booth
where he lined up early in the morning, not a word was spoken.
Everyone seemed solemn. The author then tells of walking about
most of the day, by himself, unable to work at the office, preoccupied—presumably regarding the fate of the nation. As he
walks the streets of downtown New York, he connects with sym-
bols of the American past, including Abraham Lincoln's speech
in that city one hundred years earlier, which became a turning
point in his rise to the presidency. Mr. Hamburger then goes
home to await the results, without mentioning any plans to join
anyone later in a public place.

ELECTION DAY, here in the city, is one of the quietest of all days. We
voted early. We were up and out of the house and headed for the polls
a few minutes before six. Our street was dark and silent, the air was
crisp and brilliant, and the day held promise. We don't have far to go
to reach the polls—a few steps south, past the barbershop, the hardware
shop, and the tailor shop, and a few steps east, downhill (with the river
at the foot of the hill). On our way south we saw the moon, and a faint
light in the rear of Mr. Strandbury's store (he delivers papers); his news-
stand was still bare. Turning east, we saw the river far below, and streaks
of blue and orange in the morning sky. We vote in a luggage shop barely
the size of a steamer trunk—a cramped, cluttered establishment, its floor
covered with suitcases, handbags, and piles of old belts, its walls inex-
plicably plastered, from floor to ceiling, with photographs of stars of
stage, screen, and television. At one minute to six, we were outside its
doors. Two people were ahead of us—a ruddy-faced man, gray at the
temples and wearing a trim brown topcoat, and a shambling, preoccupied man, coatless. "I vote at the crack of dawn because I like to vote at
the crack of dawn," volunteered the ruddy-faced man. "Besides, I work
in Brooklyn, and I've got a ride ahead of me." The coatless man had
something on his mind. "Somebody has to lose, " he said, half to himself.
We peered through the window of the store. It was ablaze with light.
Precinct workers bustled around a long table, clearing away paper cups
and cartons of coffee and opening long, narrow registration books. We

spied Jackie Gleason on the wall, smiling, and Bing Crosby beside him. Crosby looked serious. "We Can't Please Everybody But We Try," said a sign in the window. "Deposit Required on All Repair Work." A young policeman was hovering over the voting machine. He unlocked something on one side and tested the green curtain, and the door to the luggage shop was opened. It was precisely six o'clock.

Voting was swift and silent. The ruddy-faced man was a man of decision—in and out and off to Brooklyn. The coatless man took a moment longer, but merely a moment. Then he, too, was off, still preoccupied, still pondering. Our turn came next. For us, voting is a moment of controlled breathlessness. We promise ourself each time to be calm, collected, master of the machine and ourself, and yet when the curtain closes and we are alone, we pull down the levers with passionate haste. In a moment, we were again outside the booth, having voted. A line had formed behind us, bursting the confines of the luggage shop and spreading out to the street. Nobody said anything.

Day had reached the city with the swiftness of our vote. The sun was over the river's edge now, and the orange-and-blue streaks were becoming a deep and satisfying blue. We walked around for quite a while. It seems to us now that we must have walked around most of the day, as preoccupied as the man who had preceded us into the booth. Fruit stores were the first to open, displaying their seasonal riches—the purple grapes, the shiny red apples. The fruit stands seemed to hold promise. Next, the flower stores opened, and we saw row upon row of mellow, rust-colored pompons. The streets were still silent, and the traffic was light. People were coming out of the apartment houses now, silent and determined, aloof and subdued, acting very much alone even when they were walking with others. We looked in on many schoolhouses, with long lines edging toward the green curtains and the levers and the moment of doing what one thinks is right, and it seemed to us that this was also, perhaps, one of the most private of all days, each man an impressive island unto himself and yet each man a part of the whole. We went down to the office and tried working, but it was no go. The silence of the city, the thought of all those lines edging forward, was too much with us, and we started to wander again. A minor errand (made work, really) took us down to Astor Place, and we passed Cooper Union, shut tight, its Great Hall closed. We stopped to read a plaque commemorating the appearance there of Lincoln, not yet nominated, in 1860. He had come East in a new, ill-fitting broadcloth suit to plead, with eloquence and hard facts, the cause of the Union. Lincoln, we thought, would have been comforted by the long lines at the many polling places, and by the solemn faces of the people. One thought leads to another (work was now out of the question), and we strolled uptown, past lines in front of schools, churches, and shops, and into the American Wing of the Metropolitan. Our thoughts stretched ahead into the future, but we wanted to touch the past. We walked through the proud old rooms from Ipswich, and King George County, in Virginia, and Albany, and looked at the bright handmade silver, the Gilbert Stuarts, the mantelpieces, and the gleaming gold mirrors surmounted by eagles. Dusk was settling in when we left the Museum, and our path home took us again past those long, silent lines. When the polls closed, we settled down to await the returns.

Source: Philip Hamburger, "Lonely Day," *The New Yorker*, November 19, 1960, 45–46. Reprinted by permission of the author and *The New Yorker*; © 1960 The New Yorker Magazine, Inc. Originally published in *The New Yorker*. All rights reserved. "Lonely Day" was recently republished in Philip Hamburger's book *Matters of State*.

---

(55) Nixon Concedes to Kennedy after Long Night—Los Angeles, 1960

One of the closest presidential races in the twentieth century occurred in 1960 when Democratic senator John F. Kennedy challenged Republican vice president Richard M. Nixon. Kennedy and Nixon, destined to be two of the most talked-about political figures of their time, did not differ on the issues—both were seen as Cold Warriors—as much as they did in style. Nixon, who had risen to prominence from modest beginnings, often seemed nervous and insecure in public settings, whereas the wealthy, Harvard-educated Kennedy always appeared cool and confident. This contrast can be observed on both the day and night of the election. Kennedy, upon voting early with his wife in Boston, flew to the family compound in Hyannis Port and took a long nap, emerging publicly only after five P.M., apparently rested and relaxed. That evening, downstairs at campaign manager Robert Kennedy's house, which had been turned into a command center with banks of telephones, many people were scurrying about; Jack, though saying little, was described as "the calmest person in the room." Nixon, on the other hand, was very tense following his trip to the polls in southern California. Seeking to ease the tension and pass the time, Nixon along with a few associates traveled by car all the way to Tijuana, Mexico, before returning that evening to Los Angeles, when the results began to come in. Election night is often an "emotional roller coaster ride" for a candidate, as Nixon noted in his memoirs. But for him this was the most tantalizing and

frustrating election experience of his entire career. The overall
trend seemed to favor Kennedy at first, but by midnight Nixon
appeared to be making a comeback, only to fall short. The accompanying article describes the agonies Nixon faced that night
and early the next morning.

Vice President Richard M. Nixon today formally conceded the election
of Senator John F. Kennedy.

The dramatic concession announcement came at 9:47 A.M., a few
minutes after Kennedy had cinched election by winning Minnesota's 11
electoral votes.

Nixon sent this telegram to his Democratic rival:

"I want to repeat through this wire congratulations and best wishes I
extended to you on television last night. I know you will have the united
support of all Americans as you lead the nation in the cause of peace
and freedom in the next four years."

Nixon, the Republican nominee, had virtually conceded shortly after
midnight. He said then that if "the present trend continues, Senator Kennedy will be the next president of the United States."

The concession telegram, sent to Kennedy at his home in Hyannis Port,
Mass., was read to newsmen—and to a nationwide television audience—
by Herbert G. Klein, Nixon's press secretary.

Asked whether Nixon, who was up at 6:30 A.M. after only about five
hours' sleep, had an opportunity to analyze the election outcome, Klein
replied:

"I think the time to analyze on a more scientific basis is when you
have complete results from all the states."

Klein went on to say that the margin of popular votes was at the time
he spoke, less than 1 per cent.

Klein's conference was held shortly after Minnesota, after seesawing
all through the night and morning, gave Kennedy its electoral vote. That
was enough to put him over the top. His total was at that point was 272,
with 269 needed.

Illinois and California were still uncertain, but Kennedy did not need
them.

Source: "How Nixon Conceded Election," Associated Press, November 9, 1960.

---

(56) Hawaiians Engage in Their First Presidential Election— Honolulu, 1960

Election Day in 1960 was notable for a variety of reasons, one
of which was the initial participation of the new states of Alaska

and Hawaii in a national contest. The Hawaiian islands had gained statehood in August 1959, and in the following year, as the report below indicates, voters streamed to the polls in unprecedented numbers as they cast ballots for a president for the first time. On the island of Maui, bells rang in the churches of all denominations at 8:00 A.M. to mark the start of the occasion. There as well as elsewhere voting was especially heavy in the first couple of hours; in some places, half the expected vote was accounted for by noon. By the end of the day, 94 percent of the registered voters had participated, the highest figure in the entire nation. The state also had the closest race, with only a hundred votes or so separating the two candidates as the tabulations were made. On Wednesday morning it appeared Kennedy was ahead, but then Nixon took the lead and was subsequently declared the winner. Days later, after a partial recount, Kennedy finally triumphed, by a margin of 115 votes out of the 184,705 cast.

Hawaii's voters were streaming to the polls in apparently unprecedented numbers today to take advantage of their first chance to vote for a president.

Reports late in the morning indicate that 40 to 50 per cent of the voters had already cast their ballots.

Election officials on all Islands predicted record turnouts, that will easily top last year's record of 171,383.

Sunny skies and the presidential race brought citizens out in what election observers called a "steady flow."

Voting was orderly, with little "electioneering" spotted.

Although all precincts covered on Oahu were voting heavily, a significant trend was noted in the predominantly Republican 17th district where several precincts were turning out 30 per cent of the vote in the first two hours.

Democrats have claimed a majority of new registered voters as their own, but the Republicans apparently were going to the polls in huge numbers.

Voters, who are balloting for a president and congressman and 35 local offices, were a little confused about the presidential ballot.

Some wanted to split their vote between presidential and vice-presidential candidates. Others felt they had to mark an X after both the presidential and vice-presidential candidates.

Youngsters were peeking under the voting curtains and their parents clustered around the voting booths to discuss the presidential race.

One person lost his right to vote at Koko Head Elementary School because he became so excited talking to Governor William F. Quinn that he placed his ballot in the box without marking it.

County clerks on all Islands are predicting huge vote totals.

On Oahu, City Clerk Paul Chung forecast that more than 130,000 of 147,000 registered voters would go to the polls.

Some precincts said people who never voted before have been lured into the booths by the presidential battle between Senator John F. Kennedy and Vice-President Richard M. Nixon.

Absentee voting on the Big Island topped all records with 1,176 voting compared to last year's high of 1,005.

On Oahu, Waialae Shopping Center (17th District, 14th Precinct) reported 30 percent voting early. In Niu Valley Elementary School (17th District, 8th precinct), 40 per cent of the registered 1,602 voters had voted by 9:45 A.M. Some 150 votes rolled in within 60 minutes.

Democratic areas in the 12th District were turning out heavy voting.

At Harrington High School (12th, 1st precinct), 30 per cent of 916 registered voters had cast ballots by 9:30 A.M.

Almost 40 per cent of 1,420 registered voters had voted at Sacred Heart Convent (12th, 4th precinct) by 10 A.M.

In 11th District precincts, almost one-fourth of the voters had gone to the polls by 9 A.M.

The voting wasn't spectacular. There were very few huge lines.

But it was pouring in steadily and surely toward new records.

Church bells of all denominations rang at 8 A.M. on Maui heralding the first presidential election on the Valley Isle.

The three-hour pre-dawn rain yielded to sunshine when the polls opened at 7 A.M.

In central Maui districts, about 20 per cent of the registered voters had gone to the polls in the first hour.

On Kauai at Kapaa, 772 of 2,244 registered voters or more than one-third voted in the first two hours. Officials expected a 50 per cent turnout by noon.

The Big Island was expected to vote more than 24,000 of 26,000 registered voters.

On Windward Oahu, the turnout was almost 30 per cent by 10 A.M.

Source: "Record Island Vote," *Honolulu Star-Bulletin*, November 8, 1960, 1. Reprinted by permission of the *Honolulu Star-Bulletin*.

---

(57) Illinois Republicans Demand a Recount—Chicago, 1960

Hawaii was not the only state where Kennedy and Nixon were separated by relatively few votes. Several others would be de-

cided by small margins, and in the days after the election top
Republican officials would demand recounts and charge the
Democrats with fraud. Nowhere was this more evident than in
the state of Illinois, which Nixon lost by less than 5,500 votes
out of a total of 4.5 million. Although they did not specifically
name him, Republican leaders accused Chicago mayor and
Cook County political boss Richard Daley of engineering whole-
sale fraud in a number of precincts to give Kennedy and the
Democratic ticket enormous majorities. The margin in some of
the Chicago "river wards" was as much as three or four to one.
The document below discusses efforts by a committee of Republican volunteers in Illinois to raise funds to underwrite the
cost of a recount. Nevertheless, the movement for massive recounts did not get very far, partly because Nixon did not think
that it would be in the best interest of the country (or himself)
to proceed in that direction. For one thing, it was questionable
whether the accusations of fraud could ever be proven; also, the
vice president did not want to be seen as a sore loser. (It was
also noted later on by Democrats that Nixon had won a few
counties upstate by what seemed improbably large totals.) In
addition, even if the GOP's claims in Illinois had been upheld,
Kennedy still had enough votes in the Electoral College to confirm the original outcome.

A public appeal for funds to finance a recount of Tuesday's Presidential
balloting here was made yesterday following a final tabulation of votes
showing that Vice President Nixon lost Illinois by only 5,490 votes. William H. Fetridge, chairman of Midwest Volunteers for Nixon, directed
his appeal to the "people interested in fair play and honest elections,"
asking that they contribute $1 each to pay for the recount of Chicago
wards where fraud had been charged. Fetridge said supporters of the
Vice President had formed a Nixon Recount committee to handle the
fund raising and insure that a recount is held. . . . The Fetridge appeal
came within hours after Sen. Thruston Morton, national Republican
chairman, approved legal maneuvers looking to possible recounts in 11
states, including Illinois. The figures disclosed yesterday showed that
Nixon received 2,366,082 votes in Illinois while Sen. John F. Kennedy got
2,371,572—a difference of only 5,490 with 13 Cook county precincts still
unreported.

Fetridge said the money would be used to finance a recount and pay
for G.O.P. watchers at the official vote canvass. A recount costs $2 per
precinct where voting machines are used and $5 per precinct where pa-
per ballots are used. Fetridge's announcement came as Frank J. Durham,
. . . chairman of the Committee on Honest Elections, charged that the

Democratic machine had "stolen" the election from Nixon and State's Atty. Adam Adamowski. Durham said he had never seen fraudulent practices more "vicious" in his 25 years of poll watching. He charged that the 5,490 difference in votes between Nixon and Kennedy had been easily stolen in the so-called Chicago river wards. He pointed to the "fantastic" pluralities rolled up for the Democratic candidates—Kennedy and Daniel P. Ward, Adamowski's opponent—and further charged that his staff had found as many as 45 fraudulent registrations last Saturday in two apartment buildings in the 4th ward. . . .

Here is a tabulation of 10 wards in which Kennedy scored huge pluralities:

Ward	Kennedy	Nixon
1	16,984	4,182
2	21,072	5,447
3	19,978	4,998
4	25,770	7,120
5	18,835	7,795
6	24,600	7,646
11	20,105	6,052
17	22,100	6,591
20	21,307	6,565
24	24,206	2,130

Source: "Republicans Seek Recounts," Chicago Tribune, November 12, 1960, 1, 4.

(58) The First Presidential Vote in the District of Columbia—Washington, D.C., 1964

Just as Hawaiians cast their first presidential votes in 1960, so the inhabitants of the District of Columbia first cast theirs in 1964, thanks to the passage of the Twenty-third Amendment to the Constitution in the intervening years. District residents, who had previously been disenfranchised from presidential elections, had clearly looked forward to the event. Indeed, close to 200,000 persons would come to the polls that day, a total that would not be surpassed in the nation's capital for another two decades. For many lifelong residents of Washington, D.C., this was their first vote anywhere. Some older citizens, in fact, had been waiting for this moment for more than half a century. In the account below one can observe the sense of pride these people felt as they approached voting booths for the first time to cast ballots in the Lyndon Johnson–Barry Goldwater presidential contest. Interestingly, some longtime Republicans in the District supported the Democratic candidate, Johnson, on this occasion because of Goldwater's apparent "extremism." Johnson would receive more than 85 percent of the vote, and the District, with its heavily black population, would continue to be overwhelmingly Democratic thereafter. In subsequent years, Washington, D.C., which had been governed totally under the auspices of Congress, would begin to elect its own school board (1968), designate a nonvoting delegate to the House of Representatives (1970), and choose its own mayor and district council (1974).

Moody Garner's eyes twinkled behind his horn-rimmed glasses.

"I feel like a man," he glowed. "Like a citizen."

Garner is 72 and a Negro. He had just come out of a voting booth.

Washington had a choice instead of an echo yesterday. For Garner and thousands of others—rich, poor and in-between—it was the first time they ever had a say about who was to be President of the United States.

"I hope the Lord'll give me the right man," Garner said with a smile. "I hope the Democrats give me the right man." He voted for Lyndon Johnson.

Garner remembers his father voting when they lived on a North Carolina farm around the turn of the century.

"His last vote was around McKinley's time," he recalled. "They were disenfranchised when I grew up."

A retired municipal truck driver, Garner got his first job during World War I and had been disenfranchised ever since.

It was different yesterday.

Voters poured to the polls as soon as they opened at 8 A.M., dwindled away during the day and came back strong in the evening.

Elections Board officials said many precincts reported taking ballots from 75 per cent of the voters they had on the books by dinner time. Some experts predicted an 80 per cent or better turnout from the 219,687 that had registered.

Despite the shortest and simplest ballot in the Nation, the long morning lines touched off waits of one to three hours in many polling spots.

District Commissioner John B. Duncan took one look at Precinct 22 in the Rudolph School and left to meet a speaking engagement. He came back later when the line was shorter.

Washington-born District Commissioner Walter N. Tobriner showed up in his black limousine 15 minutes after the polls opened at the Lafayette School in Precinct 15. He was luckier.

"I've waited 41 years for this day," he said. "I've voted in primaries before," the 62-year-old Commissioner added, "but this is the first time in an election that really counts."

Source: George Lardner, Jr., "With Sense of Pride, D.C. Residents Troop to Polls," *Washington Post*, November 4, 1964, B1.

---

(59) What Goes on at the Polling Place—Evanston, Illinois, 1964

An earlier document presented what happened on Election Day from the point of view of an election judge in the nineteenth century. The following document provides an understanding of the duties performed by an election judge in more recent times, integrating the experience of Frank Hanfelder, an election official in Evanston, Illinois, in the mid-1960s with a description of the procedures followed when the polls were open and afterward as the results were recorded. The article mentions that a judge's responsibilities were broad and complicated, and that each was encouraged to attend a voluntary instructional session beforehand and take an examination regarding their duties. The article also describes the delivery of numerous supplies on election eve and how on the morning of the election the judges— in this case five in number—prepared for the day's events. The author notes the very precise rules that were to be adhered to— rules regarding the swearing-in of the judges, the unlocking of the machines, the arrangement of the room so that voting booths and ballot boxes were always in the judges' view. One comes to appreciate the hard and often tedious work that election officials undertake for little or no remuneration. Clearly, they are the unsung heroes of Election Day.

Frank H. Hanfelder of Evanston, Illinois, considers himself to be an ordinary suburbanite. Tall, graying, soft-spoken, the 63-year-old Hanfelder on most mornings gets up just in time to dress, eat breakfast, and negotiate rush-hour traffic to his job as purchasing agent for a Chicago area steel-casting company.

On November 3, election day, however, Hanfelder's schedule will be entirely different. With the permission of his company, he will not report for work at all. Instead, he will get up at 4:30 A.M., then walk to a polling place at nearby Frances Willard School. There, for the next 16 hours he will serve in a vast army of ordinary American citizens who will oversee the largest free election in the world.

Their jobs will be opening polling places, supervising voting, tabulating results precinct by precinct—a stupendous, sometimes controversial job costing millions of dollars (some $4 million in New York City alone). But despite this massive machinery and the precious privilege that it represents, large numbers of Americans will not take advantage of it. . . . Still, the marvelous machinery of free elections is there.

Take Frank Hanfelder's suburban polling place. People who vote there may assume that voter lists, ballots, voting machines, and final election tabulations somehow just appear magically. Hanfelder and thousands of other election workers . . . know better.

Actually, preparations for the election in that precinct began last winter, when the clerk of Cook County . . . selected polling places for every precinct in his jurisdiction and negotiated a rental for each. At the same time, members of civic groups, party organizations and others submitted nominations for precinct election judges. Five are required for each polling place, three from one party, two from the other, with the numerical advantage alternated among precincts. In addition, each party is permitted two poll-watchers in every precinct. For his day's work, the county pays Hanfelder $25—which he promptly donates to charity.

"I don't regard this as something you do for money," he says. "To me, it's something that you owe your country, your community, and your political party."

Hanfelder and other judges are invited to attend a voluntary evening instructional session and take an optional examination about election procedures. For this they are paid $5. Though Hanfelder has worked in primaries and general elections for five years, he attends the sessions and takes the tests.

"Election procedure is as simple as they can make it," he says, "but there always are details on which to bone up."

One this year concerns balloting for members of the Illinois House of Representatives. Due to a reapportionment of state legislative districts, all 177 members of the House must be elected at large. Because this ballot alone is some three feet long, it will be handled by a special procedure apart from regular balloting. Voters will mark their choices for House seats on a special large orange ballot, then place it in a special orange ballot box. After the polls close the boxes will be sealed and transported to designated tabulating centers. . . .

On election eve, or a day or two before, keys for voting machines, binders containing voters' registration cards, tally sheets, and other supplies are delivered to one of the precinct election judges—in Hanfelder's precinct usually to him. Receipt of all such material must be acknowledged by signing for it, and at the close of balloting, returned or accounted for otherwise.

Then Hanfelder's longest day begins. About five A.M., an hour before the polls are to open, he arrives at the school, which the building custodian already has opened. There he meets the other four precinct judges, some for the first time. One judge swears in the other four, then is sworn in by one of them, and an intricate routine begins.

Together the judges determine that all necessary supplies are on hand. This includes eight different forms for situations such as challenging voters, or taking a voter's oath that he is illiterate and therefore entitled to assistance in voting. Emergency delivery is arranged for anything that is missing.

They unlock the two voting machines used in their precinct, confirm that necessary seals on the machine are intact, record numbers on several counting mechanisms, plug in each machine, light it, hang curtains across the front, and set out a model of the machine's face which voters may examine before they enter.

They post a "Polling Place Here" card outside the front entrance, place an American flag there, post cards describing who can vote, how to use voting machines, and a specimen paper ballot. They arrange the room so that voting machines, voting booths, and ballot boxes always will be in view of all five election judges. They agree on a division of duties for the day and a schedule of rotating assignments. They put on identification badges, admit poll-watchers who have proper credentials, and then, after a final check to determine that all is in order, at six A.M., one of them opens the door and says, "The polls now are open."

During the day, as voters arrive from throughout the precinct, the legality of every vote is assured by adherence to a carefully prescribed routine. First, one judge issues an Application for Ballot, on which the voter must sign both his name and address. The judge then reads the name aloud and prints the voter's name and address elsewhere on the card.

Next, two judges, one representing each political party, compare the voter's signature with that on his registration card in the precinct binder. Then another judge, after determining that the Application for Ballot is approved, initials a ballot and hands it to the voter or, if a voting machine is to be used, admits him to a voting machine. The fifth judge, meanwhile, files the approved Application for Ballot in a binder with other applications, which he numbers consecutively.

The voter, before leaving, places every ballot issued in a designated ballot box or, if unused, returns it to an election judge—eliminating possible "chain-balloting," a procedure that still helps big-city political bosses maintain power. After obtaining a blank ballot, the boss or his hireling would mark it in a prearranged fashion, then pay an individual

about to vote to drop it in the ballot box, and bring back a blank ballot
with which to continue the "chain."

There are other technicalities. In Illinois, for example, the only legal
way to hand-mark a ballot is with a cross in the circle or square opposite
the candidate's name. Or, if the vote is a write-in, the name of the person
for whom the write-in is cast must be written on the ballot. Judges are
not allowed to count votes cast by a written "yes," a check mark, or a
cross whose lines do not intersect inside the voting circle.

Judges also must know the procedure for vote-challenging. That is, a
judge, poll-watcher, or other registered voter in the polling place may
challenge the voting right of any individual he believes to be improperly
registered or already to have voted. If a majority of judges are satisfied
as to the voter's eligibility, he may be allowed to vote promptly. If not,
before voting he must complete a "challenged voter's affidavit"—making
him liable to prosecution if he has acted falsely.

There are specific rules concerning spoiled ballots. If a voter errs while
marking his ballot, for instance, he may change it for another. But a judge
must immediately mark it "Spoiled" and place it with other items to be
turned in to election officials.

In addition, to preserve secrecy and freedom of action in the voting
booth, there are stringent restrictions on judges helping voters. It is legal
for a judge to explain specimen ballots posted on the wall or a model
voting machine, and two judges of opposite political parties may enter
a machine together to instruct a voter if they first part the curtains so
that all in the room may observe. A friend or a relative may assist a
paraplegic or a blind person. Physical help in marking anyone else's
ballot is strictly prohibited. However, this violation is one of the more
common irregularities in elections.

Access to the vote-registering and vote-counting mechanism of voting
machines also is severely controlled. Certain parts are sealed and can be
reached only by breaking the seal, for which one can be prosecuted on
a charge of tampering. Other portions can be unlocked only with a special key, and in some cases only once. The day's vote tabulation, for
instance, cannot be seen until a certain key is turned, and once turned,
the key is locked in that position until reset by higher-level officials.

There are both a "protective" counter which registers a cumulative
vote from election to election, and a "public" counter, which is set at
zero before each election. Nobody can cast a vote on the machine until
a lever is pulled closing the curtains, and an election judge pulls a control
latch at the side that allows the machine to be operated. As a further
check against tampering, judges examine the face of the voting machine
before and after each voter uses it.

All day the voters come—housewives, tradesmen, executives, young
people casting their first vote, the elderly—sometimes in a flood, at other

times a trickle. There are serious moments, silent moments, moments of friendly banter. At times there also are crises, as when a voting machine jams and emergency help must be summoned.

Finally about dinner time comes the last rush, a tide of homeward-bound office and shop-workers, deliverymen in uniform, and executives carrying attache cases. At 5:30 P.M., according to procedure, one judge makes his way through the crowd to the front door and announces, "The polls close in half an hour." At six P.M. he proclaims the polls closed. Everyone in line inside is allowed to vote. Then the door is locked and the last, most dramatic stage of the election begins: determining the outcome of the all-day vote.

Tired but exhilarated, the judges work rapidly now. One of them turns the key that exposes the election results on each voting machine. Then, monitored by a judge representing the opposition political party, he reads the vote registered for each candidate. Other judges record it on multiple copies of tally sheets and poll-watchers keep a record to turn in at party headquarters. In the same way, a paper roll for write-in votes is exposed and any write-in votes recorded. Then the roll is removed and folded into a labeled envelope to be transported to local election officials' offices along with other supplies.

Absentee ballots, which have been sealed in an envelope all day, then are counted, along with any other paper ballots not to have been handled previously. Ballots which are to be counted at special centers—those used in Illinois' at-large election for the House—are sealed in their boxes to await delivery. Paper ballots improperly marked are invalidated by the judges labeling them "Defective" or "Objected to," and signing their names along with the reason for invalidation. They, too, go into labeled envelopes or bundles to be turned in.

When all vote totals are recorded and cross-checked, the used paper ballots are securely bound in a heavy paper box on which the judges sign their names. It then is sealed by wrapping transparent adhesive tape length-wise and cross-wise around the box so that nothing can be removed without disturbing the signatures. Voting machines are closed and locked, and other supplies are assembled. Ballots, tally sheets, and all supplies not to be left for later pick-up are taken by one or more judges to a collection point in the community. Then they are turned in, and a receipt obtained—and the precinct election results are ready to be swept into a tidal wave of returns awaited by the public.

Source: Alfred Balk, "What Happens to Your Ballot on Election Day?" *Today's Health* (November 1964), 32–35, 86.

Disengagement and Declining Interest, 1968–2001

After the mid-1960s, the next few decades would witness a considerable decline in interest in Election Day. Although the size of the potential electorate would continue to expand, with the addition of young persons between ages eighteen and twenty-one and the elimination of legal obstacles that had barred certain minority groups, the proportion of those actually voting would gradually fall. Political parties grew weaker and proved less able to mobilize electors. Many Americans began to experience a distrust of government as a result of the Vietnam War and the Watergate scandal. Younger voters in particular were "turned off" by the political system, which they saw as indifferent to their needs; others too felt that it did not really matter who was in office. As the vote declined, reformers sought new ways to get people back into the elective process—through greater use of absentee ballots, the inauguration of early voting, and even mail-in ballots in a few states. In the late 1990s, studies would be made regarding the possibility of voting via the Internet. Yet, as some commentators pointed out, in the absence of a link between voting and any form of public celebration, it would remain a cold, lonely act, a fact that would hamper efforts to restore interest among large segments of the populace. While a bare majority of those eligible would continue to vote in presidential elections, they did not display the enthusiasm and excitement visible among participants of earlier periods.

(60) Hippies and Yippies Protest against Both Parties—
San Francisco, 1968

All the materials presented so far have dealt with people who were part of the electoral process and with people seeking to be part of the process. Even those in the past who broke the rules on Election Day and engaged in improper behavior were not usually taking stands against the entire system; they were only trying to bend the system and gain victory for their sides. However, in the late 1960s, some Americans, especially among the younger generation, began to oppose traditional authority and reject many of the prevailing values of society; soon they were condemning the whole existing political apparatus. As the government continued to support heavy U.S. involvement in the Vietnam War and offered no quick solutions to societal injustices at home, certain "antiestablishment" groups would use Election Day in 1968 not to vote for an alternative ticket but to demonstrate against the major parties and their policies. The parties were seen as tools of corporate America and electoral participation was sharply ridiculed. Although such activities were not common nationwide, vigorous protests organized by "hippies," "yippies," and other leftists did occur outside both Democratic and Republican headquarters in a few large cities, such as San Francisco, as the following newspaper report indicates. Whether these outbursts had any impact is hard to tell, though over the next few decades more and more individuals, and not just those on the extreme Left, would become disenchanted with the political process and decline to vote.

Yippies, hippies and old-fashioned anti-war demonstrators by the hundreds paraded through downtown San Francisco yesterday in what amounted to an all-day election protest.

By the end of the day, a smaller band of 100 protesters returned to Civic Center, where it all began, for an election-night vigil in front of City Hall. The vigil was more orderly than sorties earlier in the protest but some 30 police officers were on hand in case of new trouble.

Before long, however, protesters at the vigil gave up and went home. The weather was just too cold to stay up all night, one said.

In the course of the day, by 8 P.M., about two dozen demonstrators were arrested on charges ranging from disturbing the peace to lighting bonfires and inciting to riot.

On the way back from a late afternoon invasion of the financial district by some 400 to 500 demonstrators, bands of protesters stopped at Humphrey and Nixon headquarters on Market street, and yelled anti-war slogans and obscenities at staffers.

"We're here because the election is shucked," said one 15-year-old parader. "We're doing our voting by being here on the streets."

During the financial district invasion, a score of the protesters were arrested as 200 police struggled to keep traffic from being brought to a standstill. Charges here were mostly for obstructing traffic.

The demonstration centered around Montgomery and Sutter streets. The demonstrators sat on the sidewalks, built bonfires, scattered stage money around and filled the air with Indian war whoops.

An American flag was burned at the Civic Center, as a rock band blared over amplifiers. One bearded man added a dollar bill to the fire and four others tossed on their draft cards.

The rally and Montgomery street demonstration were staged by Students for a Democratic Society, whose officials brought two pigs to Civic Center as "our candidates for president and vice president."

Plainclothes police and FBI agents hovered around the fringes, apprehensive that the demonstrators might try to interfere with voting. The announcement of the rally had called for creating disturbances at the polls.

Two humane officers also were on the scene to see that the pigs were not mistreated.

In urging the hippies at the rally to troop down to Montgomery street, an unidentified speaker told them over the amplifying system, "We're going to play Monopoly."

"Our lives are completely channeled," he said. "We are choked by the plastic money factories."

"We're not gonna change that by voting; we're gonna have to do it ourselves. We're playing Monopoly today. They do it every day."

Four women—ranging in age from 18 to 30—were among the 21 demonstrators arrested during the day of protest.

For a time, members of the police tactical squad kept the general public from entering City Hall last night. The common practice of awaiting election results there was restored as soon as the protesters left the area.

Source: "Yippies Invade Downtown," *San Francisco Chronicle*, November 6, 1968, 3.

(61) Blacks Begin to Win Office in the South—Pritchard, Alabama, 1972

Before the Voting Rights Act (1965) and other civil rights laws in the mid-1960s were passed by Congress, few African Americans cast ballots in the Deep South, and Election Day had little importance in the black community. Even after that legislation passed, change was not immediate. Generations of oppression and intimidation had left a legacy of voter apathy. Many blacks continued to believe that politics was the business of "white folks" and that participation in the electoral process would not make any difference in their lives. Yet in less than a decade blacks in some locales did become more active on Election Day. Black candidates began to run for office in an effective manner, and black organizations worked harder to register people and to get out the vote. By the 1970s, blacks were starting to win local elections in places where whites had always been politically dominant. One such community was the small city of Pritchard, Alabama, not far from Mobile. In the 1972 mayoral contest, a twenty-eight-year-old black lawyer, Algernon Johnson (Jay) Cooper, with the help of several outside consultants and many resident volunteers, defeated a three-term white incumbent, first in the general election and then in the runoff. Cooper's volunteers, though given only brief training, learned how to canvass neighborhoods, operate phone banks, serve as poll watchers, and provide voters with transportation to the polls. As later reported by campaign manager John Dean, on the day of the general election "no operational units failed to perform their duties." The selection below describes the actions taken by the phone-bank, transportation, and poll-watcher units, whose efforts greatly contributed to the day's success.

Election Day Activities

A final strategy meeting was held with the campaign coordinators the night before election to outline with charts all of the things their units had done in preparing for their responsibilities on election day. Any remaining tasks which had to be accomplished before or during election day were also charted. The deputy campaign manager was given overall supervision of election day activities.

Phone Bank/Transportation

This unit's day began with 6:00 A.M. calls to all poll watchers, drivers, canvassers, and day care supervisors to remind them of their final briefings at headquarters that morning. The bank spent the remainder of the day calling voters urging them to get to the polls, calling the previously assembled list of those needing a ride to the polls and accepting calls from others who needed rides.

Because of the functions, transportation operations were transferred to the phone bank for election day. When drivers reported in that morning for their final instructions, a car control log was established so the campaign would know where each car was at all times. Drivers were sent to the church centers from their area. The church centers were also checked by the coordinator periodically during the day to insure they were functioning properly. The 20 drivers that did show up on election day gave the campaign a ratio of one car per 2,000 residents which was about half of the normally ideal ratio of one car per 1,000 residents, but certainly far short of the 100 cars projected for the election.

As voting patterns became more established, and based on intelligence called in from the polling places, the bank was directed to blanket those neighborhoods where there was low voter turnout with calls.

Poll Watchers

The watcher's kits were handed out by the deputy manager at their morning briefing. Each kit contained a manual, a voting machine diagram, the voting machine identification data sheet for that ward, the election official's list for that ward and the watcher's authorization certificate. The watchers were also given a one-page summary of the key points in their manuals and the tally sheet with instructions for taking the final count from each machine.

One chief poll watcher was designated for each ward and he was given that ward's voting list. A roster of the 75 watchers who reported was drawn up to show their poll assignments with whatever minimal shift changes that could be made. The chief watchers were instructed to locate primary and back-up phones at or near their polls for reporting to headquarters. The campaign coordinators, one of whom was a lawyer, were assigned to tour specific polling places all day as flying trouble shooters to back up the watchers.

This was the first time the city of Pritchard had seen any candidate field the total number of poll watchers he was authorized by law to have—one poll watcher per voting machine. Their very presence and superior knowledge of election procedures intimidated most of the election officials for most of the day. As the time wore on, however, some officials became obstructive. In some places, poll watchers were not allowed to stand close enough to sign-in tables to verify from their voter list those who were voting. Instances of graveyard voting, voting by persons who were no longer residents of the city and the voting by unauthorized persons under a real voter name were reported. There were also problems with the illegal instruction of voters by some election officials inside the voting booth and some newly registered voters whose names were not on the voting lists had their voter registration certificates taken when they voted.

All campaign coordinators whose units were not specifically involved in election day activities and local staff were re-assigned to the above units and were required to report at designated intervals to headquarters. With the exception of the lawyers at the phones and the campaign manager in the command center, no other personnel were allowed in the headquarters office. During the day, no operational units failed to perform their duties. Election day was a quiet day at headquarters and there was time to plan the press conference to follow the official tallying of the vote and the receptions for the public and the staff.

Source: John Dean, *The Making of a Black Mayor* (Washington, D.C.: Joint Center for Political Studies, 1973), 22–25.

---

(62) Youths Vote for First Time in Presidential Election— New Haven, Connecticut, 1972

An important constitutional change further expanded the number of potential Election Day participants in the early 1970s; it lowered the minimum age for voting to eighteen. After many years of deliberation, Congress passed a statute granting eighteen-year-olds the right to vote in national, state, and local elections. When the Supreme Court ruled that a federal law could affect voting only in national elections, the Twenty-sixth Amendment was enacted, extending the right to state and local elections as well. Young people, especially young men, had often taken part in previous elections as paraders and poll watchers, but now they could be actual voters. It had long been argued that anyone old enough to go to war or to graduate from high school ought to be able to participate in the electoral process. Yet traditionalists had always rejected this view; only a few states, beginning with Georgia during World War II, had accepted the argument. But as other formerly disfranchised groups obtained voting rights advocates for the youth vote on a national basis finally won their case. However, as the accompanying article points out, enthusiasm among young people toward their first presidential contest in 1972 was not very high, even among Ivy League college students (perhaps partly due to the one-sidedness of the Nixon-McGovern race that year). Nationwide, the turnout of young voters on that occasion would, in fact, be lower than that for all other age cohorts up to age sixty-five. Even during more competitive elections over the next few decades, the vote of young people would remain low. Indeed, the turnout of people under twenty-four in 1996 was only 32 percent. In addition, the youth vote would not be as liberal as expected. Although left-of-center candidate McGovern had hoped to win two-thirds of the under-twenty-four vote, he wound up with barely half, even in many college towns, a trend that plagued other Democrats through the 1980s. The report below focuses on Yale University and New Haven, Connecticut, where McGovern gained a majority, but only a small one.

"There is no sense of this being a historical occasion," said 18-year-old Fred Krupp, a Yale freshman. "Everybody just takes it for granted."

As on campuses elsewhere around the country today, there were no bullhorns, no placards, no rallies at Yale University. There was also no discernible student exuberance to mark the enfranchisement of those under 21, who were being allowed to vote in a Presidential election for the first time.

Nevertheless students here, like those on other campuses, were apparently exercising their new power. A number of polls conducted at Yale in recent weeks showed that 75 to 85 per cent of the nearly 5,000 undergraduates had registered to vote.

Of these, the overwhelming majority had registered in their home towns and were voting by absentee ballot. Some 450 registered in New Haven. The polls conducted by student activists were confirmed by . . . conversations with students here in the last two days.

Despite the student registration, which seemed to be 20 percentage points above the national average, the most significant thing about political attitudes at Yale, according to most students here, was the low-key campaign.

The McGovern support on campus contributed somewhat to the Senator's victory in New Haven. Mr. McGovern managed to eke out a 5,000-vote margin, although he ran well behind local Democratic candidates. Four years ago, Hubert Humphrey, without the benefit of a youth vote, took the city by 14,000 votes.

In the early evening, small groups of students gathered around television sets in the dorms. Some studied as commentators told of a Nixon sweep. There were no tears and none seemed shocked by the results.

When Illinois was declared a Nixon gain, one denim-clad youth announced quietly, "Well, I guess it's going to be humiliating."

Another student in the room remarked: "I've been down all month, I can't get more depressed."

[The article concludes by noting that the students could have done more for the McGovern ticket but had somehow lost some of their crusading spirit during the course of the campaign.]

Source: Michael T. Kaufman, "First-Time Yale Voters Show Little Exuberance," New York Times, November 8, 1972, 33.

---

(63) Westerners Protest against Network Projections—San Francisco, 1980

As television coverage further dominated Election Day proceedings and modern polling techniques more accurately predicted the outcomes of political races, turnout at the voting booths continued to diminish. In this connection, one issue that increasingly bothered prospective voters was that the major networks' competitive desire to forecast the outcome of presidential races as early as possible threatened to make many votes, especially those in the West, meaningless. This issue became particularly controversial starting with the election of 1980, when the Republican presidential candidate, Ronald Reagan, was projected by mid-afternoon to be the winner over incumbent Democrat Jimmy Carter; at that point many people on the West Coast had not yet cast their votes. The network projections caused a great deal of anger; thousands called TV station switchboards in protest. Most of the callers felt that such projections interfered with the democratic process. "We're supposed to decide, not the media," one woman complained. Indeed, there was a tremendous fall-off in the western vote by late afternoon, as many who might have gone to the polls decided it was not worth the effort. In the aftermath of the election, various solutions were suggested— restricting network projections, establishing a set of uniform voting hours across the country—but the problem would continue over the next two decades. It remains unresolved. The accompanying article describes the frustration of voters in the San Francisco Bay area on Election Day in 1980.

All over the Bay Area last night, people fumed because radio and television crowned Ronald Reagan long before polls closed in the West.

Angry listeners swamped local media switch boards with phone calls, spitting out their rage at the Reagan victory predictions that began by mid-afternoon.

And the politicians, including San Francisco Mayor Dianne Feinstein sharply criticized the electronic news media for becoming kingmakers rather than reporters.

Lucille Hughes, a nursing registry coordinator, echoed many people's resentment as she waited on a downtown San Francisco street for her bus to San Bruno.

"We're supposed to decide, not the media," she said, as she headed home to vote anyway.

In a San Francisco laundromat, Andrea Patterson folded her clothes in neat stacks and said she decided not to vote when she heard Ronald Reagan was winning in the South.

In a bar at Masonic Avenue and Geary Boulevard, fireman Ron Parker said he decided against voting for President Carter when television anointed Reagan the victor. He voted instead for [independent candidate] John Anderson.

Dozens of people interviewed on the streets, who voted for various candidates, agreed that they thought the media were playing the improper role of kingmaker by heralding results so early.

Some people said they knew what television was saying, but they would still vote anyway because they cared about other issues. But the media blitz was simply too much for others.

"I just decided it was pointless to go down and vote. I would have voted for Carter against Reagan. When you hear half the country has already voted against him, it seems hopeless," Patterson said as she and her 12-year-old son, Jay, piled up rows of socks, blouses and jeans under the harsh white light of a Castro Street laundromat.

Source: Susan Sward, "Voters Irked by Media's Projections," *San Francisco Chronicle*, November 5, 1980, 9.

---

(64) Woman Candidate Seeks Votes on Election Day— Maine, 1984

One of the greatest changes in politics in recent decades has been the increasing number of women involved. Although the Nineteenth Amendment was ratified in 1920, women were slow to use the vote, and slower still to be active on other political levels. To be sure, some individuals became associated with the League of Women Voters or joined lobbying groups for various causes. Others served as clerical workers or precinct walkers during campaigns. They also volunteered as poll watchers and drivers on Election Day. But few stood as candidates or sought other high-profile positions in either major party. However, by the early 1970s that had begun to change. As the modern feminist movement developed, many more women made their presence felt on Election Day, voting in proportionately larger numbers, operating in high-level party posts, and even running for office. ("Women's place is in the House—or the Senate," became a popular slogan.) One of those female office seekers was Barbara Trafton of Maine, a Democratic National Committeewoman and for several terms a member of the state legislature. In the selection below, taken from her book *Women Winning*, we can see how her thoroughness as a candidate paid off and how she used Election Day as the most crucial time for acquiring additional votes. As Trafton notes, not every office seeker has had the same philosophy—many have preferred to relax and let the chips fall where they may—but quite a few of the most successful ones have used Election Day to further their candidacies.

When election eve arrives, some candidates and many members of the public seem to think that the election is over. If you haven't convinced the voters of the merits of your candidacy by now, what more can you possibly do?

In fact, election eve and day should be the busiest times of the whole campaign. Opinion polls may have you winning or losing, but the outcome will be determined not by what people think but by what they do at the ballot box if they get there. It is critical that you make every effort to get your supporters to the polls. Elections can be won and lost by a mere handful of votes.

One reason for my success is my conviction that the "next" vote is the winning one. Although my elections have never been that close, I work as if they are until the polls close. My typical routine on election day began with a distribution of leaflets at each factory gate in the city; I work several of the larger gates personally and assign supporters to the rest. When that job is finished, at 7:00 A.M., I swing through the district making sure my signs are still standing at locations close to the polls. If time permits I then leaflet some of the larger trailer parks in the rural areas. At eight the polls open. I vote early and encourage all my supporters to do the same. It is not uncommon for an involved campaign worker to forget to vote herself!

Before election day I've identified some supporters in need of transportation. I drive several groups to the polls in the morning. I really enjoy this personal contact with my supporters. Often I help an elderly voter into the polling place. This gives me a chance to say hello to the election workers in each ward. Throughout the day I am on call to collect absentee ballots, transport people to the polls, and register voters. From 3:30 P.M. on I greet voters at the polling place in Ward 5, as the enrollment is heavily weighted to my party. In the late afternoon I gather a seasoned canvassing team to go door to door in this ward, encouraging voters to go to the polls. As soon as the polls close at 8:00 P.M., my supporters and I collect all my campaign signs.

Source: Barbara Trafton, *Women Winning* (Boston, Mass.: Harvard Common Press, 1984), 136–38.

---

(65) Voting in Rural America—Highland County, Virginia, 1985

The vast majority of voting today takes place in urban or suburban settings, with balloting done on voting machines and fairly large numbers of individuals—several hundred or more—coming to each polling site over the course of the day. However, a small amount of voting still occurs in sparsely populated rural areas with tiny precincts, where some of the modern rules for casting ballots—rules usually made for big, urban precincts—do not "sit too well." The following essay on Election Day during the mid-1980s at the Headwaters Precinct in Highland County, Virginia—which listed only sixty-eight persons on the registration book (the whole county contained a total population of less than six hundred)—tells a different kind of story than most of the other narratives included in this collection. Not only were there far fewer people registered in this locale, the turnout on this occasion would be quite small due to the heavy rain and flooding. Indeed, the polling place had to be moved from its normal spot at an individual residence to the local church, which was on drier ground. Even then just a handful of eligible voters showed up to cast ballots—paper ballots inserted into a ballot box—for this statewide election. This lower than usual turnout happened despite the fact that a black man was running for a high office in the state for the first time (Douglas Wilder seeking the lieutenant governorship), and a woman was listed on the ticket for the post of attorney general. As the author points out, bad weather, not politics, was the main topic of conversation for people of the region that day.

The Monday before Election Day was abnormally quiet here in Highland County. Usually, opening day of the Virginia Turkey season is a ruckus of shots and halloos, but today the great black-and-tan birds roosted in the dripping hemlocks or squabbled through the autumn olive unmolested. You couldn't get to them. It had been raining all weekend, and the Simmonses' rain gauge, which Nelson Simmons emptied Sunday night at bedtime, overflowed Monday. It's a good deep rain gauge, too: twelve inches. The turkey hunters stayed in camp or prowled the roads, restless and discouraged. By noon they couldn't cross any watercourse in the county except where the state bridges cross. The Cowpasture River divides our farm. Monday morning you could hear it roar half a mile away.

It's not really something you expect. Probably a half-dozen times a year the TV broadcasts flood warnings. The worst it gets is deep puddles in Laurel Gap where the road dips beside the river, so maybe you postpone your trip to town until the next day. Most of the people who died in this flood died of disbelief. They really couldn't believe it was happening.

I was worried about the election. It's twelve miles from our farm to the Varners' house in Headwaters, where the precinct votes. I'm Headwaters' precinct captain. In a precinct that votes sixty-eight souls, being captain isn't a real *big* job; but it does mean you have to drive up to Monterey, the county seat, the Saturday before Election Day so Maxine Huffman, the registrar, can give all the captains cardboard boxes containing ballots, poll books, summaries of results, forms for "Disputed Voters," forms for "Absentees Who Wish to Vote in Person," the *Handbook for Election Officials*, two pencils, two blue ball-points, and one red one.

Usually, the night before the election, I make up a lunch and fill a thermos of coffee. Country manners say we shouldn't count on a supper invitation from Orpha Mae Varner, but come 6:00 P.M. the three election officials are invariably seated at table with the Varner family, enjoying country-fried steak with gravy and Orpha Mae's homemade rolls. If a voter comes in during supper, we excuse ourselves from the table and go into the living room to vote him.

I generally figure on rising at five, election morning, and get to Headwaters by half-past, plenty of time to set up the ballot box and do the necessary swearing in. But this year it looked like Election Day morning would be poor traveling. Maybe I'd have to take the Power Wagon. Our 1951 Dodge Power Wagon has four-wheel drive and is high enough off the road that the running boards tap a tall man's knees. Its top speed is about 45 mph, and it gets 8 miles a gallon at any speed. Nothing much stops it, but it rides more like a buck board than a limousine. Tomorrow, in that old monster, grinding along wet roads in poor visibility, I'd want to leave half an hour early.

The rain was steady but not hard as my stockdog Pip and I went down to the river field where our ewes were grazing. The perimeter ditches were over my rubber boots and running fast. The river was out of its banks; it had climbed to within a foot of our line fence, running brown, loud, and ugly. Sheep hate to cross running water, and I thought I'd get them to higher ground before things got worse. Under the low, drizzly sky, the rye fields were as green as an Irish whiskey ad. I felt silly, overprudent, as Pip and I chivvied the bouncing sheep through the running ditches and out of the field. After the flood waters dropped I found dead fish in those fields, and all my fences were gone.

Our up-the-road neighbors were in town, across the mountain in Harrisonburg, and they'd arranged for their children to be dropped off with us after school. At 3:15 the school bus driver's wife called to say he couldn't get through. Since our neighbors' kids were the last on the bus, he'd keep them at his house until the water went down.

The Varners' farm, where Headwaters Precinct usually votes, is an especially well kept sheep-and-cattle operation of 114 acres. Their house is a neat two-story frame with modest gingerbread at the eaves. Elmo Varner subscribes to all the farming journals, and when I'm being precinct captain, I usually browse through them in the long waits between voters.

Virginia's election laws are designed for great urban precincts, with voting machines and thousands of voters. They can be bruisingly awkward in Highland County, where the biggest precinct votes less than six hundred souls. Recently the man from the state election commissioner's office inspected Elmo's house and said Elmo'd need to install a wheelchair ramp for the use of handicapped voters. Since Headwaters Precinct doesn't have any handicapped voters, that didn't sit too well. And even if we did, why, we'd be more than willing to go out and vote them in their cars. The state man said Elmo's half-closet polling booth was acceptable, but we'd have to shift his couch and armchair to make room for a long table where the three election officials could sit elbow-to-elbow. That didn't sit too well, either.

Elections are serious here, and voter turnout is high. At the last presidential election we'd voted every single registered voter by early afternoon, except for two farmers who'd taken a load of calves to market, and young Corrine Stewart. The farmers would stop by and vote on their way home. Corrinne had moved out to Colorado with her boyfriend and hadn't (somebody noted) written home in six months, but we had enjoyed speculating about what we'd do if Corrinne did drop out of the sky to cast her ballot. With all the registered voters voted, could we count up and go home?

Four o'clock Monday, the river trickled into our lower fields. I decided to inspect our absent neighbors' farm, just two miles east of us upriver.

The Power Wagon was built for rough conditions, and I confess to a modest thrill firing up my machine. The sky had lowered, got sullen, and I put my headlights on.

The river was within three feet of the struts of the iron bridge and across the road in Laurel Gap. Landscape features were altered, and I couldn't know whether what I was rolling across was road or jumble-tumble river bottom. I slipped the Power Wagon into low-range four-wheel drive, and we grumped along slower than a man walks. The water climbed over the running board and lapped around my feet. I heard it hiss as it spattered the engine block. The murky half-river-half-road continued on ahead as far as I could see. I put my macho machine in reverse and puttered back out of that water somewhat quicker than I'd come into it.

That night, before we lost our long-distance lines, I talked to my fellow precinct worker June Clevinger, who told me the Varners were at the Clevingers' tonight because the Varner house was under four feet of water. "Elmo just keeps getting up and looking out. He can see his rooftop from my kitchen window." June said the election would be in the church if the water didn't get it, too.

Before the power went out, about seven o'clock, the river was across the road in Williamsville, downstream from us. In Slim's Store, they moved most of the goods to upper shelves. Old Mrs. Marshall had to leave her house to stay with her daughter-in-law.

Election morning, the water at last receded, and by noon, I reached Headwaters, where we had to set up the polls.

Elmo Varner had plenty of neighbors at his house. The wall-to-wall carpet was lying in cut-up pieces on the front lawn. The TV was on the living-room couch which Orpha Mae had reupholstered herself. Elmo's big John Deere tractor was powering an electric generator for the industrial vacuum cleaners and hoses being used to clear water, mud, and trash out of the devastated house.

Elmo looked as genial as a man can who hasn't slept in the last thirty hours. He said he knew he was lucky, but wished the water hadn't got into the TV.

Miller's store was closed. Without power for his coolers or gas pumps, Ronnie Miller was out of business. The water had barely lapped over the floorboards of his store, though, so he was lucky, too.

I set up the Restricted Area signs outside the Presbyterian Church just as it says to do in the manual for election officers. June Clevinger was trying to get a fire going. The Church has twin Warm Morning heating stoves connected by a single over-head U pipe. Normally, Orpha Mae fired these stoves an hour before services. Services are held here on alternate Sundays. According to the hymn board, attendance last week was three.

Carl Clevinger, June's husband, arranged the choir loft as a voting booth. We put our wooden pencils on one pew, figuring voters could write on the back of the pew in front of them.

For forty-seven of his seventy-three years Carl Clevinger was a miner in Buchanan County. He retired to his Highland hunt camp eleven years ago with his wife, June. Carl has the black lung and takes spells. June Clevinger wears glasses with Coke-bottle lenses. When they go out coon hunting at night, June does all the driving. She drives slow.

We had a couple voters waiting on us while I swore in June Clevinger and we both signed the poll book in the spaces provided. We held up the ballot box to show it was empty before we padlocked it. The voters waited while we counted the ballots to make sure there weren't more or less than sixty-eight, which, fortunately, there weren't. There's a form you have to fill out when you're given too many ballots.

We checked voters off in the poll book, and after each voted, we took the ballot and dropped it into the green steel ballot box. Thus we ascertained that nobody had smuggled in a hundred dummy ballots with which to stuff our ballot box.

Usually Maxine Huffman gets down early with the absentee ballots, but she didn't come today. She might not have known we were open. Mrs. Simmons, the third precinct worker, called Ronnie Miller at one o'clock to say she'd be in as soon as state bulldozers cleared the landslide that had cut their house off. She arrived not much later.

Except for the moment each of us voted, I don't really think any of us gave a thought to the election. All our talk was flood. Douglas Wilder, the first black man to run for lieutenant governor in Virginia since Reconstruction, was on the ballot, as was Mary Sue Terry, the first woman candidate for attorney general, but our conversation was of US 250— how it had been washed out in Ramsey's Draft and how much worse flooding must be in Roanoke, downstream. We wondered when we'd get our power back.

Our neighbors came running in at three o'clock, and I told them where to find their children. They'd drowned their new diesel pickup yesterday trying to get through, and had spent a bad night worrying. They did vote.

"How many does that make?" Mrs. Simmons asked.

June Clevinger counted the red checks in the poll books. "That's nine," she said.

As the afternoon wore on, the church warmed, and all the flies came out to bat at the windows. Motorists stopped at Ronnie Miller's for gas, but he explained he had no way of pumping it. They asked how bad was it ahead. People were looking after their kin and their worldly goods. Nobody was traveling for pleasure.

The voters trickled in. Neither of the Varners came in, though they are usually faithful. The tractor chugged, and the cleaners worked on their house. June offered me a cheese sandwich and a cup of coffee. She had, she said, made extra.

We heard about Ivan Stone, whose neighbors had at first refused evacuation from their new home. There is a man, two women, and a child on that rooftop when they changed their minds and begged Ivan to please see if he could get through to take them off. Ivan tried to reach them on his tractor, but he was swept away. The family on the rooftop was lost soon afterward.

Last night about ten o'clock, Mrs. Dickenson called Bill Obaugh, the undertaker, and said her husband is dead, couldn't Bill come and get him? Bill got the volunteer fire department, and half a dozen men forded waters and scrambled along brushy hillsides to reach Mrs. Dickenson's house. At the approach of the drenched but mannerly undertaker and his team, Jack Dickenson sat up in bed and used vile language on them.

"They say he drinks a lot," Mrs. Simmons said.

Somebody spoke of a minister's wife and baby granddaughter who'd tried to get down through Franklin. They found the car but hadn't found them yet.

There wasn't much traffic on US 250, but not many voters, either.

At dusk Carl Clevinger carried in a couple of kerosene lamps. They hadn't been used recently, and one was too smoky. So we had just the one lamp, which threw enough light to let us mark the poll book. If any more voters came tonight, we'd have to abandon our station so they could see to mark their ballots.

At 7:01 by the fastest watch among us we closed the polls, and all officials signed the poll books. By yellow lantern light we opened and counted the ballots. On November 5, 1985, Virginia elected Jerry Baliles, Governor; Douglas Wilder, Lieutenant Governor; and Mary Sue Terry, Attorney General. I am pleased to note that Headwaters Precinct concurred with wisdom of the greater electorate by a margin of nine to five.

Source: Donald McCaig, "Democracy," *Country Journal* (November 1986), 14–19.

(66) Americans Choose Candidates in Harry's New York Bar—Paris, France, 1988

What has Election Day been like for the many Americans who happen to be abroad on that occasion? It would appear that those living or visiting in most Western European countries voted earlier than those back home (through special absentee ballots) and went about their business as usual during the day and evening. Then, after midnight or 1:00 A.M., depending on the time difference from the United States, many of them would gather at a prominent hotel ballroom (the Savoy in London) or nightspot (such as the legendary Harry's New York Bar in Paris) to celebrate and await the results, which they would announce or place on blackboards at certain intervals. In all the major European capitals, hundreds of VIPs would be invited to the American embassy to hear the returns while consuming American-style food and drink. Meanwhile, those who did not wish to attend any of the public festivities could celebrate at home and listen to news of the election on the various national radio networks or, in a country like Great Britain, watch the outcome on special late-night telecasts. The following report tells of the George H.W. Bush–Michael Dukakis presidential election in 1988, as seen from the vantage point of Harry's Bar in Paris.

PARIS—George Bush picked up an early victory yesterday in the 15th presidential straw poll at Harry's New York Bar, birthplace of the Bloody Mary and 1920s hangout of Ernest Hemingway and F. Scott Fitzgerald.

Bush racked up a 579–471 victory over Gov. Michael S. Dukakis in a poll of 1,050 American patrons who filled out printed ballots at Harry's.

Duncan Mac Elhone, an American who manages the family owned business, said the early results are nearly as reliable as the New Hampshire primary in predicting presidential winners.

"We've only been wrong once, when Carter won against [Gerald] Ford," Mac Elhone said. "We had Ford winning by 2 votes."

Harry's patrons accurately predicted Calvin Coolidge's victory in the bar's first straw poll, which was held in 1924 before absentee ballots were available, Mac Elhone said.

"Americans felt detached from home in those days, when mail arrived twice a week by steamer. So the vote was a real gel in the American community here," said Mac Elhone, who learned the history of the bar from his father and grandfather.

The polls have been held once every four years since, except for two election years during World War II.

Harry's takes credit for inventing the Bloody Mary and serving the first hot dog in France in 1925.

Founded in 1911, the bar became a favorite hangout for American volunteers during World War I and picked up legendary patrons such as writers Hemingway and Fitzgerald during the Roaring '20s.

In London, Ron Pollard, a spokesman for Ladbrokes, the country's largest bookmaking chain, said Tuesday the final odds on Bush winning were 1 to 8 "on," meaning that on an $8 bet the gambler would make $1 given a Bush victory.

The final odds on Dukakis were 4 to 1, giving the gambler a $4 return on a $1 bet for the Democrat.

Source: "Abroad, a Prescient Bistro Goes for Bush," *Boston Globe*, November 9, 1988.

---

(67) Controversy over "Street Money"—Atlanta, Georgia, 1994

One of the biggest controversies regarding Election Day practices in recent times has revolved around the allocation of "street money." Street money, or "walking-around money," as it is also called, is money distributed by the political parties to get out the vote in the inner city. It is nowadays especially aimed at black and other minority voters who have traditionally gone to the polls in lesser numbers than other groups. It has become controversial because the money is disbursed in cash and is therefore not easily accountable. Street money actually has a long history in urban America. As noted in document 33, above, a party functionary a century ago remarked that black men in her district had to be paid in some form in order to vote, and she provided them with food, cigars, and other small rewards. Today, the principle is basically the same—offering incentives to get individuals to the polls. However, the amount of money involved has skyrocketed. Instead of a handful of dollars, many thousands are earmarked for each locale, and there have been rumors of large payoffs, not to voters but to consultants and campaign organizers. Defenders of the practice claim that the amounts are not really that large compared to other election costs, such as advertising. They also argue that campaign workers who struggle hard to get out the vote deserve to be paid for their services, and that this is where the bulk of such money is spent. Critics, on the other hand, see this process as a blatant example of modern-day political corruption. A discussion of the street-money issue in Atlanta, Georgia, during the 1994 state-wide campaign follows.

The Democrats last month paid $30,000 to a firm with no offices that lists a mail drop on Monroe Drive as its place of business.

The company, Concerned Community Development Corp., is owned by a black political consultant, Munson Steed, who is helping to carry on a tradition in American politics—last-ditch efforts to get out the vote.

Critics refer to the money paid to boost black turnout as "street money" or "walking around money" because it often is distributed in small cash payments that are nearly impossible to track.

State party chairman Ed Sims said Democrats don't do that. "There's no street money that the Democratic party is paying out in 1994," Sims said.

But the only specific example he could give of Steed's work is the printing of T-shirts. Steed did not return repeated telephone calls for this article.

Paying for turning out voters is a sensitive subject for both parties. Georgia's Republicans have drawn most of the attention this year because of their agreement to pay the company of Democratic state Rep. Tyrone Brooks of Atlanta $52,000 to drum up support for Republican gubernatorial nominee Guy Millner.

Those types of payments have drawn increased interest since last year's governor's election in New Jersey, when Republicans were alleged to have paid black leaders to discourage black turnout.

But it is the Democrats who are the primary practitioners of spreading money to maximize black turnout because black voters have long been a crucial constituency for Democrats. That is no less true this year for the party and Gov. Zell Miller.

Rep. Calvin Smyre (D-Columbus), chairman of the Democrats' state-wide coordinated campaign, refused to say how much the party would spend this year. But Brooks, although he is working with the Republicans, put the figure at upward of $300,000. . . .

"Street money" is a bad term," Brooks said. "It's campaign funds to mobilize your troops and give you exposure just like it is when they write checks to buy ads in your newspaper and put commercials on television."

He also described how the money is typically spent: "When we hire people, we usually have to pay them by cash. Most of these people don't write checks. But we will send the party a bill to say, 'this is how we disbursed your funds.'"

Source: Mark Sherman, "Street Money: Both Parties Spread It among Black Voters," *Atlanta Journal-Constitution*, November 5, 1994. Reprinted with permission from The Atlanta Journal and The Atlanta Constitution.

---

(68) The Movement toward Early Voting—Texas et al., 1994

Perhaps the biggest change in regard to casting ballots in recent times has been the movement toward early voting—that is, voting prior to Election Day, either through the increased use of absentee ballots or actually going to a polling place in the days or weeks before the traditional vote is cast. A century ago, it was almost impossible to vote anywhere except at the polls on the one designated day. Absentee balloting, introduced in some states early in the twentieth century, especially around the time of World War I, remained a limited phenomenon for many decades. It was meant mainly for military personnel, business travelers, and those confined to the home by illness or old age. However, in the late 1970s, spurred by the movement to democratize the system and to make voting more accessible to an increasingly mobile population, two major states, California and Virginia, created systems whereby individuals of any kind could apply for an absentee ballot and vote in the twenty-nine days before the election. Only Fairfax County in Virginia set up satellite absentee voting sites in government buildings where residents could actually cast an absentee ballot starting two and a half weeks before Election Day. But by the end of the next decade, Texas had introduced early on-site voting in many counties in the twenty days preceding the official Election Day. In 1992, one-third of the fifteen most populous counties in that state saw 40 percent of registered voters casting ballots early. By 1994 nine states had established provisions for voting before the regular election day. A 1994 article describing the new phenomenon follows.

There was a time when elections were one day sales. Campaign sweat, tears, money and motion were directed toward a single day when all culminated in either victory or defeat.

But in many states and counties across the nation, election day has become days, now that new laws allow voters to start marking ballots as early as six weeks before the "real" election day. These new rules will change not only the timing of campaigning but will also increase the importance of targeting turnout efforts aimed at early voters so the votes of reliable supporters are "put in the bank" before the last-minute mudslinging begins.

Interestingly, many state and local law changes have gone virtually unnoticed by not only the public and press but by campaign pros. Recent revisions of the Hatch Act and passage of national motor-voter legislation will alter voting and political participation in subtle yet vital ways. Too little attention has been directed to understanding the federal mandates and the regulation of the time, manner and place of elections. Also getting short shrift are the practical implications of statutory changes involving all-mail elections, election-day voter registration, voting by facsimile and early voting.

Nine states now have provisions for voting before the official election day, in addition to traditional absentee balloting. Three of them have new rules that are being implemented for the first time during this election cycle.

Early voting and other revisions which radically expand the methods of early voting could lead to increased voter fraud. Recently in Philadelphia, Democrat William Stinson was stripped of his state senate seat after a federal judge ruled that his campaign obtained hundreds of illegal absentee ballots. This seemingly minor incident had a tremendous impact because the reversal gave Republicans control of the Pennsylvania state senate. However, stuffing the ballot box is not an uncommon phenomenon.

Voting procedure liberalization should be scrutinized to ensure each "reform" is not vulnerable to fraud—a decades-old affliction. North Dakota does not even require citizens to register for federal elections. Minnesota, Wisconsin and Wyoming now permit election day registration at the polls. But of all the state election "reforms" taking place, early voting will have the greatest effect on campaigns.

Early voting is basically unrestricted absentee voting. It originated in Texas in 1991 and several states have followed the Texas model. Voters may now take advantage of some form of early voting within the following nine states: Texas, California, Virginia, Iowa, Colorado, Arizona, Nevada, New Mexico and Tennessee. Early voting proposals were rejected by Kansas in 1991 and Georgia in 1994. Ballots resulting from early voting are neither individually identifiable nor individually challenged.

Early voting takes place in general polling places or in satellite locations with provisions for extended weekend and weekday hours. To be productive it must be widely publicized.

However, not all states conform to standard, strict definitions. Virginia's process restricts voters to specific classes and restricts satellite sites to government buildings. Colorado counties have neither provided early voting satellite sites nor extended hours for voting. Iowa requires that an application be attached to each ballot. Although both Nevada and Arizona allow for early voting without variations, these states have not fully implemented the procedures. This lack of implementation is due to the absence of a state mandate for county compliance.

Source: Edwina Rogers, "Election Daze: Is Early Voting Coming to a State Near You?" *Campaigns & Elections* (September 1994), 36–37. Reprinted by permission of *Campaigns & Elections*.

(69) Balloting by Mail—Portland, Oregon, 1996

While Election Day has always been synonymous with voters going out to the polling place to cast ballots, a look at a special Oregon senatorial contest in early 1996 to fill the seat vacated by Republican Bob Packwood gives us a glimpse at how elections in many locales may be conducted in the near future. The voting was done entirely by mail-in ballots. Voting by mail can be seen as an extension of the concept of absentee balloting, which has come into widespread use in recent years. In fact, nearly 20 percent of the vote in certain states such as California was cast in this fashion by the 1990s. As a result, the idea of having everyone vote by mail began to be seriously debated, both as a way to increase participation and also to reduce costs. Although voting by mail was opposed by leading members of both parties—Republicans fearing increased fraud, Democrats fearing underusage by their constituents—the government of Oregon, hoping to save money and simplify the voting process, decided to experiment on a state-wide basis. In the senate race, prospective voters were given three weeks to send in their ballots. Many people voted in the first few days; others, like the author of the following article, procrastinated until the end. As it turned out, more voters participated than usual (57 percent of those eligible and 65 percent of those registered), and only a few complaints were heard about fraudulent or lost ballots. The state ended up saving a million dollars. And oh yes—the underdog Democratic candidate won. The author recounts his own experience with the new system.

For me, the big difference between a vote-by-mail election and a regular one is that, once arrived, the ballot in a vote-by-mail election feels more like homework than a civic responsibility, more like a bill to pay. Granted, it's easier than taking out the garbage: you fill in the little oval next to the name of the candidate of your choice using a No.2 pencil, the pencil preferred by the state; seal the ballot in the "secrecy envelope"; sign another envelope, put a stamp on it, drop it in the mail and wait to find out who gets to fill Bob Packwood's Senate seat. So simple is it that about half the people who voted in Oregon's vote-by-mail elections mailed in their ballots within the first few days, only very rarely forgetting to sign it. But in my own electoral universe, the three-week voting window closed with supernatural speed; I hung onto the ballot half for political purposes—suppose a revealing fact about the candidate comes up after I drop my ballot in the mail box?—and half for purposes of procrastination. In previous vote-by-mail elections (this was the first statewide one), I have waited until the last half hour, when I end up rushing down to drop my ballot at the county elections office. By the time I get home—I tend to stop at the store on the way back—the election has been called on the news.

For elections officials, vote-by-mail is like a giant absentee ballot vote, an electoral pleasure. "I love it! I love it!" says Vicki Ervin, the director of Multnomah County elections. Never mind that Bill Lunch, a political science professor at Oregon State University, and an opponent of vote-by-mail, argues that the thirty-two-cent stamp amounts to a poll tax and may be unconstitutional. It was in part because of vote-by-mail's similarity to absentee balloting that the national Democratic Party so vehemently opposed it when it was first considered last summer. The White House even put pressure on Governor John Kitzhaber, a Democrat, to veto the bill that would have made vote-by-mail law. (Kitzhaber deemed it an experiment.) During the last congressional elections here, absentee votes were Republicans' strong card and quietly pushed congressional Republican candidates over the edge in close races. The DNC's [Democratic National Committee's] concerns also stemmed from self-doubt: despite the fact that vote-by-mail has increased turnouts in local Oregon elections by as much as 20 percent and that larger turnouts tend to help Democrats, Democrats consider themselves less likely than Republicans to send in the ballots.

Some of the more fretful opponents of vote-by-mail raised the specter of fraud and illegal influence. A Ron Wyden campaign member I spoke with in the weeks before the primary campaign was sounding paranoid about what might take place in rural—and conservative—churches. Republicans, meanwhile, were gloating about laser-printed letter capabilities, about expensive, out-of-state phone banks.

So it was that at the end of November, when the first ballots were scheduled to arrive in Portland at the Multnomah County elections office, there were scores of observers from the campaigns of Congressmen Wyden and Peter DeFazio, waiting to identify fraud as soon as it turned up in the hands of the mostly elderly women who are the lifeblood of the American political system. The ballots came in; they were accounted for; the signatures were verified with the help of a computer system that called up a scanned signature for every voter in the county. No whistles were blown. Within an hour, most of the observers had gone out for coffee. "They found out how boring it is," Ervin said.

Throughout the primary's three-week balloting period, I realized the same thing. A few days into it, I met a woman who happened to be a graphologist and was observing the election on behalf of the Wyden campaign, and she said she noticed a few signatures that indicated possible stress on the part of women who, she theorized, might have been influenced by their husbands, or vice versa. All told, however, the problem ballots numbered only about 300. The most significant development was the creation of our nation's first vote-by-mail non-postal drop off booths. The one constructed by Multnomah County was a ten-foot-tall red, white and blue box that looked like a phone booth and had just enough room for two election officials and a space heater. "We're very proud of this," Ervin said.

On the last night of the primary, late in the afternoon, as she emerged from the sealed-off vote-counting room, Donna Knutson, the county official in charge of vote tallies, seemed embarrassed to admit that the major problem for the counting machines was food stuck to the ballots—many voters had apparently filled theirs out at the kitchen table. Finally, at a few minutes after 8:00, more than 90 percent of the votes were counted, and the results were announced. Secretary of State Phil Keisling, a Democrat and the number-one fan of vote-by-mail, announced that, in addition to a high turnout (at 57 percent, the highest nonpresidential primary turnout ever in the state), participation by registered Democrats seemed to have increased by a percentage point or two.

The general election—a contest between Wyden and State Senator and frozen-vegetable magnate Gordon Smith—was one long and grueling telemarketing campaign. The initial negative ads quickly dashed hopes that vote-by-mail would somehow make campaigning cleaner in tone. Then, it seemed as if everyone in Portland got a call from somebody. In both the primary and the general election, the campaigns first made voter ID calls, to determine who their likely supporters were, then followed up with copious mailings. After a few days, the campaigns began to purchase the county's computerized records of exactly who had voted. This turned out to be a formatting nightmare, with counties using everything from SyQuest disks to old keypunch cards while the campaigns split fairly evenly along party lines between more modern Macs and IBMs.

In the final days, the race appeared to be too close to call—local news editors agreed not to publish results of the voting thus far—and the money was leaning toward Smith, whose mailings and TV ads had been exemplary in their Bob Robertsian slickness. Some people I know were called more than once, others were called after they had already voted. People were beginning to feel accosted; at least one woman left a message on her answering machine announcing that she had already voted. In the end, it was as if Ron Wyden was MCI Friends and Family Calling, Gordon Smith was AT&T.

On election day, if it can still be called that, Wyden supporters lined busy intersections in Portland, but the events were mainly exercises in anti-climax. At a little after 8:00, when Wyden appeared to have edged ahead, the 1 percent margin that would stand over the next few days had already been calculated. Yet the TV reporters continued to chant the phrases "We're still waiting for the rural vote to come in" and "It's going to be a long night" as if reading from the old script. In fact, the rural county figures were likely to have been tallied first, the majority of their votes having come in days before. It was a short night. Wyden had won, and the predominant thinking was that the Republican strategy had backfired, that the negative ads had induced all those people with loaded ballots at hand to vote. In the two key counties in the metropolitan area, Wyden was able to edge by in part with an environmental vote, after reminding voters that Smith's frozen-vegetable factory has a tendency to leak frozen-vegetable tailings.

When my political party called me, I considered their offer to drop by and pick up my vote at the last minute; it was so cold out that our car door was frozen shut. My friend Jim thought I was crazy. "I wouldn't trust my ballot to anyone," he said. And my wife wondered if the party workers could figure out where we live since delivery people never can. So I drove down to the elections office again, which was fun. The last night of a vote-by-mail election is a new civic phenomenon entirely. People hand off ballots from their car windows to shivering election workers, like voting football stars. It's tax night without the taxes. By the time I got home, I had a quart of milk, some D batteries, tortilla chips and a brand-new senator. Now Senator Mark Hatfield has announced his resignation, and, like all of Oregon, I am bracing for another wave of phone calls.

Source: Robert Sullivan, "Mail Order," *The New Republic* (February 26, 1996), 14, 16. Reprinted by permission of THE NEW REPUBLIC, © 1996, The New Republic, Inc.

(70) Voting on the Internet—Arizona, 2000

As the country moved toward the twenty-first century and more and more people were using the Internet to conduct business and handle other matters in their daily lives, it naturally occurred to political leaders to consider its possible use for future voting. Especially as there has been a search for ways of increasing turnout, the idea of Internet voting seemed a logical solution. It would remove the inconvenience of going to the polls and waiting in line. One could cast a ballot without leaving home, simply by turning on a machine and clicking a mouse. Public officials realized that if voting online was successful it would also save millions of dollars and speed up calculation of the returns.

As a result of rising interest in the possibility of Internet voting, California secretary of state Bill Jones commissioned a panel of experts to study the subject. At the end of 1999, a report was released with a series of recommendations. The task force concluded that while it was not "practically or fiscally feasible to develop a comprehensive remote Internet voting system" in the immediate future, online voting on a limited basis could be implemented soon, while technical concerns regarding the security and secrecy of Internet ballots was being worked out.

Meanwhile, throwing caution to the wind, the Arizona Democratic party went ahead and introduced the concept of Internet voting in the state's presidential primary in March 2000. As the authors of the article presented below point out, opinion was sharply divided about whether the experiment was a success. While the state party chairman was highly enthusiastic about the increase in participation, one critic saw the Internet as a deterrent to future voting and creating a greater divide between the haves and have nots in society.

Click on Arizona for conflicting views about the Internet's political future.

Last month, 39,942 Arizona Democrats went online to cast their votes in the state's primary. It was the largest demonstration yet of how the Internet might be used in public elections. But the results remain a Rorschach test, open to radically different interpretations.

For Arizona Democratic Party officials, the vote sparked celebration. The number of voters hit a record since the party began conducting primaries in 1984. The state's party chairman, Mark Fleisher, boasted that Internet voting was "the first thing to come along to motivate people to vote since the repeal of the poll tax."

But for some analysts such as Curtis Gans of the Center for the Study of the American Electorate, the Arizona results are less impressive than meets the eye and a potential warning sign.

"There are a whole slew of reasons why Internet voting is a bad idea," Gans said, citing concerns that the Internet ultimately may deter voter participation and the fear that "this promotes the digital divide that is already exacerbating class politics in our democracy."

Without question, election officials nationwide are trying to unscramble Internet implications. California Secretary of State Bill Jones recently accepted a comprehensive report from his own Internet voting task force. The National Science Foundation is preparing its own assessment of Internet voting at President Clinton's request.

Several private elections already have been conducted or planned for using the Internet, from a Boeing union election in mid-March to an upcoming Sierra Club election.

"We think there are going to be a lot of opportunities in the future, whether they're school board races or mayoral races," said Andy Berenblum, vice president of the New York-based Election.com. "This really exceeded our expectations."

Election.com ran the Internet portion of the Arizona election, and its officers are eager to portray the vote as a success. Registered voters could vote via mail or the Internet for a four-day period prior to March 10. The e-voters were assigned a personal identification number as protection against fraud.

One of several businesses attempting to carve out a niche in the Internet election field is Election.com. Its officers invested staff time and advertising dollars to stimulate as large an Arizona turnout as possible.

By the company's accounting, they succeeded: a total of 86,907 Democrats voted this year, compared with 12,844 in the 1996 primary and 36,072 in the 1992 primary. Nearly half of this year's voters cast their ballots via the Internet.

But remember this: 1996 was an uncontested primary, and thus boring to most voters, while this year Democrat Bill Bradley was still in the race until March 9. Though he wasn't part of the Democratic primary, Arizona's own John McCain also attracted more attention to the overall presidential race.

Even with the six-fold voting increase, only about 10% of registered Arizona Democrats voted this year, and less than 5% of the registered Democrats voted via the Internet.

"This doesn't compare to a normal election in that state," Gans said. "That's no test."

Still, the novelty of the Arizona election, the inherent buzz surrounding any dot-com suffixed political activity and the interests of the Internet-election firms themselves combine to build up significance of the Arizona experience.

"This will be a very profitable area for commercial firms," predicted R. Michael Alvarez, associate professor of political science at the California Institute of Technology. "And these firms have clear incentives to prod reluctant governmental agencies to move quickly on Internet voting. . . . [It's] clear to me that Internet voting will probably happen faster than anyone predicted, and will happen faster than is good for our political system."

Alvarez served on the California Internet Voting Task Force, whose report . . . urged gradual adoption of full Internet voting so technical and political concerns could be addressed. California officials are evaluating a system designed by an Election.com competitor, called VoteHere.net, for the state's own potential Internet voting.

"Internet voting must be put to the test, and Arizona takes us one step closer in that direction," said Christy Adkinson, marketing director for VoteHere.net. "But before victory is declared in Arizona, and we assume that public officials and the public at large embrace Internet voting, important questions must be answered."

The abiding technical questions include ballot security and the ability to remain up and running. Berenblum said his company's encrypted system survived the Arizona election and, except for some Macintosh computers, he said users confronted no system problems.

But Alfie Charles, who was chairman of the California Internet Voting Task Force, noted that a power outage temporarily shut down the Arizona voting. Potential voters had difficulty getting professional help. And California officials, he cautioned, are uncomfortable with Arizona allowing votes from possibly virus-prone home computers.

"We can't approve a system in California until one is developed that's more secure than the one they used in Arizona," Charles said.

The technical issues, moreover, may be a snap compared to the broader social and political ramifications.

Gans, for one, fears Internet voting is another step toward a "plebiscitary democracy" marked by instant-gratification referenda.

Worse, he said the idea distracts from more important factors determining participation.

"The Internet idea suggests that problems with turnout are mechanical rather than motivational," Gans said. "We need to work on things like civic education, values, the nature of political campaigns and the way the news media covers them."

Source: Michael Doyle and Tom Hamburger, "Polls Haven't Closed on Internet Voting," *Fresno Bee*, April 3, 2000, 1. Reprinted by permission of the *Fresno Bee*.

---

(71) The Presidential Election of 2000—Austin, Nashville, and Florida

---

The presidential election of 2000 between Texas governor George W. Bush and Vice President Al Gore was one of the closest in United States history and perhaps the most controversial. The result was not finalized until after five weeks of legal haggling, public protests, on-and-off recount efforts in the state of Florida, and questionable but decisive rulings by the U. S. Supreme Court. For only the fourth time in election history the nominee with the higher popular vote wound up losing in the Electoral College. It was an election in which a third-party candidate—Ralph Nader of the Green party—proved to be a spoiler. Although Nader attracted less than 3 percent of the overall vote, his totals would tip the scales in a few states and enable Bush to achieve victory.

Election night itself was filled with many twists and turns and moments of high drama. There were also several unprecedented actions. After campaigning through the early morning hours of Election Day, the vice president continued to reach out to prospective voters. As noted in the article below, Democratic candidate Gore, his wife Tipper, and running mate Joseph Lieberman would be on the telephone in the early evening calling radio stations in the western states, where the polls remained open, trying to encourage people to vote. Gore seemed to be ahead at that point, especially when the TV networks projected that he would win in Florida and obtain that state's crucial twenty-five electoral votes. But an hour or two later the networks reversed themselves and declared that the state remained too close to call. The race went on neck and neck through much of the night, with a few states still undecided. Finally, at about 2:15 A.M. Eastern Time, the networks declared Bush the winner in Florida, apparently making him the overall victor. Gore soon called Bush on the telephone conceding the election and began riding to downtown Nashville to deliver his concession speech. However, before he arrived there Democratic operatives in Florida called to tell him that the race in Florida was not really decided. Gore subsequently called Bush to withdraw his concession, which marked the beginning of his five-week, ultimately unsuccessful challenge.

The first article, which went to press before all the late-night details were available, offers a glimpse of how the candidates and their supporters reacted to the situation in the early evening. The second continues the story in the early morning hours after the retraction, foreshadowing the long struggle ahead.

George W. Bush and Al Gore battled to a near draw Tuesday night as each struggled to assemble an electoral college majority in a breathtaking finish to a presidential race that hinged on a relative handful of votes.

As of late Tuesday, the fight for the 270 electoral votes needed to claim the White House was too close to call. A few states—most notably Florida—seemed destined to decide the contest. Similarly close was the nationwide popular vote....

With the race so achingly tight, Gore continued campaigning relentlessly Tuesday night, even after polls closed in the East and Midwest. Manning the phones from his hotel suite in Nashville, he joined his wife Tipper, and running mate Sen. Joseph Lieberman of Connecticut, in calling radio stations in several states where ballots were still being cast.

Early in the evening, when several television networks called the vote in Florida, Michigan and Illinois for the vice president, "cheers went up around the room" in the Gores' suite, press secretary Douglas Hattaway said. The group took a brief dinner break, he said, then got back on the phones.

But later, Florida came to symbolize the night's cliffhanging quality when the media outlets moved the state back into the too-close-to-call column.

In Bush's hometown of Austin, the chilly and wet election night had the suspense of a movie thriller. Several hundred people gathered outside the State Capitol, their mood falling and rising with projections— and corrections of those projections—by the TV networks.

Bush himself had an abrupt change of plans dictated by the changing forecasts. Originally, he intended to gather with family, friends and other invited guests to watch the returns at the Four Seasons hotel. Instead, Bush and family members, including his parents, retired to the Governor's Mansion to watch the returns in private.

"I'm going to wait until they count all the votes," he told reporters allowed in for a visit. "I think Americans ought to wait until they count all the votes."

Source: Mark Z. Barabak, "Bush, Gore Neck and Neck," Los Angeles Times, November 8, 2000, 1.[lb]

The extraordinary battle for the White House continued today, with a full recount coming in Florida to determine whether Texas Gov. George W. Bush or Vice President Gore becomes the next president.

Gore had called Bush early today to concede the election. But in a move surely unprecedented in U. S. history, he later called back to retract it, as returns showed Florida agonizingly close.

If Bush wins Florida and therefore the election, as his campaign predicts, it will mark the first time since 1888 that a candidate won the popular vote but not the all-important Electoral College vote. Gore was ahead in the nationwide popular tally by well over 200,000 votes this morning, a lead that no recount appears capable of overturning.

Lawyers and advisers for the two nominees raced to Florida this morning to investigate two potentially crucial situations. In one, Democrats claim that more than 3,000 Gore votes in Palm Beach County may have been mistakenly recorded as votes for third-party candidate Patrick Buchanan because of oversized ballots whose lines were skewed.

In the other, an unknown number of absentee ballots have yet to be tallied. Some state officials said a recount could be completed by late Thursday, but absentee ballots have 10 days to arrive. . . .

As of mid-morning, the Florida tally showed Bush leading by fewer than 2,000 votes. That includes all votes cast yesterday at polling stations, all domestic absentee ballots and all foreign absentee ballots received by 7 P.M. yesterday.

Bush campaign chairman Don Evans said he believes the governor has won the election, but Gore's chairman William Daly, said it's too close to call. . . . Florida law requires an automatic recount if the margin of difference is less than one-half of one percent, as this one clearly is.

Source: Charles Babington and Dan Balz, "Presidential Cliffhanger Awaits Florida Recount," *Washington Post*, November 8, 2000, 1.

---

(72) The Future of Voting—Riverside County, California, 2001

As mentioned earlier, the presidential election of 2000 demonstrated some of the shortcomings of the existing balloting system. Especially in some of the larger counties in Florida, where punch cards were used, the flaws were abundantly evident. The punchcard tool did not always push the perforated bit of paper, known as a chad, clearly out, particularly when the ballot was not well aligned, leaving "hanging" chads, "swinging" chads, or, if minimally touched, "dimpled" chads. In such cases the vote was not necessarily recorded. In addition, many counting machines threw out ballots containing a single irregularity, such as the voter mistakenly pressing out two spots for the same office.

New and improved technology is available. Nine percent of the nation's electors already use state-of-the-art touch-screen voting. These machines, which work like automated teller machines at a bank, prevent double voting and allow voters to change their minds about selections before the end of the process. But, as the accompanying article points out, certain problems exist regarding their adoption. The biggest is the expense; each new machine costs several thousand dollars, which is difficult for local jurisdictions to afford. There are also issues of security and the willingness of the public to accept new technology. But many public officials want to avoid the problems of election 2000 regardless of the cost, which means that it is quite likely that changes will occur in the not-too-distant future.

For anyone troubled by voting in Florida last fall, the future seems to have arrived here in this rocky, arid and chad-free stretch of development and desert about an hour's drive east of Los Angeles.

"It was very good and very simple," Cane Munsee, 67, a retired engineer, crowed as he stepped into the sunshine from his polling place in Moreno Valley on Tuesday. "You can't make a mistake. This is the only way to go. You can't say that I got cheated on my vote."

Mr. Munsee is now among the voting elite—about 9 percent of the nation's electorate—who have cast their ballots on an electronic touch screen, which works like an automatic teller machine at a bank.

As the nation searches for ways to avoid the debacle that crippled Florida last year—and as the elections equipment industry gears up to take advantage of a potential multibillion dollar market—elections officials are examining with ever more scrutiny the touch-screen option, now under the microscope here in this sprawling middle-class laboratory.

Riverside County, with 635,000 registered voters, is the largest county in the nation to have converted entirely to touch-screen voting. It spent nearly $14 million on 4,250 machines for its 714 precincts last fall, just in time for the presidential election, and deployed some of them again last week in a special election for a seat in the California Assembly.

The Assembly district covered part of Riverside and part of an adjacent county, San Bernardino, which still uses punch cards. . . . The difference? The results in Riverside came in like greased lightning.

Riverside had counted and reported all results in the 111 precincts that are part of the district by 9:17 P.M., just an hour and 17 minutes after the polls closed. At that point, San Bernardino had no returns to report. At

9:30, an elections worker in San Bernardino said forlornly into the phone, "I understand the ones from Big Bear are on their way."

The results from San Bernardino were not fully tallied until 12:27 Wednesday morning. While a slightly higher percentage of voters in San Bernardino went to the polls for this low-profile eight-way assembly race (19.2 percent, compared with 17.8 percent of the voters in Riverside), Riverside had to handle thousands more voters (21,408 compared with 13,622 in San Bernardino).

Mischelle Townshend, Riverside County's registrar of voters, proudly called the touch-screen system the "racehorse" of the field. "The equipment has served us well," she said, beaming after the votes were tallied, her expansive offices a cool sea of high-tech efficiency and tranquility on what for most election officials is a night of frenzy.

But while election-night efficiency is a worthy goal, it is not the only one or even the most important one to state and local officials, who are charged with calibrating the mechanics of democracy.

"Elections are not about speed and cost," said Lloyd Levine, a consultant for the California Assembly's committee on elections, which has been monitoring voting changes across the state. "Having your vote count, accuracy, secrecy, fairness and access to ballots—those are much more important." . . .

Needless to say, the manufacturers of Riverside's system, Sequoia Voting Systems Inc., based in Hayward, Calif., insist that their machines, which are plugged into the wall and not hooked up to a central network open to hackers, are thoroughly reliable, accurate and secure.

There were glitches in November. The tabulating machines shut down shortly after 11 P.M. with 10 percent of the ballots uncounted because the system did not have a large enough capacity. Although that was an embarrassment—delegations from as far away as Japan were observing the countywide debut—Sequoia officials said the solution was a simple matter of adjusting the software. . . .

Source: Katharine Q. Seelye, "County in California Touches Future of Voting," *New York Times*, February 12, 2001, A1, A19. Copyright © 2001 by the New York Times Co. Reprinted by permission.

Bibliographic Essay

Readers who wish to pursue further the history of Election Day will find few other published works covering to the entire subject from early times to the present. The only book-length study available is Kate Kelly, *Election Day: An American Holiday: An American History* (New York: Facts on File, 1991), which contains a great deal of original information but is somewhat lacking in scholarly rigor. There are, however, some important scholarly books and essays on specific aspects of the Election Day experience. Peter Argersinger's essay "Electoral Processes," in Jack P. Greene, ed., *Encyclopedia of American Political History* (New York: Scribners, 1984), 2: 480–500, surveys the changing nature of voting and the rules and regulations regarding it. On voting qualifications, see Alexander Keyssar, *The Right to Vote: The Difficult Path to Democracy* (New York: Basic Books, 2000). On the recent trend of voting prior to Election Day, see Robert M. Stern, "Early Voting," *Public Opinion Quarterly* 62 (1998), and Rebecca B. Morton and Kenneth Williams, *Learning by Voting: Sequential Choices in Presidential Primaries and Other Elections* (Ann Arbor: University of Michigan Press, 2001). Nicholas von Hoffman, "Voting in Cyberspace? The Pros and Cons of Casting Your Ballot Online," *Architectural Digest* 57 (November 2000), 196–200, discusses the possibilities of Internet voting.

There are also many books on the politics of particular periods of American history that contain significant material about what has occurred on Election Day. For the colonial era, the classic work by Charles Sydnor, *Gentlemen Freeholders* (Chapel Hill: University of North Carolina Press, 1952), presents a colorful and informative treatment of elections in eighteenth-century Virginia. Robert J. Dinkin, in *Voting in Provincial America* (Westport, Conn.: Greenwood, 1977), chapter 6, and in *Voting in Revolutionary America* (Westport, Conn.: Greenwood, 1982), chapter 6, provides a general overview of the electoral process prior to 1789.

Edmund S. Morgan, *Inventing the People* (New York: W. W. Norton, 1988), offers a provocative look at elections in the early republic, comparing them to European carnival celebrations. Two works by Noble Cunningham, *The Jeffersonian Republicans* (Chapel Hill: University of North Carolina Press, 1957), and *The Jeffersonian Republicans in Power* (Chapel Hill, N.C.: 1963), furnished much information about election activities from 1789 to 1808. Jean H. Baker, *Affairs of Party* (Ithaca, N.Y.: Cornell University Press, 1983), tells much about Election Day in the middle decades of the nineteenth century, while Michael McGerr, *The Decline of Popular Politics* (New York: Oxford University Press, 1986), gives us the flavor of elections in the late nineteenth century. For the twentieth century, one can sometimes find descriptions of Election Day occurrences in the periodical literature. A good example is Georges Lechartier, "Election Week in New York," *Living Age* 308 (January 22, 1921), which has the perspective of a French journalist. One can also obtain information about Election Day in books that began to be written about particular elections, such as the Dewey-Truman contest in 1948, the latest one being Gary Donaldson, *Truman Defeats Dewey* (Lexington, Ky.: University of Kentucky Press, 1999). In addition, Theodore White's series, *The Making of the President* (New York: Atheneum, 1961–73), touches on the elections of the Kennedy-Johnson-Nixon years, while the books of Jules Witcover and Jack Germond, such as *Blue Smoke and Mirrors* (New York: Viking Press, 1981) and *Mad as Hell: Revolt at the Ballot Box 1992* (New York: Warner Books, 1993), do the same for elections in the last quarter of the century. Many books will eventually be written about the election of 2000 and its aftermath; two of the earliest are Jeff Greenfield, "*Oh, Waiter! One Order of Crow! Inside the Strangest Presidential Finish in American History* (New York: G. P. Putnam's Sons, 2001), and *Deadlock: The Inside Story of America's Closest Election* by the political staff of the *Washington Post* (New York: Public Affairs, 2001).

Index

About the Author

ROBERT J. DINKIN is Professor Emeritus at California State University, Fresno. His earlier books include *Before Equal Suffrage* (Greenwood, 1995) and *Campaigning in America* (Greenwood, 1989).